ON
ND

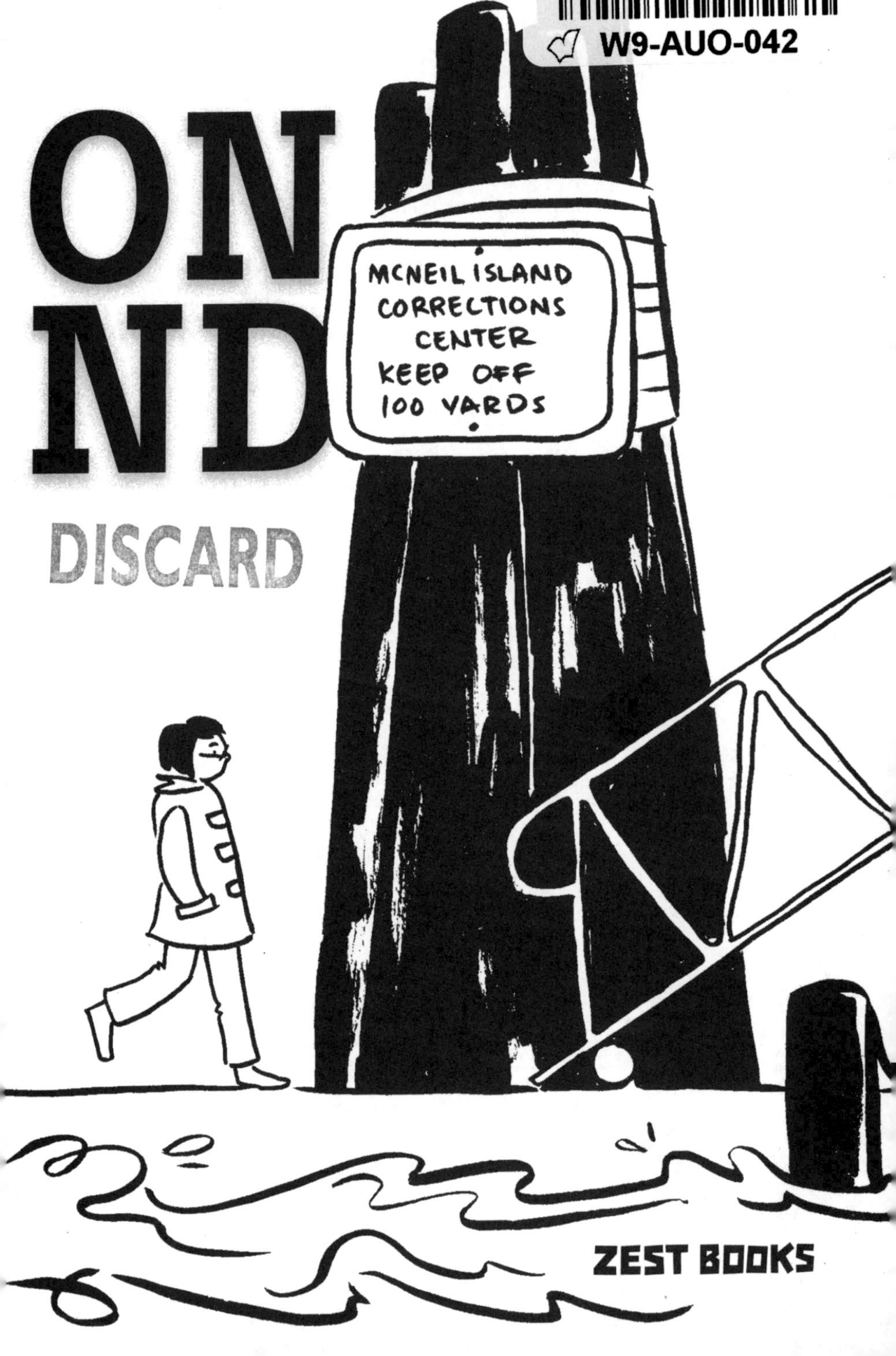
MCNEIL ISLAND
CORRECTIONS
CENTER
KEEP OFF
100 YARDS

ZEST BOOKS

DEDICATED TO:

- My Center for Cartoon Studies family
  Go CCS, you're the best!
- My McNeil Island family
  What? I always said I was going to write a book about this place.
- And my Family family
  Thanks for putting up with all this.

ZEST BOOKS

Connect with Zest!

- zestbooks.net/blog
- zestbooks.net/contests
- twitter.com/zestbooks
- facebook.com/BooksWithATwist

35 Stillman Street, Suite 121, San Francisco, CA 94107 / www.zestbooks.net

 | Nonfiction / Biography & Autobiography / Art | ISBN: 978-1-942186-02-1 | Design by Adam Grano

Manufactured in the U.S.A.
DOC 10 9 8 7 6 5 4 3 2 1
4500543046

AUTHOR'S NOTE

This book is drawn (quite literally) from my own experience. The names and distinguishing characteristics of all the people, my own family excluded, have been changed to protect their privacy.

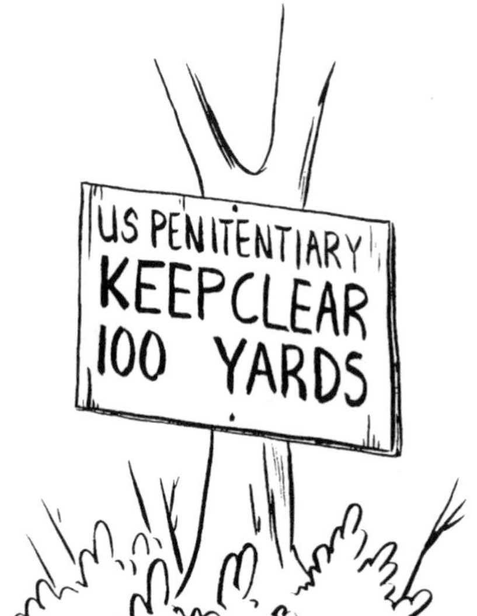
US PENITENTIARY
KEEP CLEAR
100 YARDS

CHAPTER 1

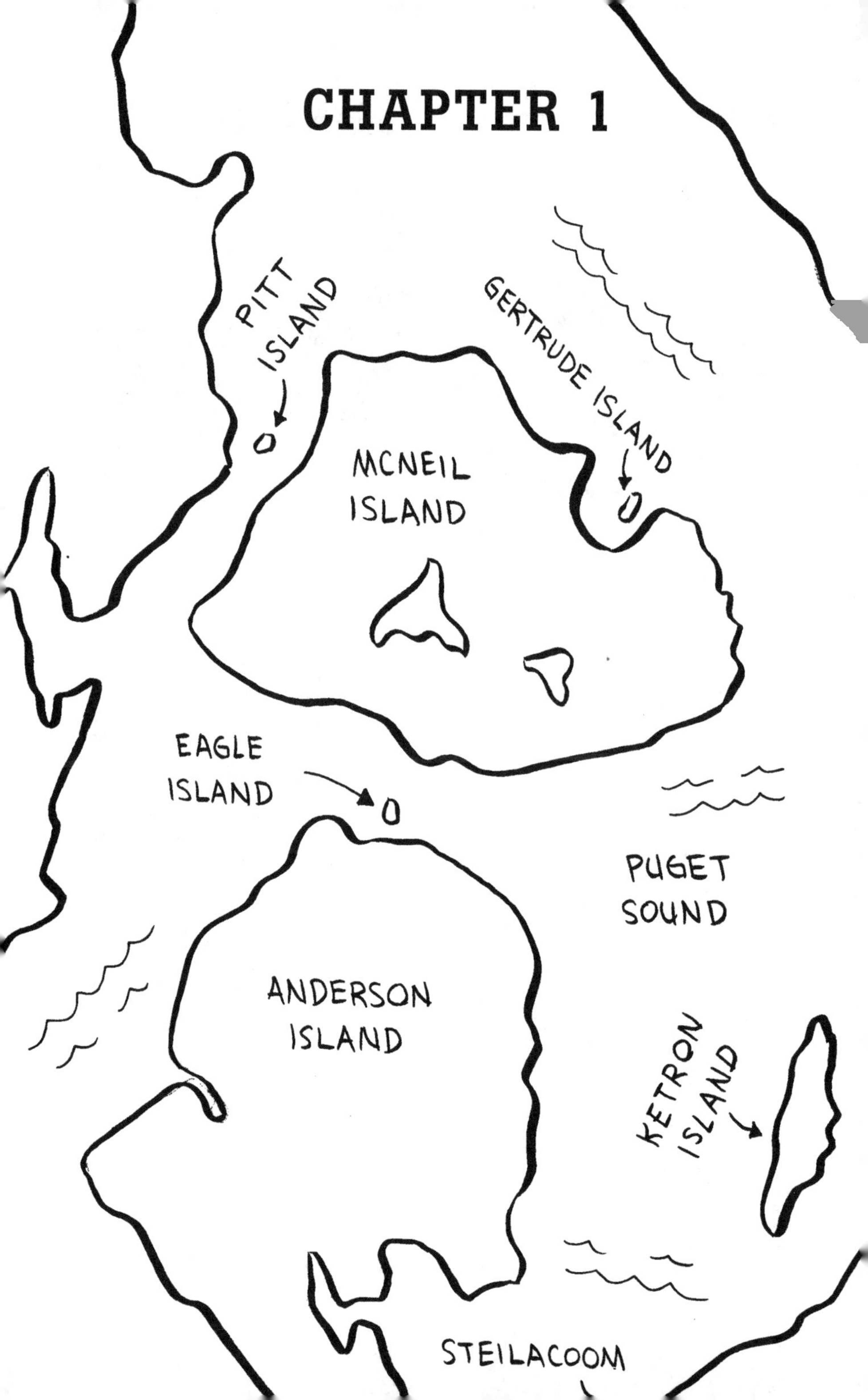

PITT ISLAND
GERTRUDE ISLAND
MCNEIL ISLAND
EAGLE ISLAND
PUGET SOUND
ANDERSON ISLAND
KETRON ISLAND
STEILACOOM

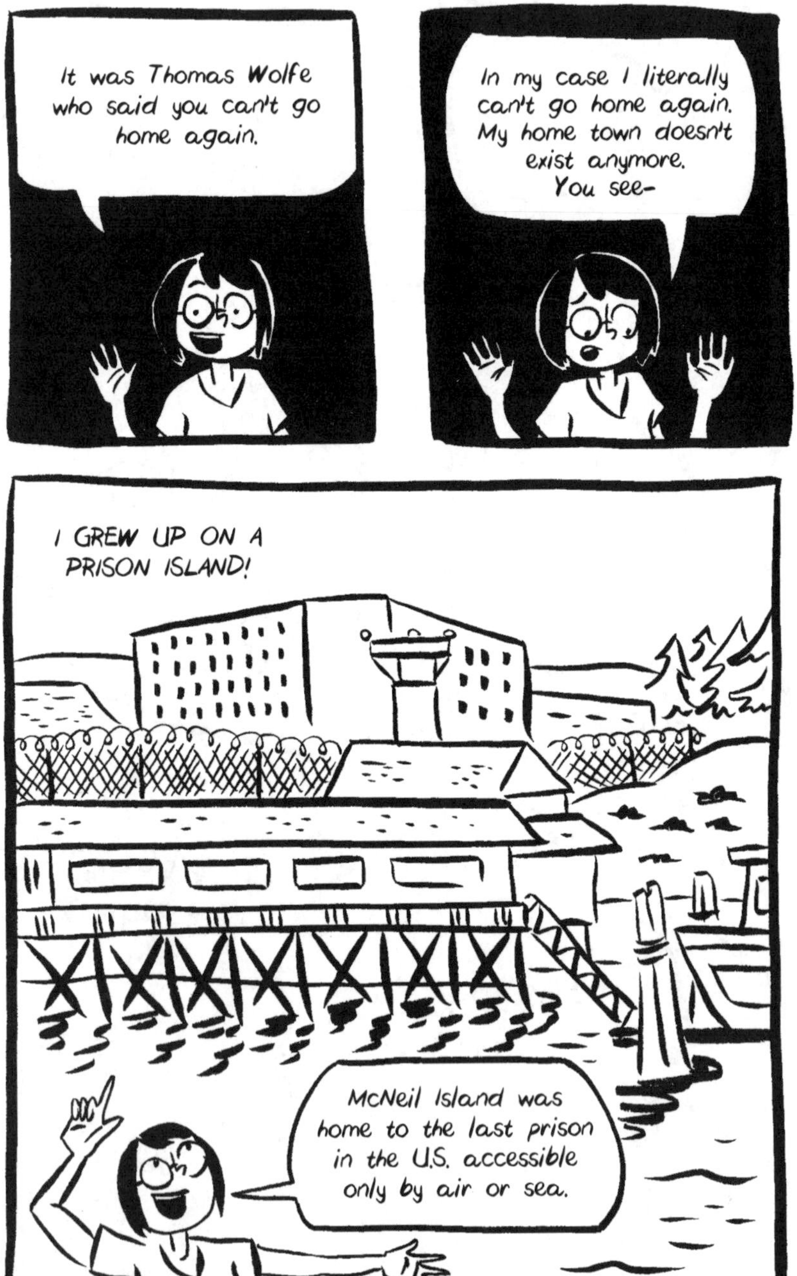
It was Thomas Wolfe who said you can't go home again.
In my case I literally can't go home again. My home town doesn't exist anymore. You see-
I GREW UP ON A PRISON ISLAND!
McNeil Island was home to the last prison in the U.S. accessible only by air or sea.

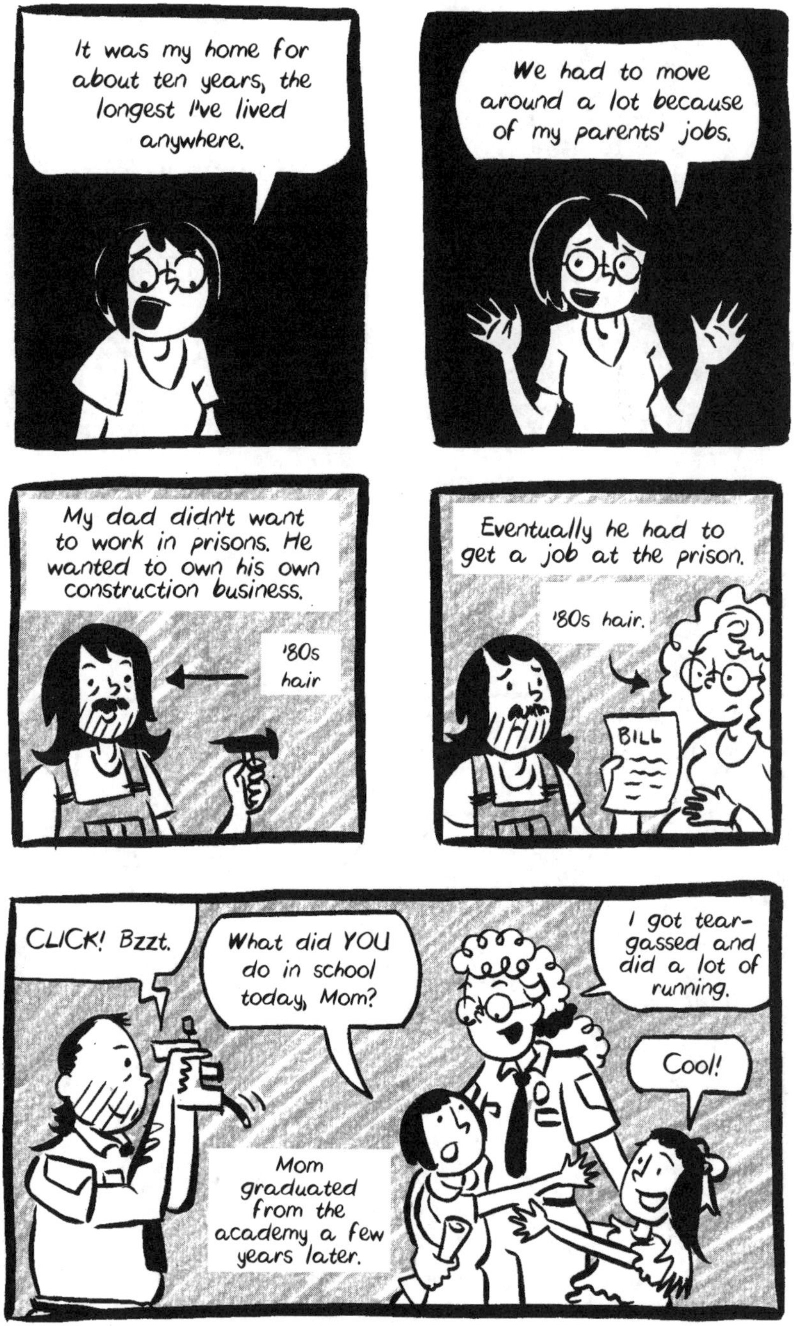
It was my home for about ten years, the longest I've lived anywhere.
We had to move around a lot because of my parents' jobs.
My dad didn't want to work in prisons. He wanted to own his own construction business.
'80s hair
Eventually he had to get a job at the prison.
'80s hair.
BILL
CLICK! Bzzt.
What did YOU do in school today, Mom?
I got tear-gassed and did a lot of running.
Cool!
Mom graduated from the academy a few years later.

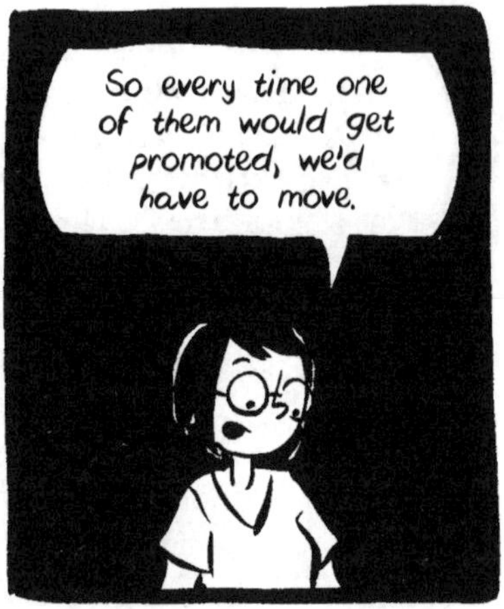
So every time one of them would get promoted, we'd have to move.

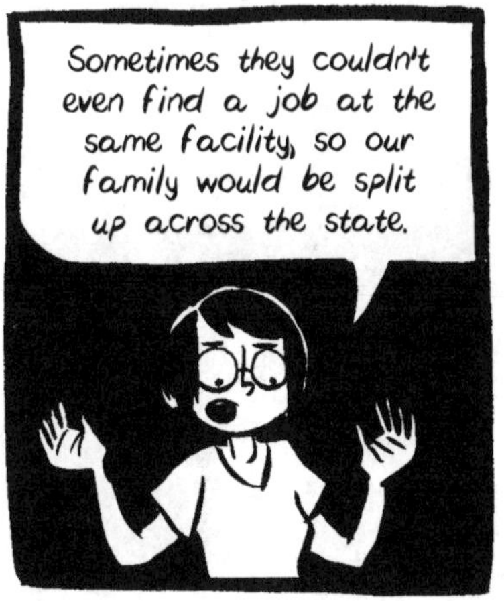
Sometimes they couldn't even find a job at the same facility, so our family would be split up across the state.

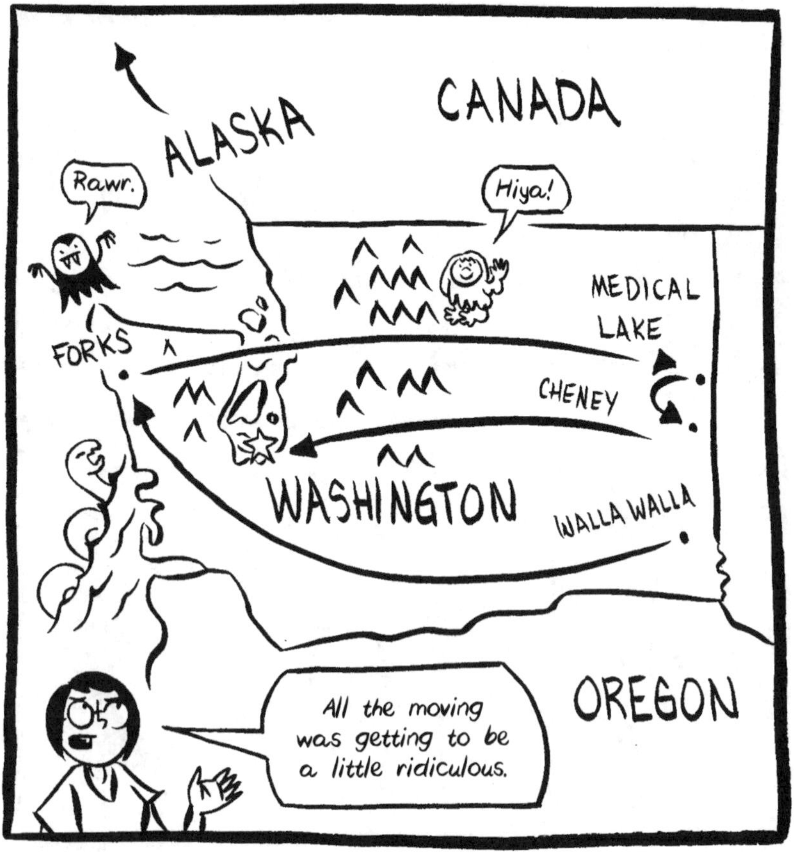
ALASKA
CANADA
Rawr.
Hiya!
MEDICAL LAKE
FORKS
CHENEY
WASHINGTON
WALLA WALLA
OREGON
All the moving was getting to be a little ridiculous.

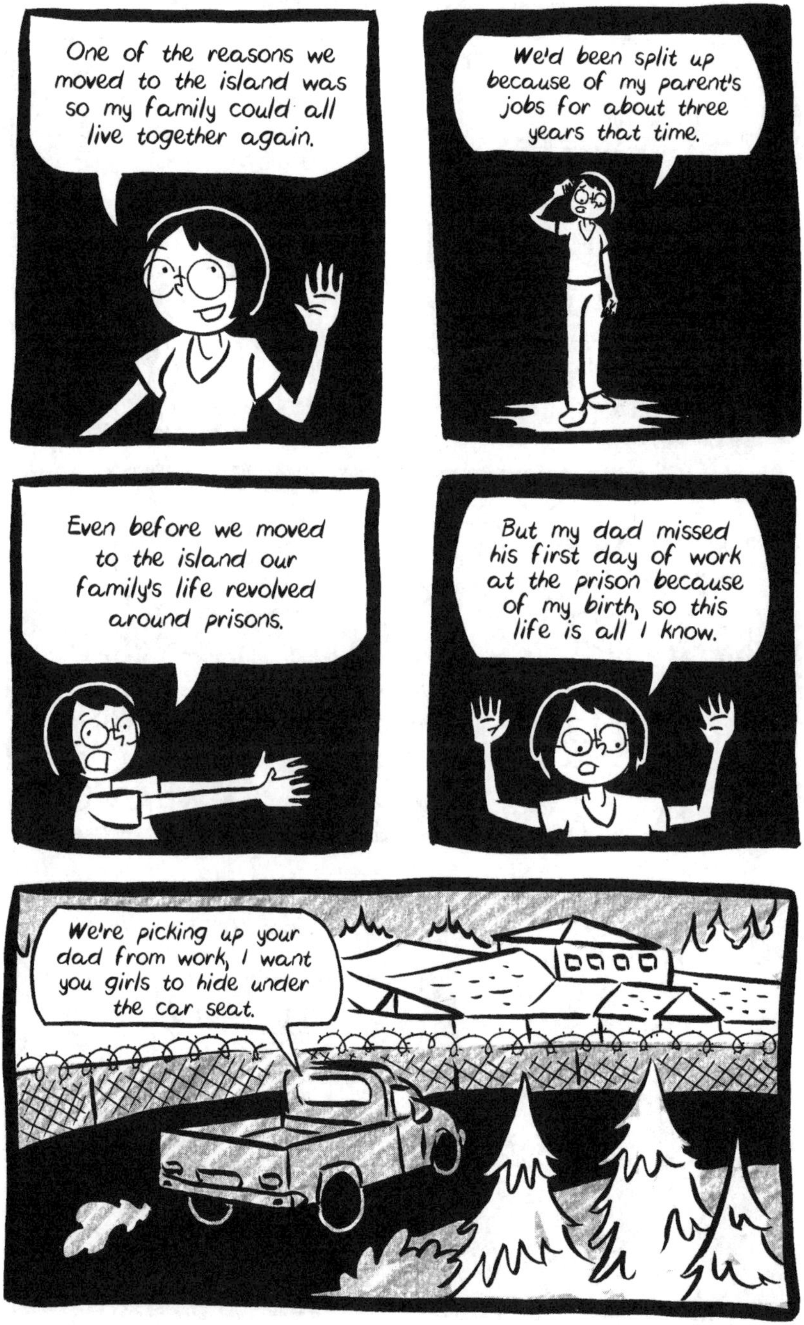
One of the reasons we moved to the island was so my family could all live together again.
We'd been split up because of my parent's jobs for about three years that time.
Even before we moved to the island our family's life revolved around prisons.
But my dad missed his first day of work at the prison because of my birth, so this life is all I know.
We're picking up your dad from work, I want you girls to hide under the car seat.

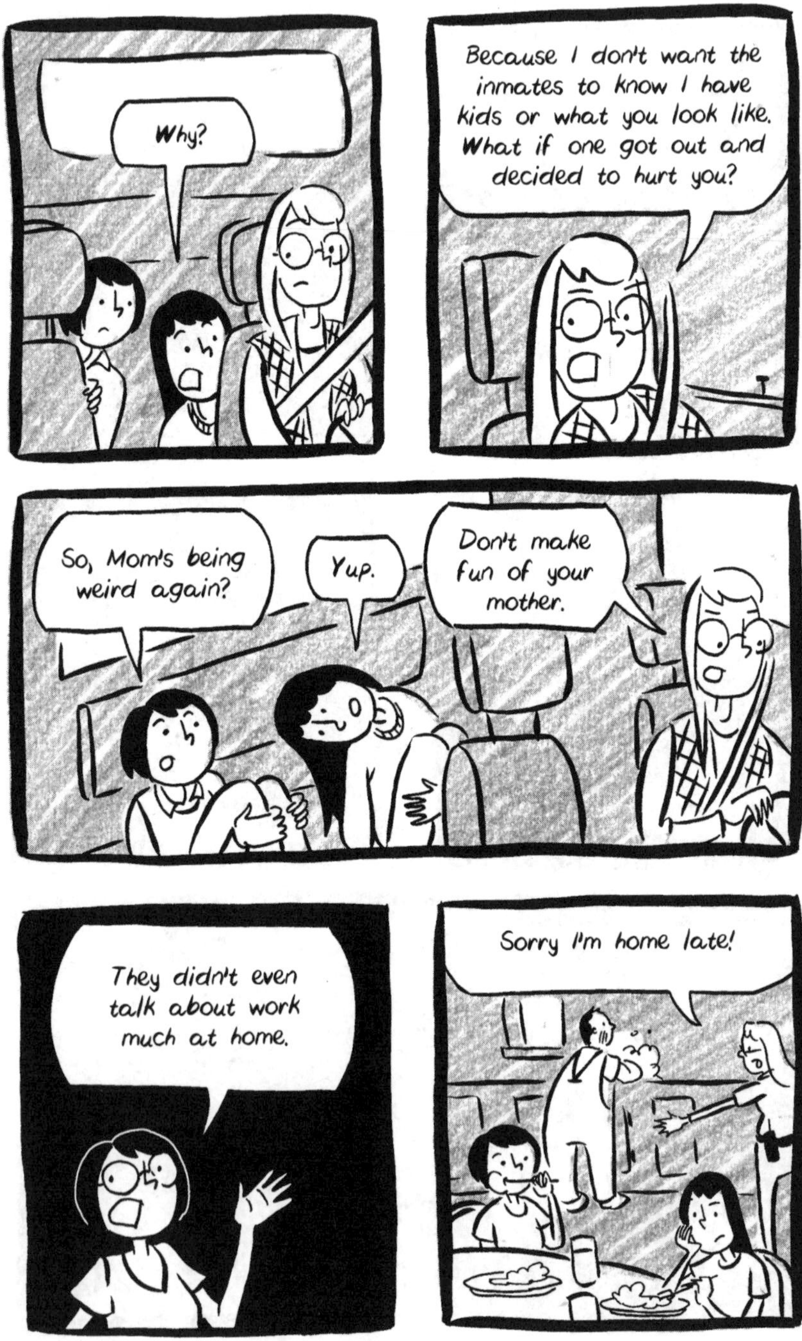
Why?
Because I don't want the inmates to know I have kids or what you look like. What if one got out and decided to hurt you?
So, Mom's being weird again?
Yup.
Don't make fun of your mother.
They didn't even talk about work much at home.
Sorry I'm home late!

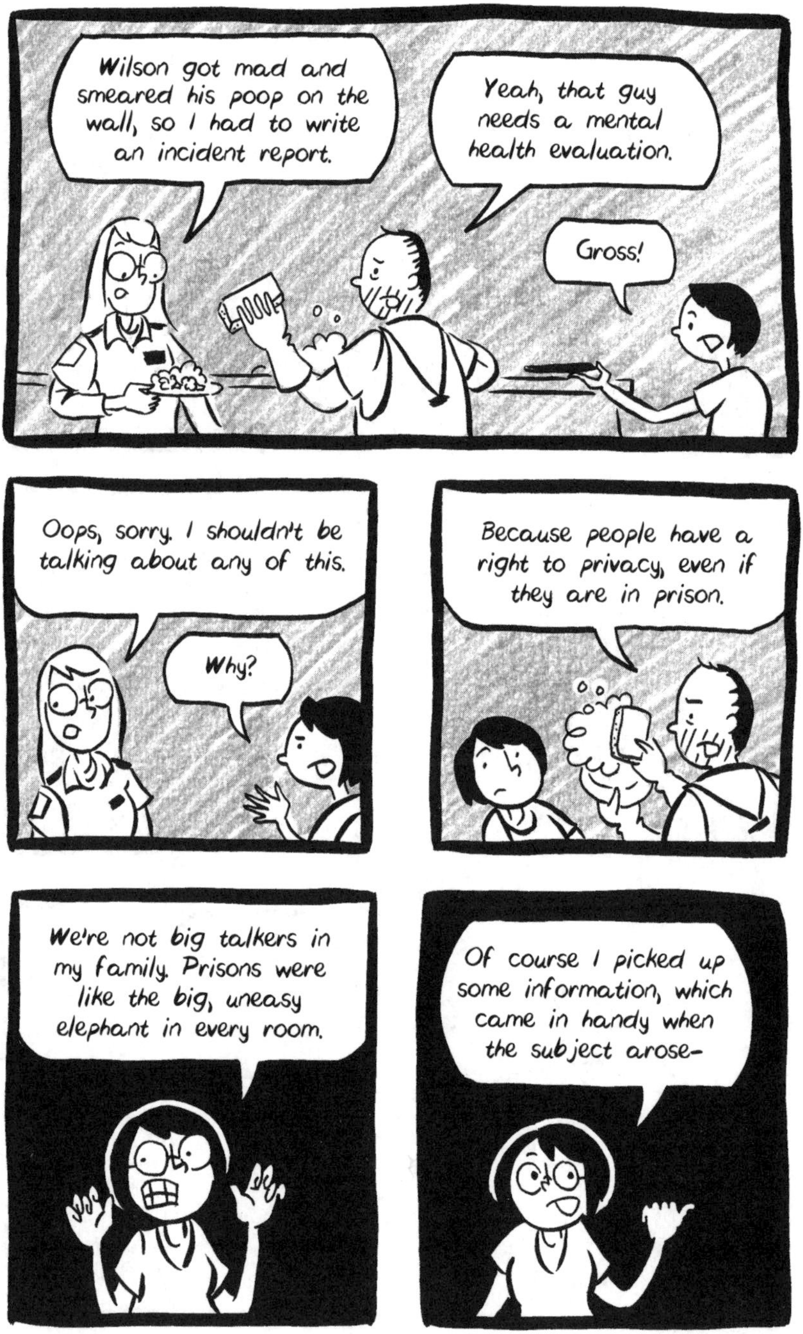
Wilson got mad and smeared his poop on the wall, so I had to write an incident report.
Yeah, that guy needs a mental health evaluation.
Gross!
Oops, sorry. I shouldn't be talking about any of this.
Why?
Because people have a right to privacy, even if they are in prison.
We're not big talkers in my family. Prisons were like the big, uneasy elephant in every room.
Of course I picked up some information, which came in handy when the subject arose-

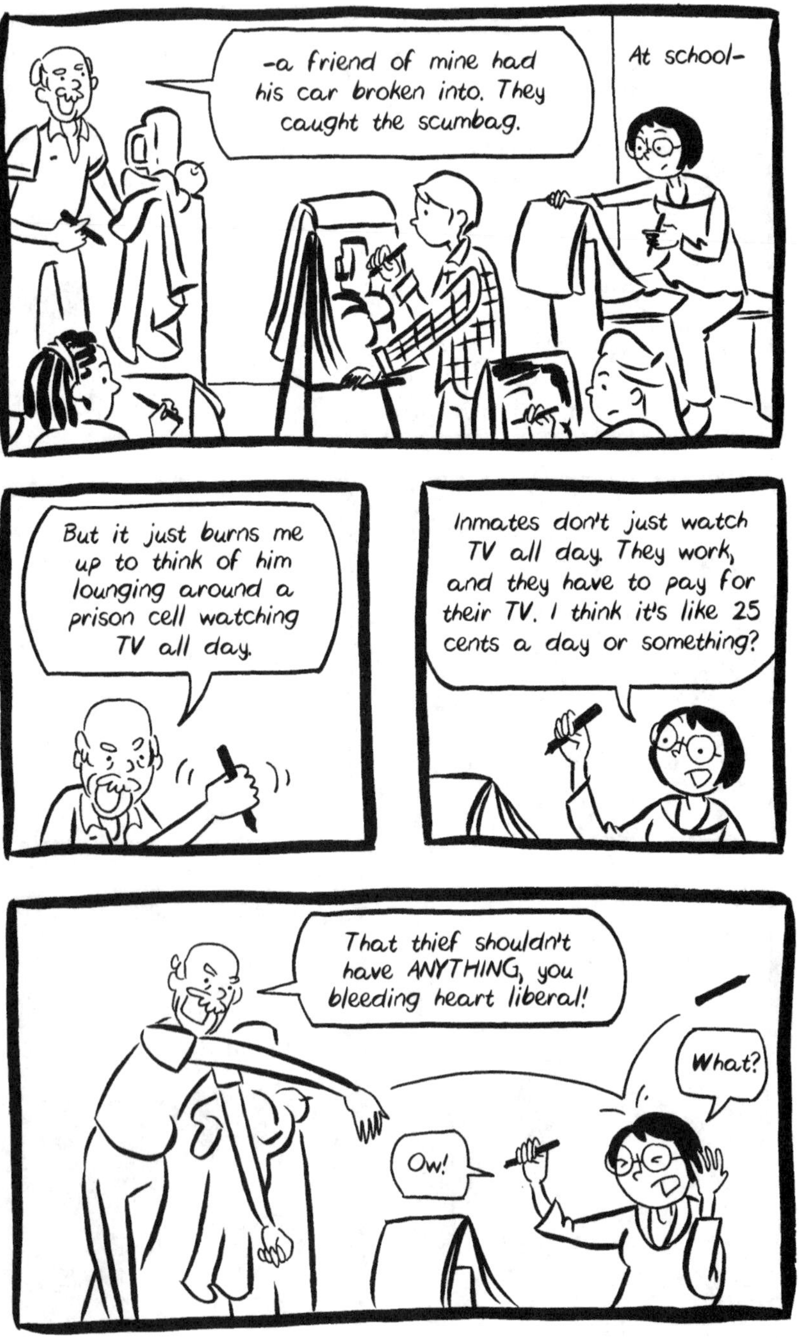
-a friend of mine had his car broken into. They caught the scumbag.
At school-
But it just burns me up to think of him lounging around a prison cell watching TV all day.
Inmates don't just watch TV all day. They work, and they have to pay for their TV. I think it's like 25 cents a day or something?
That thief shouldn't have ANYTHING, you bleeding heart liberal!
What?
Ow!

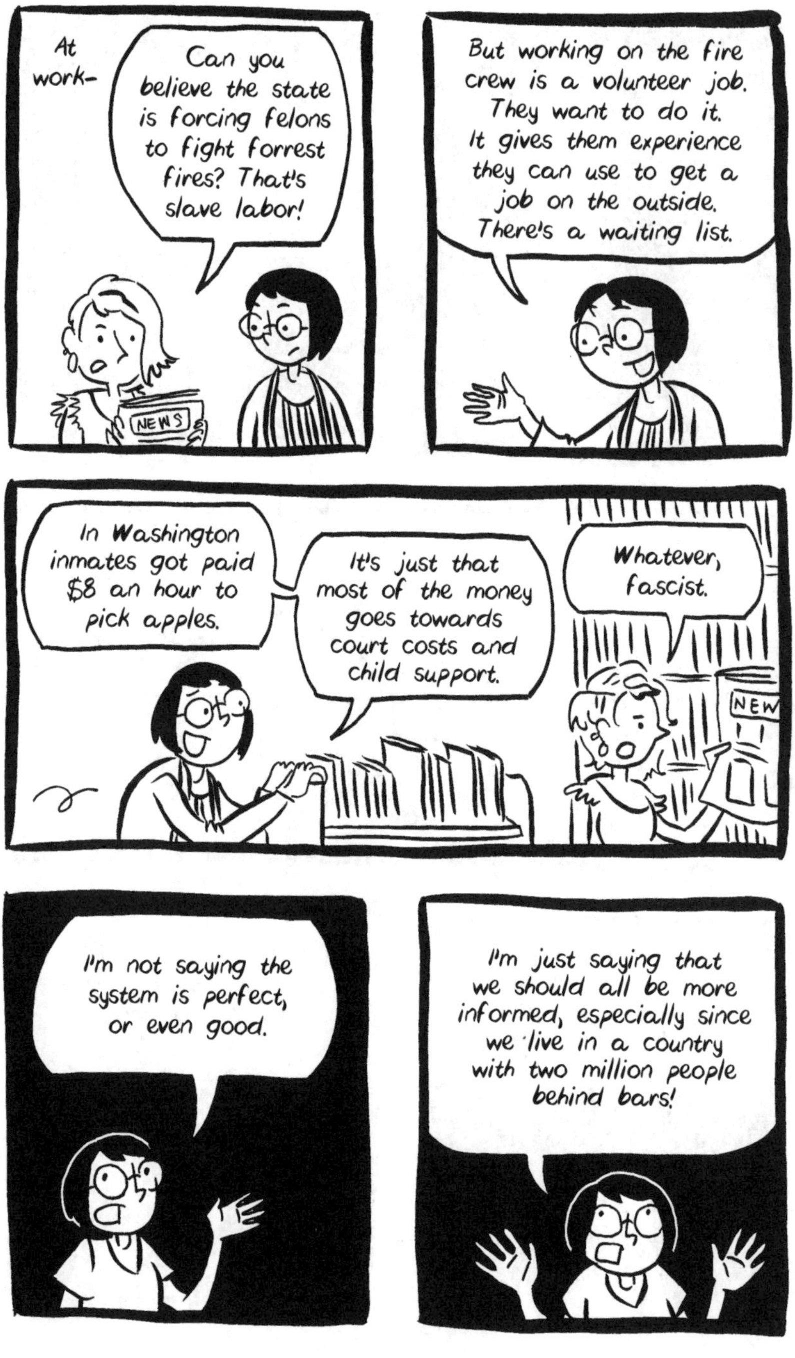
At work-
Can you believe the state is forcing felons to fight forrest fires? That's slave labor!
But working on the fire crew is a volunteer job. They want to do it. It gives them experience they can use to get a job on the outside. There's a waiting list.
NEWS
In Washington inmates got paid $8 an hour to pick apples.
It's just that most of the money goes towards court costs and child support.
Whatever, fascist.
I'm not saying the system is perfect, or even good.
I'm just saying that we should all be more informed, especially since we live in a country with two million people behind bars!

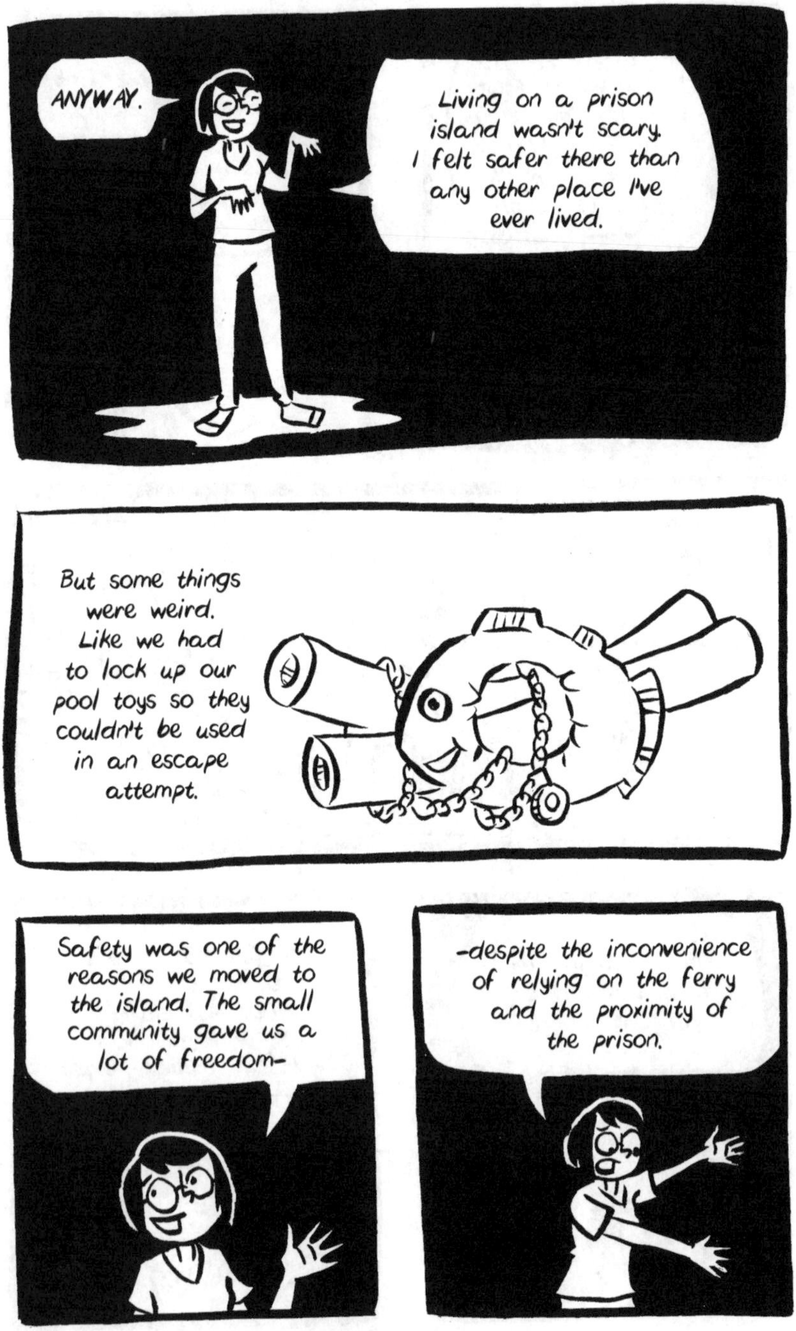
ANYWAY.
Living on a prison island wasn't scary. I felt safer there than any other place I've ever lived.
But some things were weird. Like we had to lock up our pool toys so they couldn't be used in an escape attempt.
Safety was one of the reasons we moved to the island. The small community gave us a lot of freedom-
-despite the inconvenience of relying on the ferry and the proximity of the prison.

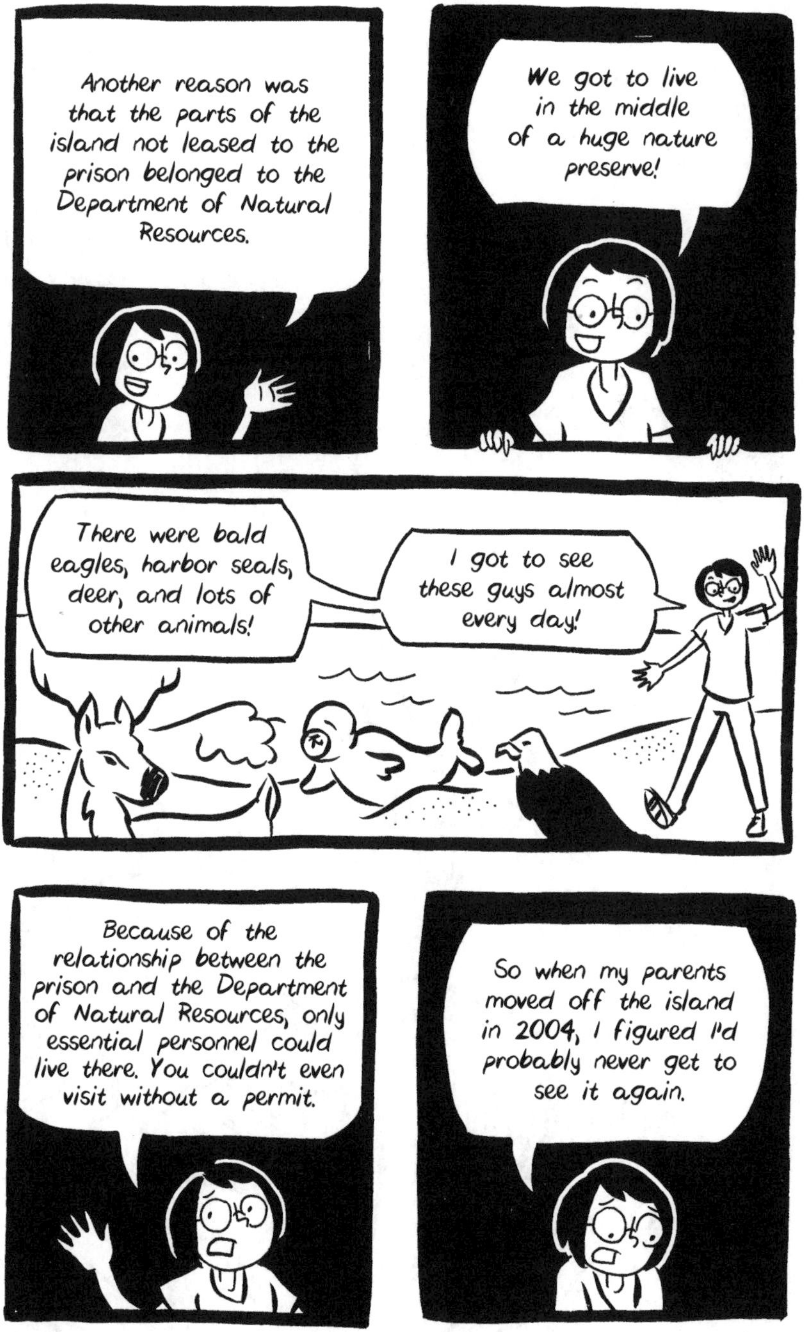
Another reason was that the parts of the island not leased to the prison belonged to the Department of Natural Resources.
We got to live in the middle of a huge nature preserve!
There were bald eagles, harbor seals, deer, and lots of other animals!
I got to see these guys almost every day!
Because of the relationship between the prison and the Department of Natural Resources, only essential personnel could live there. You couldn't even visit without a permit.
So when my parents moved off the island in 2004, I figured I'd probably never get to see it again.

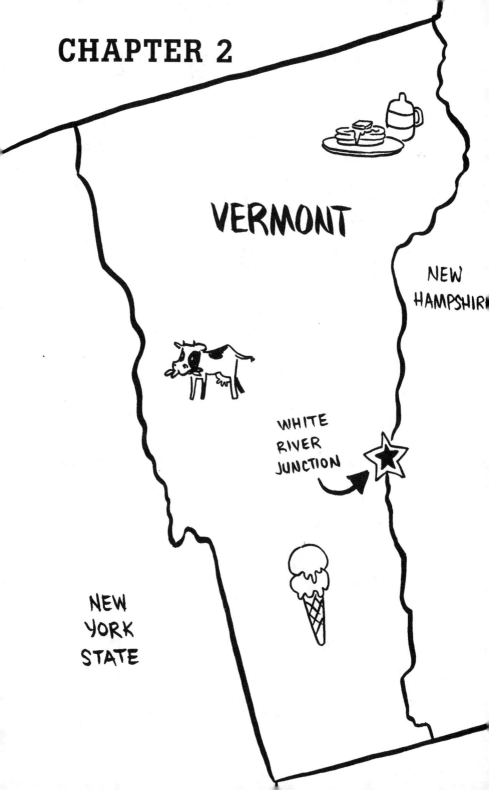

CHAPTER 2

VERMONT

NEW HAMPSHIRE

WHITE RIVER JUNCTION

NEW YORK STATE

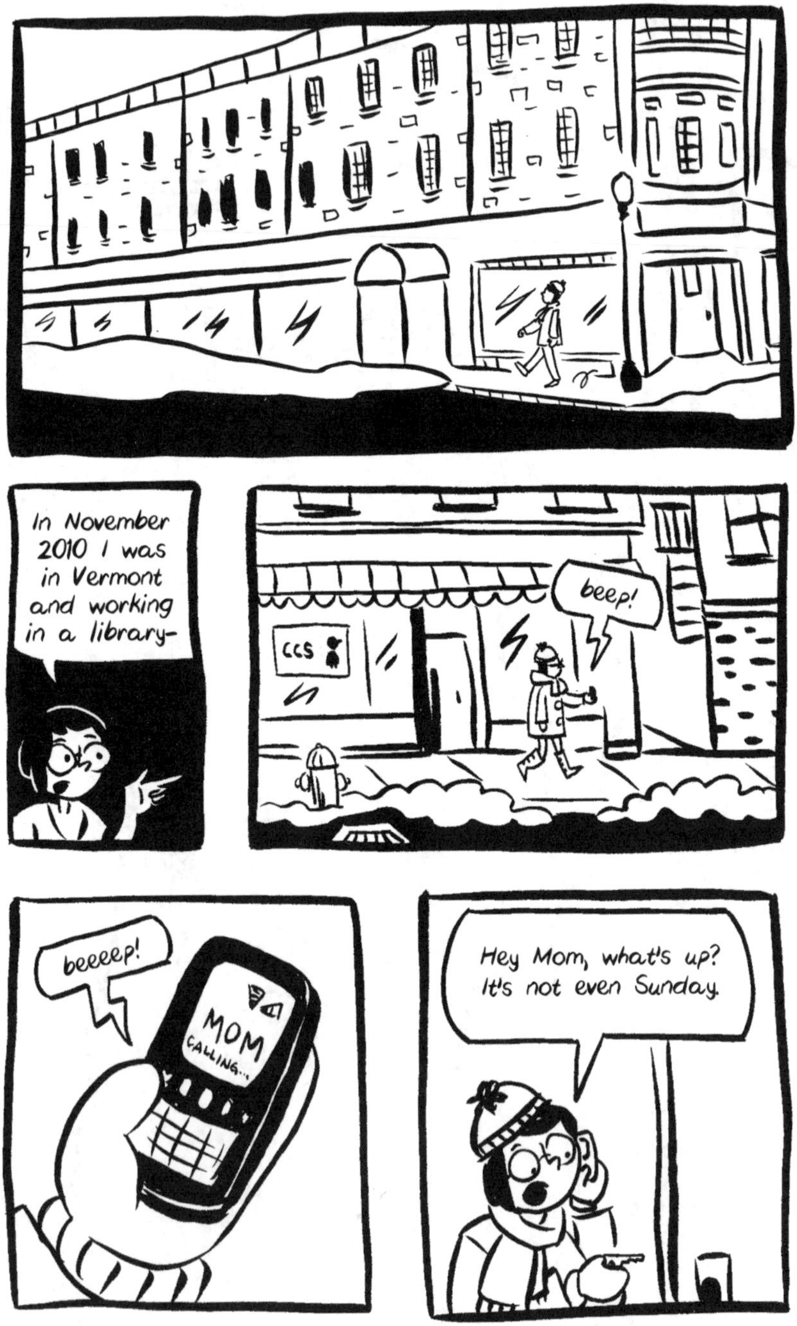
In November 2010 I was in Vermont and working in a library-
beep!
CCS
beeeep!
MOM
CALLING...
Hey Mom, what's up? It's not even Sunday.

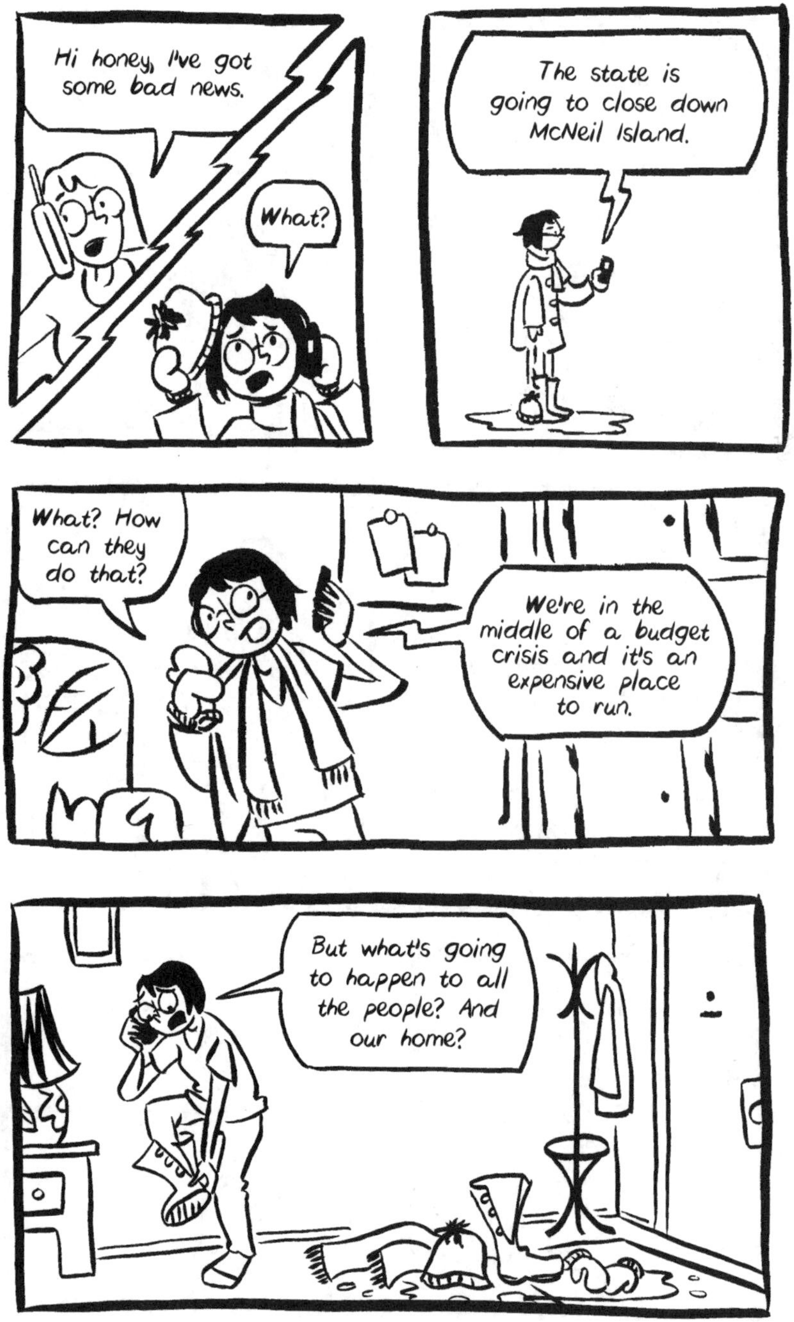
Hi honey, I've got some bad news.
What?
The state is going to close down McNeil Island.
What? How can they do that?
We're in the middle of a budget crisis and it's an expensive place to run.
But what's going to happen to all the people? And our home?

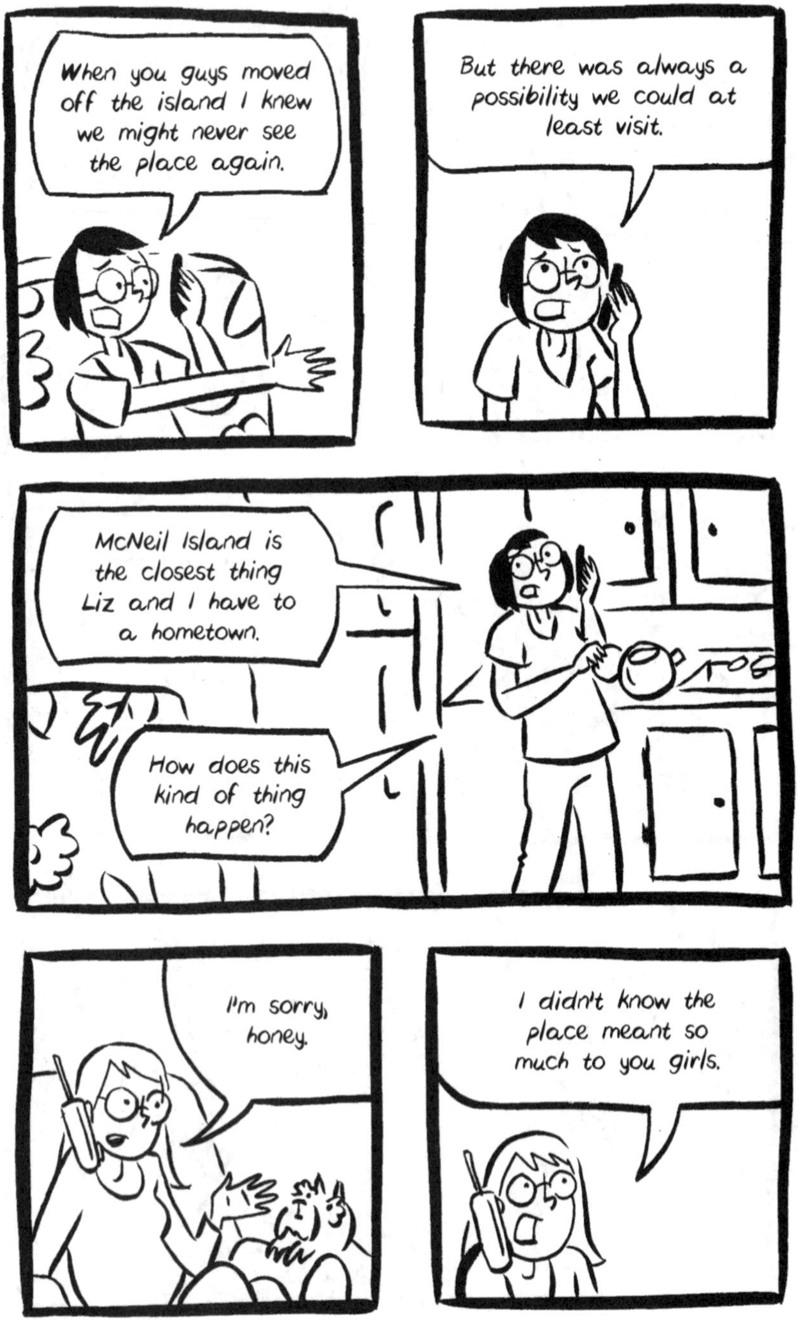
When you guys moved off the island I knew we might never see the place again.
But there was always a possibility we could at least visit.
McNeil Island is the closest thing Liz and I have to a hometown.
How does this kind of thing happen?
I'm sorry, honey.
I didn't know the place meant so much to you girls.

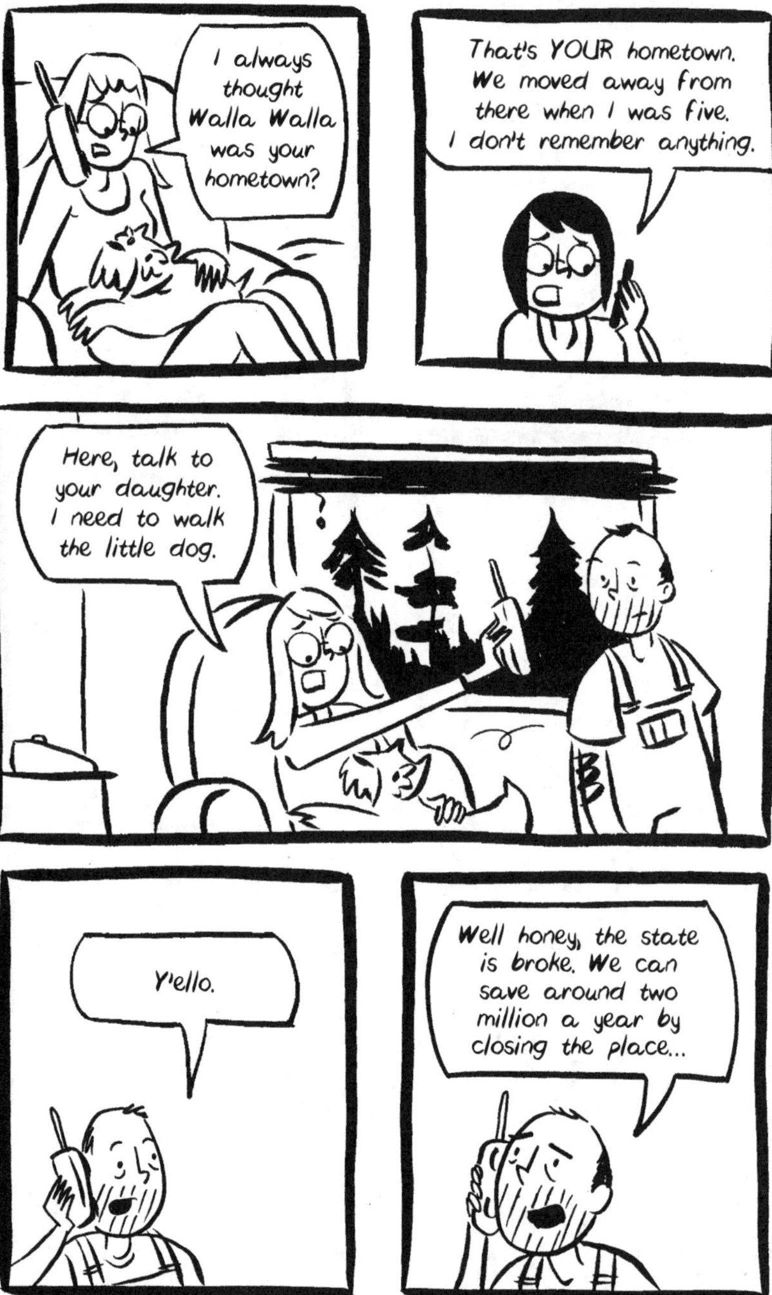
I always thought Walla Walla was your hometown?
That's YOUR hometown. We moved away from there when I was five. I don't remember anything.
Here, talk to your daughter. I need to walk the little dog.
Y'ello.
Well honey, the state is broke. We can save around two million a year by closing the place...

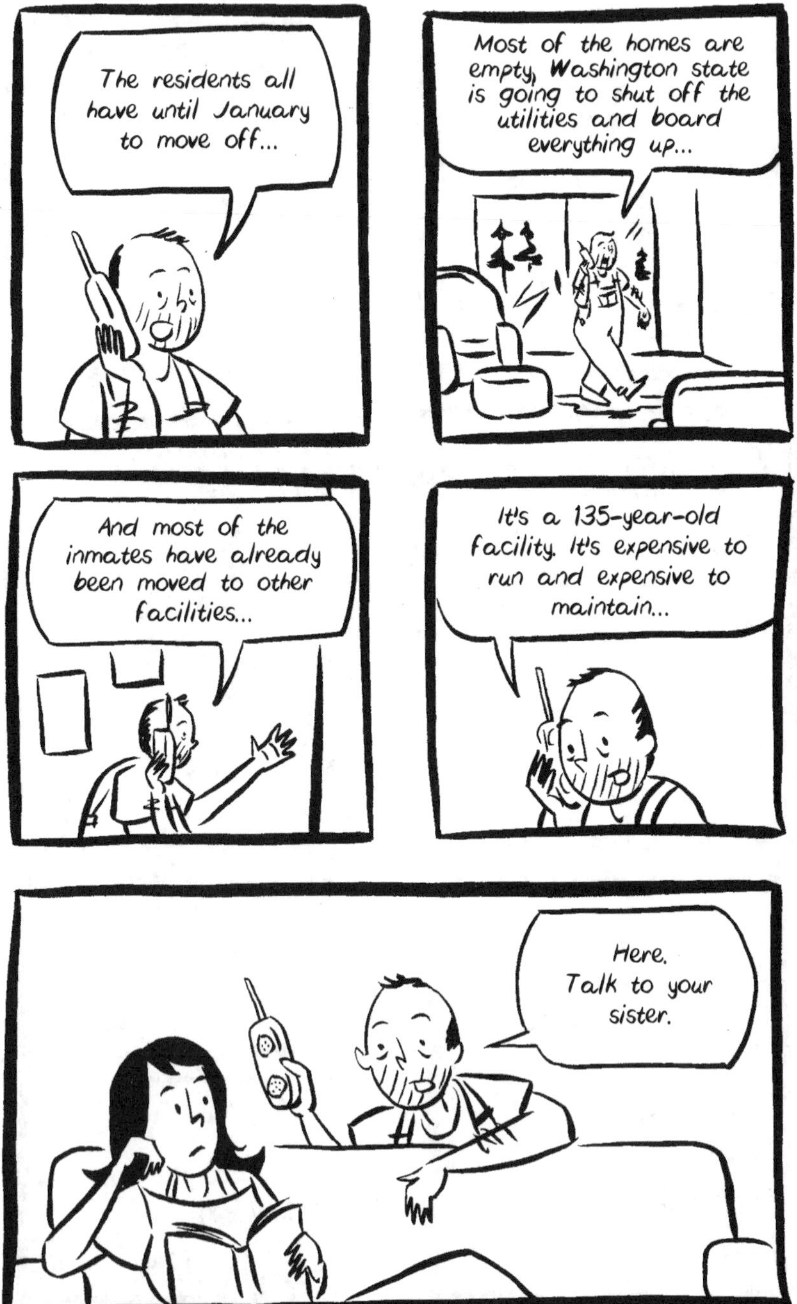
The residents all have until January to move off...
Most of the homes are empty, Washington state is going to shut off the utilities and board everything up...
And most of the inmates have already been moved to other facilities...
It's a 135-year-old facility. It's expensive to run and expensive to maintain...
Here. Talk to your sister.

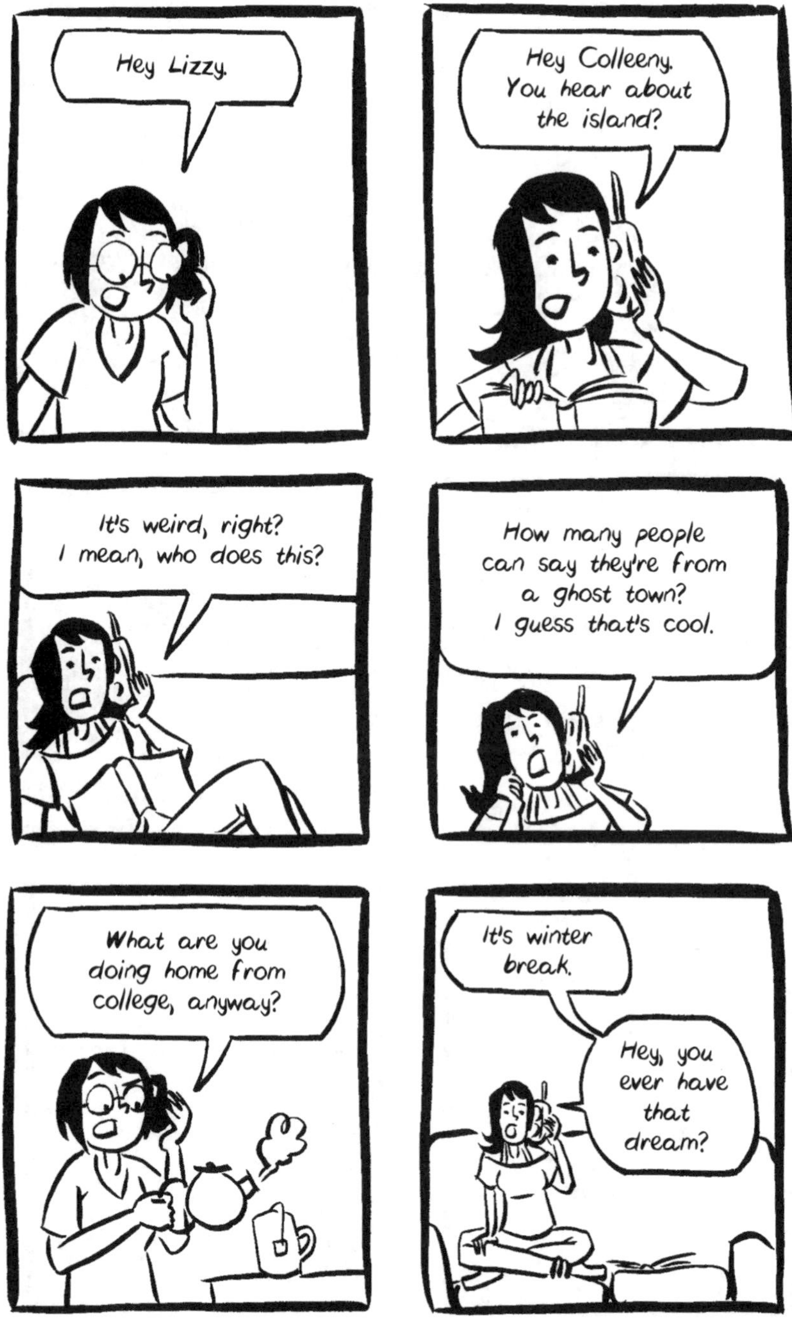
Hey Lizzy.
Hey Colleeny. You hear about the island?
It's weird, right? I mean, who does this?
How many people can say they're from a ghost town? I guess that's cool.
What are you doing home from college, anyway?
It's winter break.
Hey, you ever have that dream?

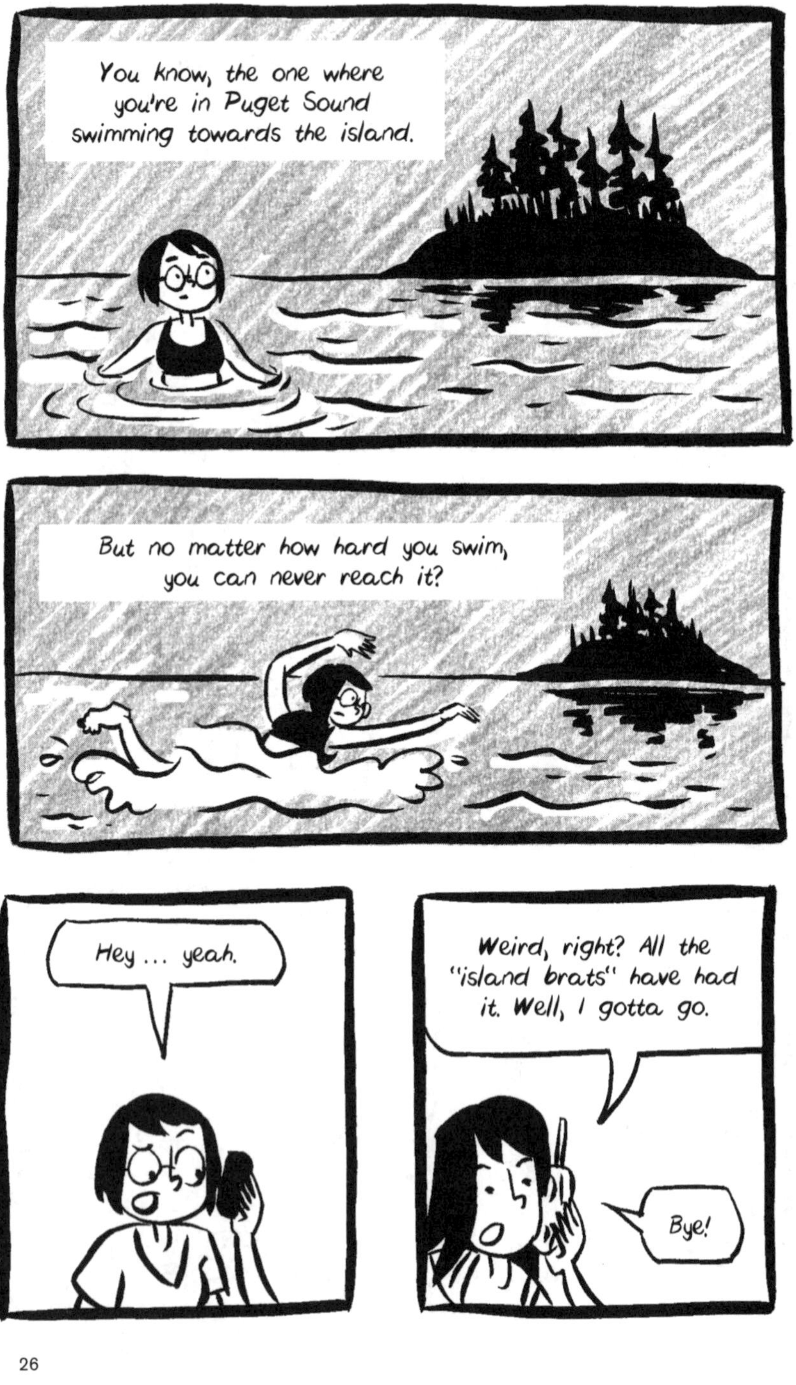
You know, the one where you're in Puget Sound swimming towards the island.
But no matter how hard you swim, you can never reach it?
Hey ... yeah.
Weird, right? All the "island brats" have had it. Well, I gotta go.
Bye!

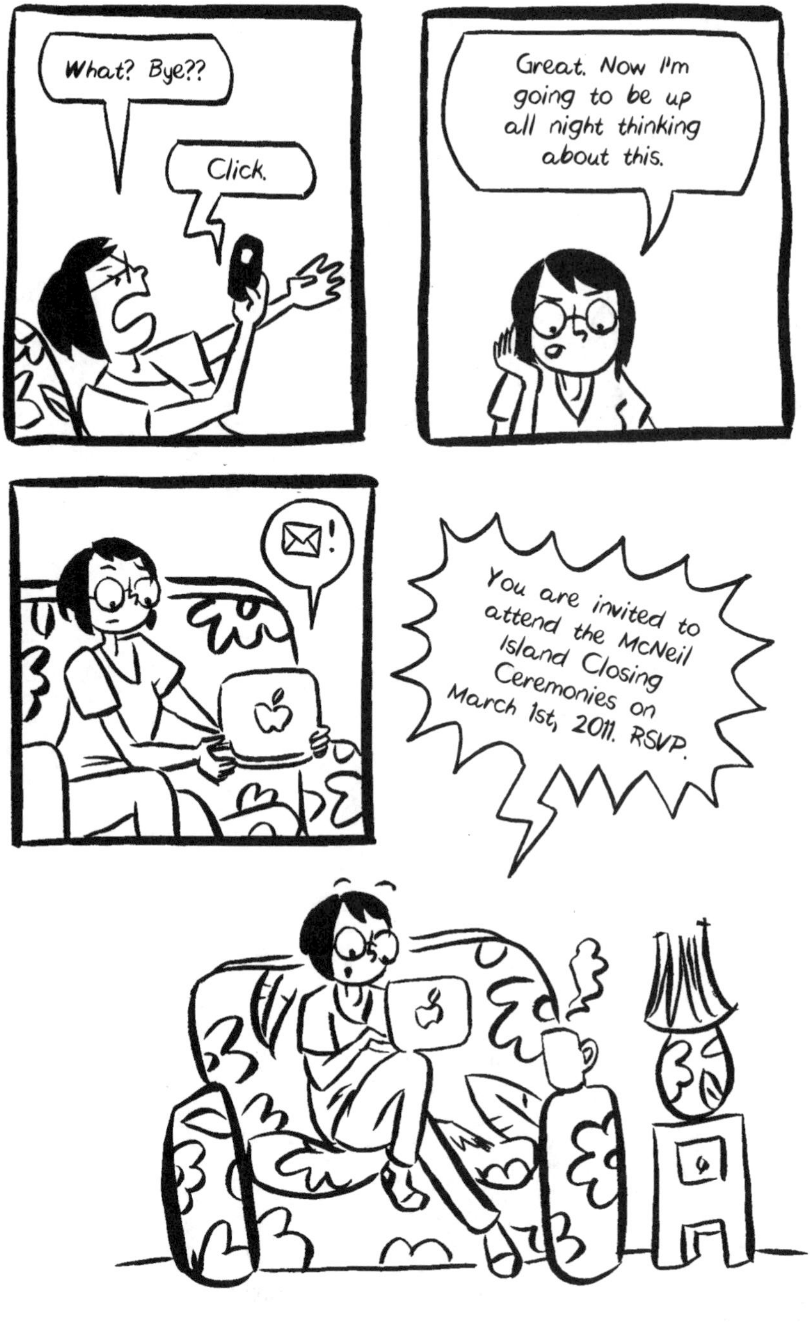
What? Bye??
Click.
Great. Now I'm going to be up all night thinking about this.
You are invited to attend the McNeil Island Closing Ceremonies on March 1st, 2011. RSVP.

CHAPTER 3

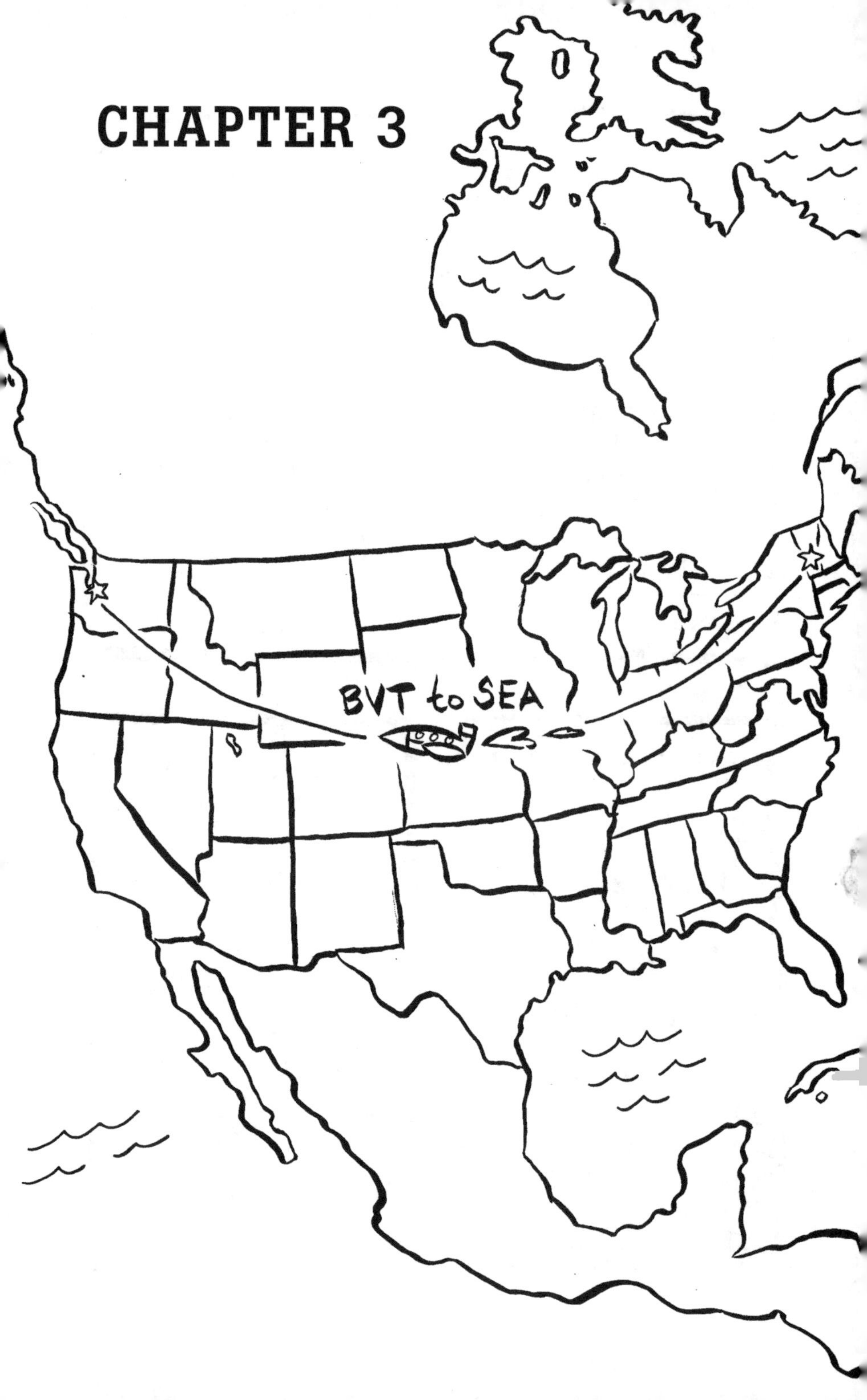
BVT to SEA

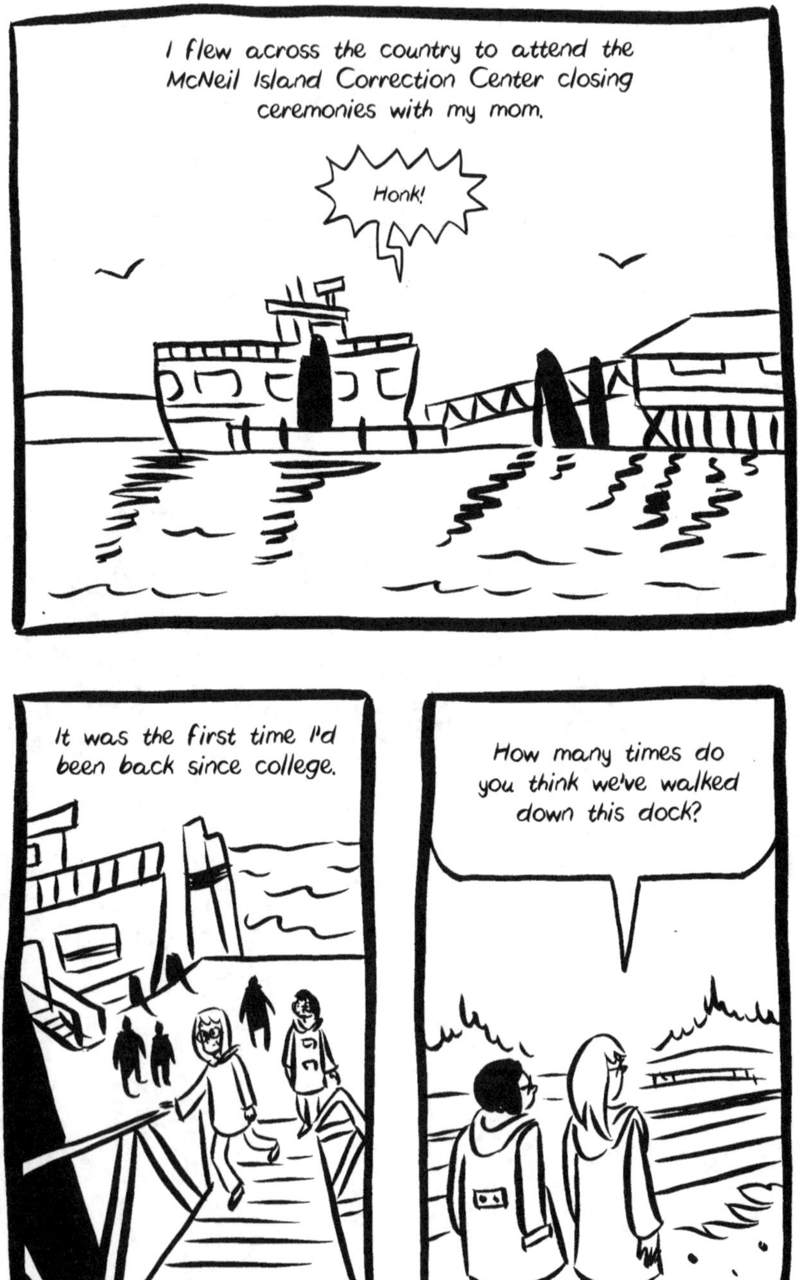
I flew across the country to attend the McNeil Island Correction Center closing ceremonies with my mom.
Honk!
It was the first time I'd been back since college.
How many times do you think we've walked down this dock?

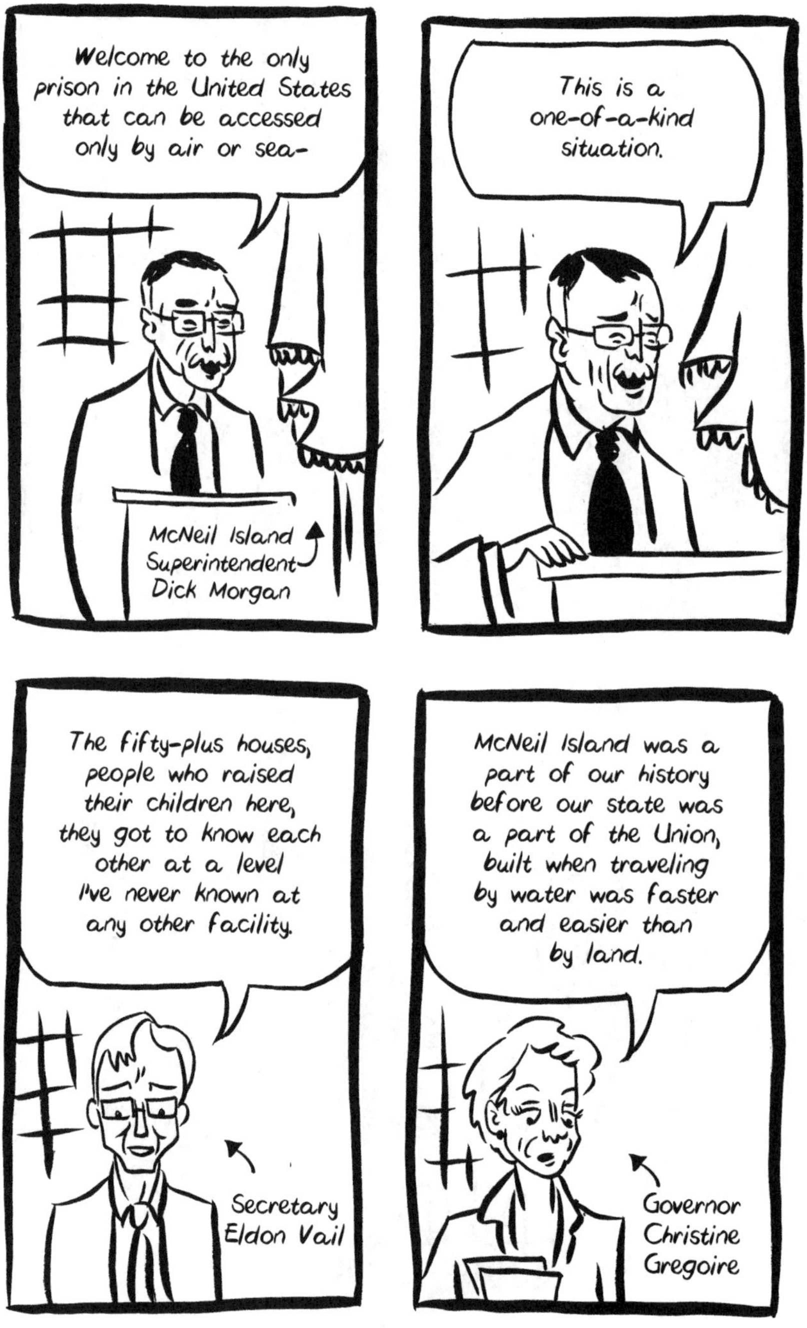
Welcome to the only prison in the United States that can be accessed only by air or sea-
McNeil Island Superintendent Dick Morgan
This is a one-of-a-kind situation.
The fifty-plus houses, people who raised their children here, they got to know each other at a level I've never known at any other facility.
Secretary Eldon Vail
McNeil Island was a part of our history before our state was a part of the Union, built when traveling by water was faster and easier than by land.
Governor Christine Gregoire

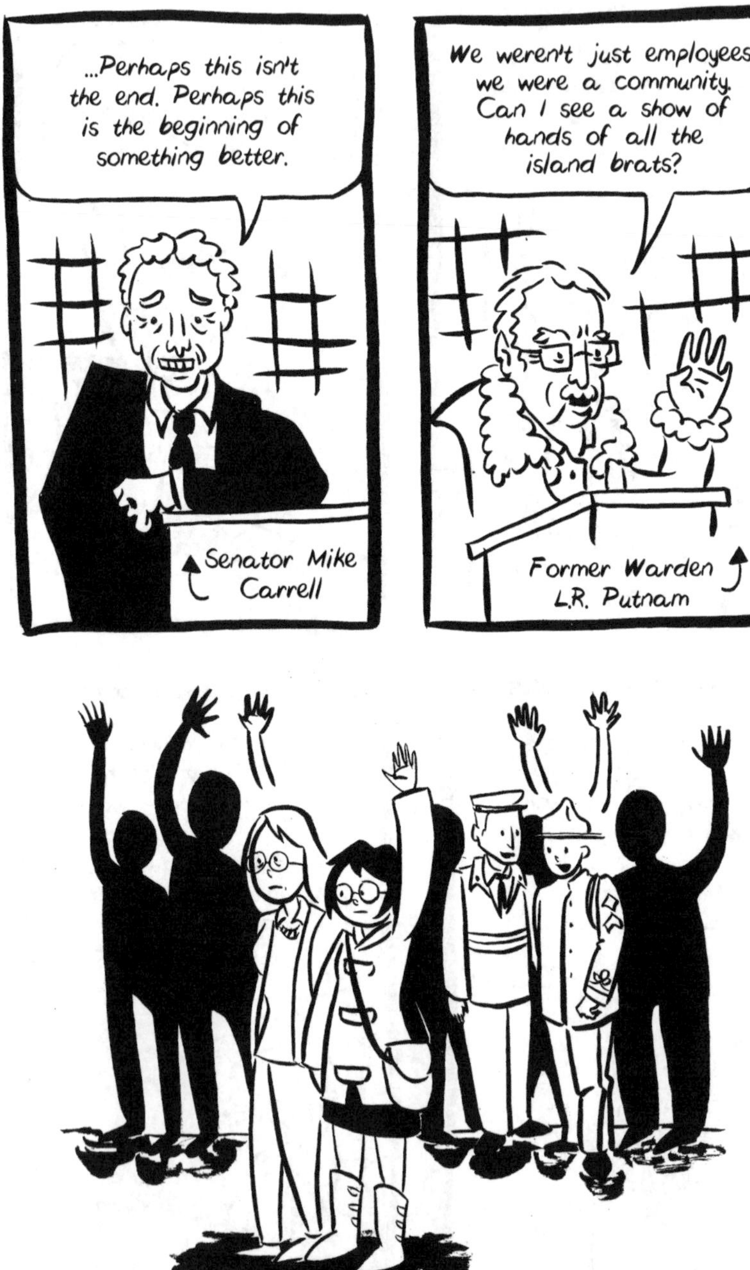
...Perhaps this isn't the end. Perhaps this is the beginning of something better.
Senator Mike Carrell
We weren't just employees, we were a community. Can I see a show of hands of all the island brats?
Former Warden L.R. Putnam

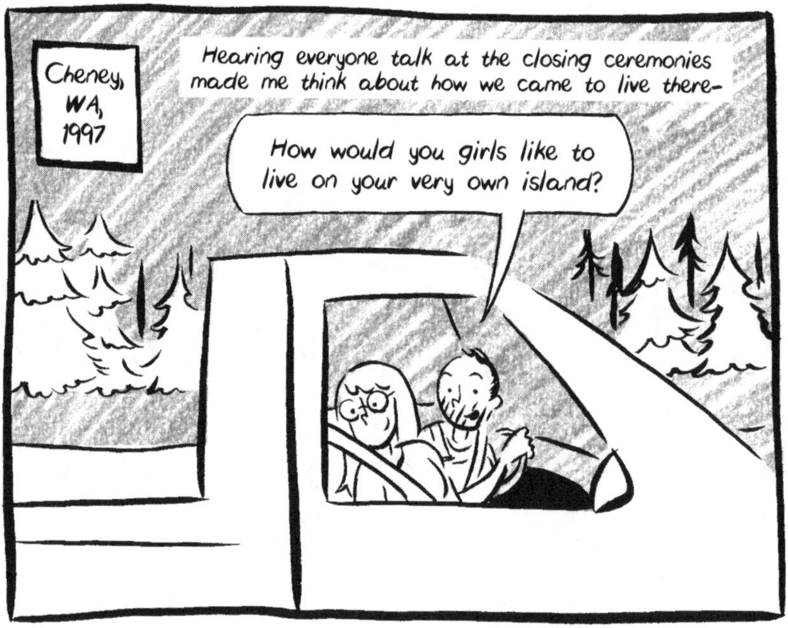
Cheney, WA, 1997
Hearing everyone talk at the closing ceremonies made me think about how we came to live there-
How would you girls like to live on your very own island?

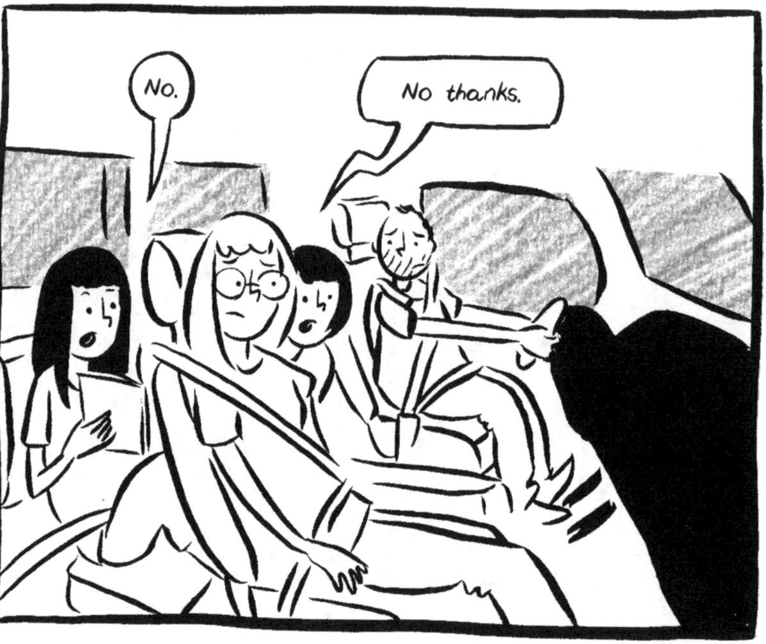
No.
No thanks.

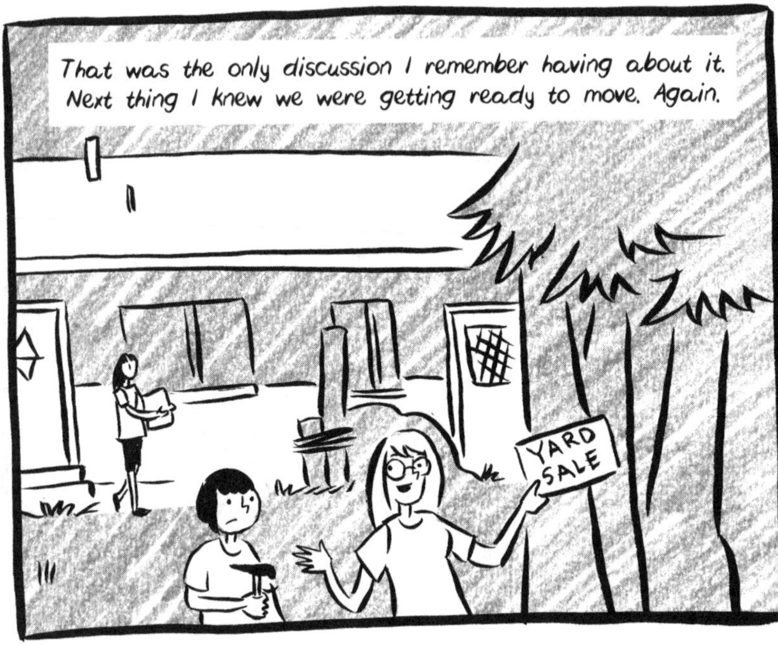
That was the only discussion I remember having about it. Next thing I knew we were getting ready to move. Again.
YARD SALE

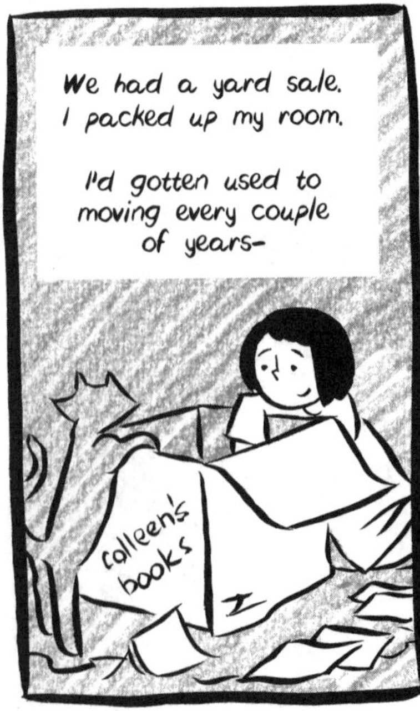
We had a yard sale. I packed up my room.
I'd gotten used to moving every couple of years-
colleen's books

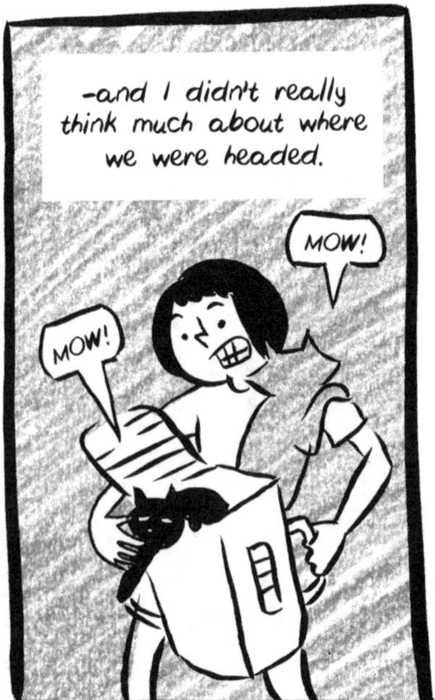
-and I didn't really think much about where we were headed.
MOW!
MOW!

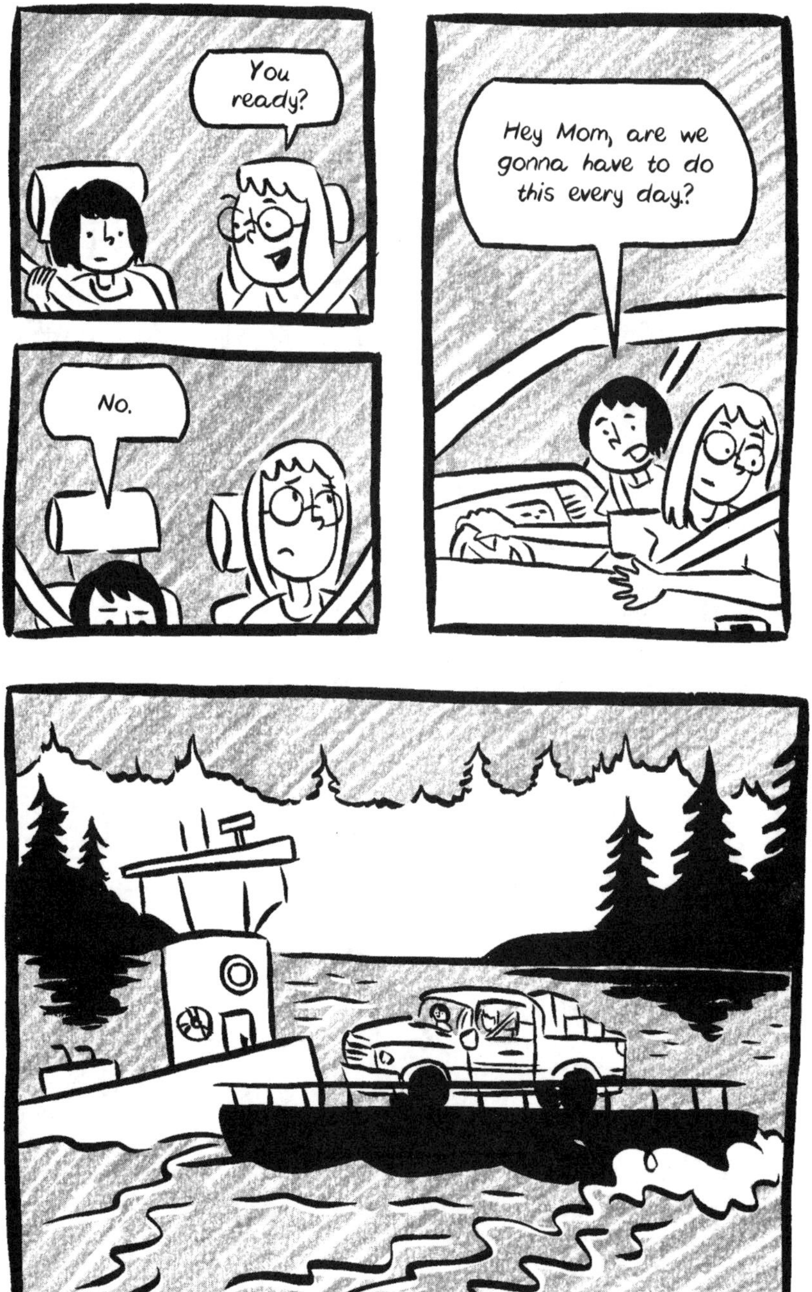
You ready?
No.
Hey Mom, are we gonna have to do this every day?

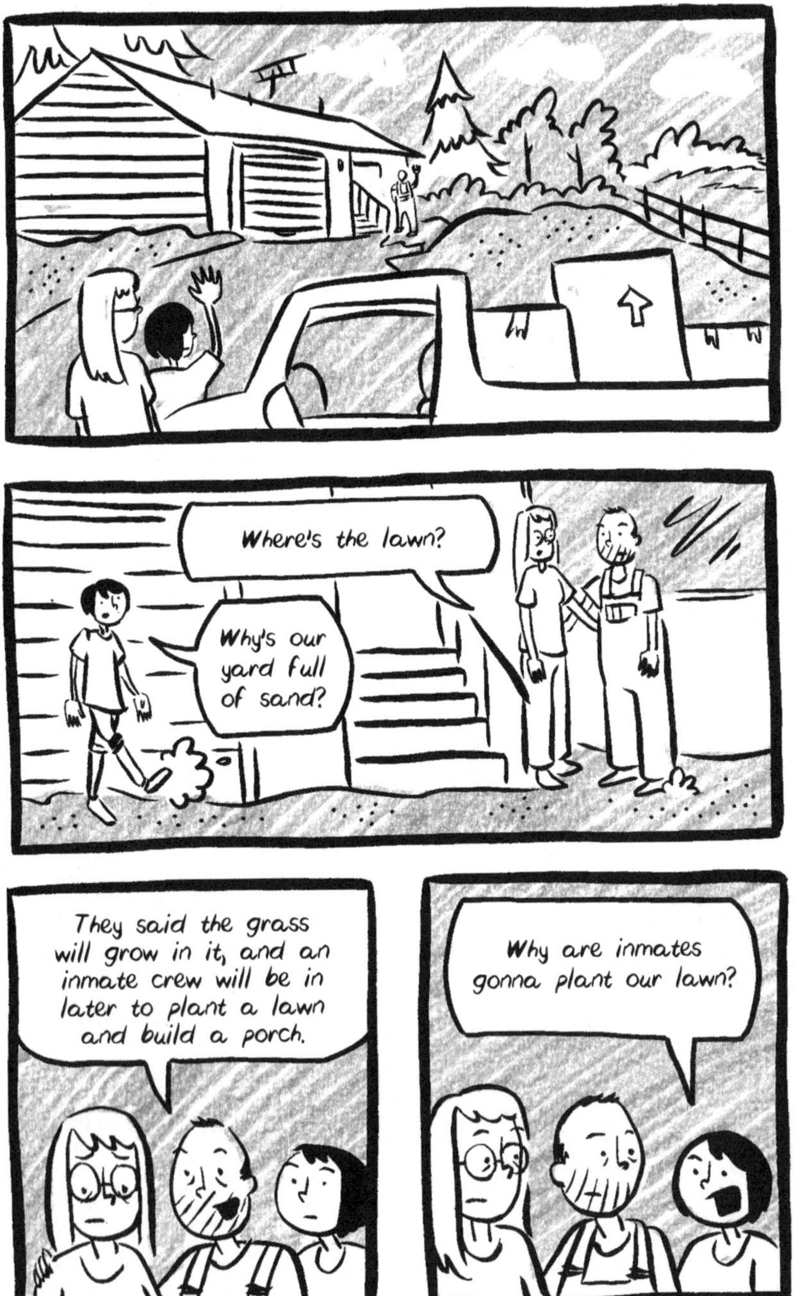
Where's the lawn?
Why's our yard full of sand?
They said the grass will grow in it, and an inmate crew will be in later to plant a lawn and build a porch.
Why are inmates gonna plant our lawn?

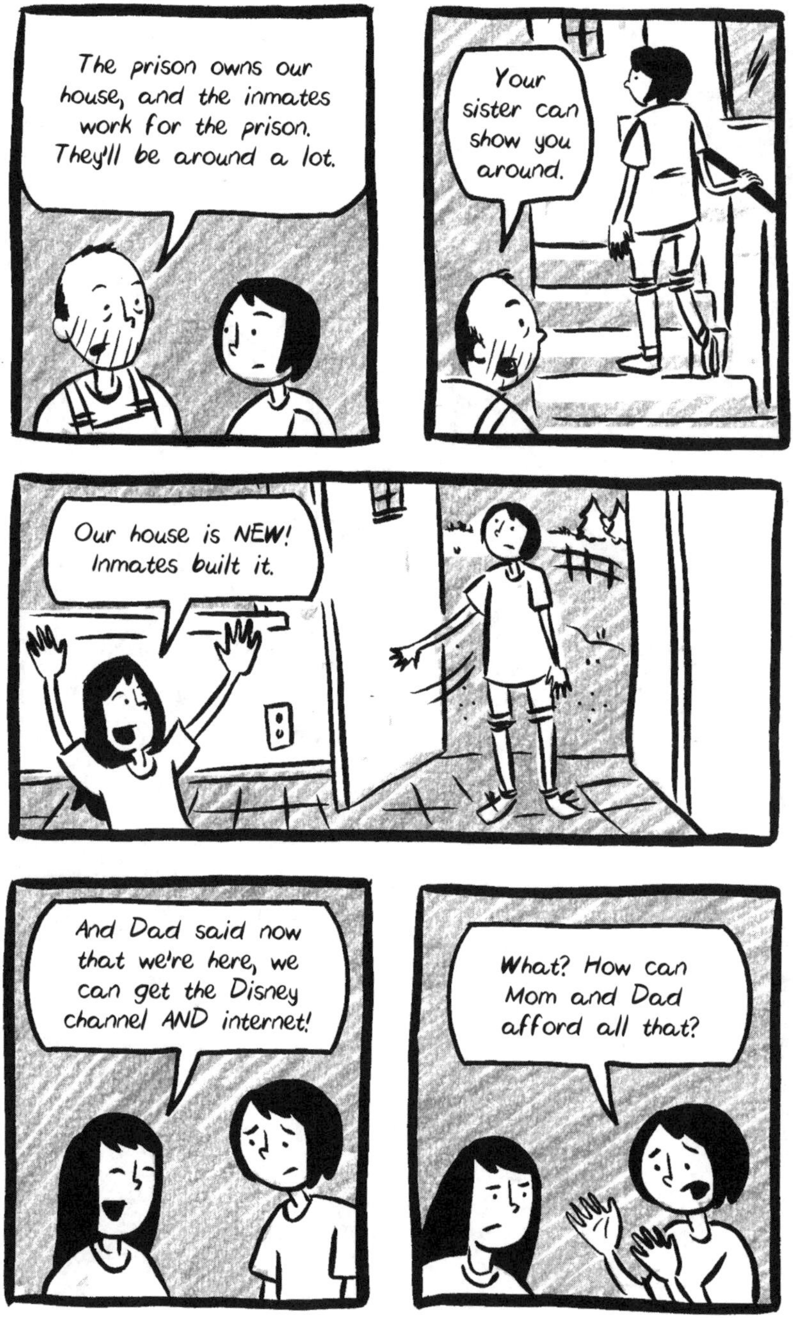
The prison owns our house, and the inmates work for the prison. They'll be around a lot.
Your sister can show you around.
Our house is NEW! Inmates built it.
And Dad said now that we're here, we can get the Disney channel AND internet!
What? How can Mom and Dad afford all that?

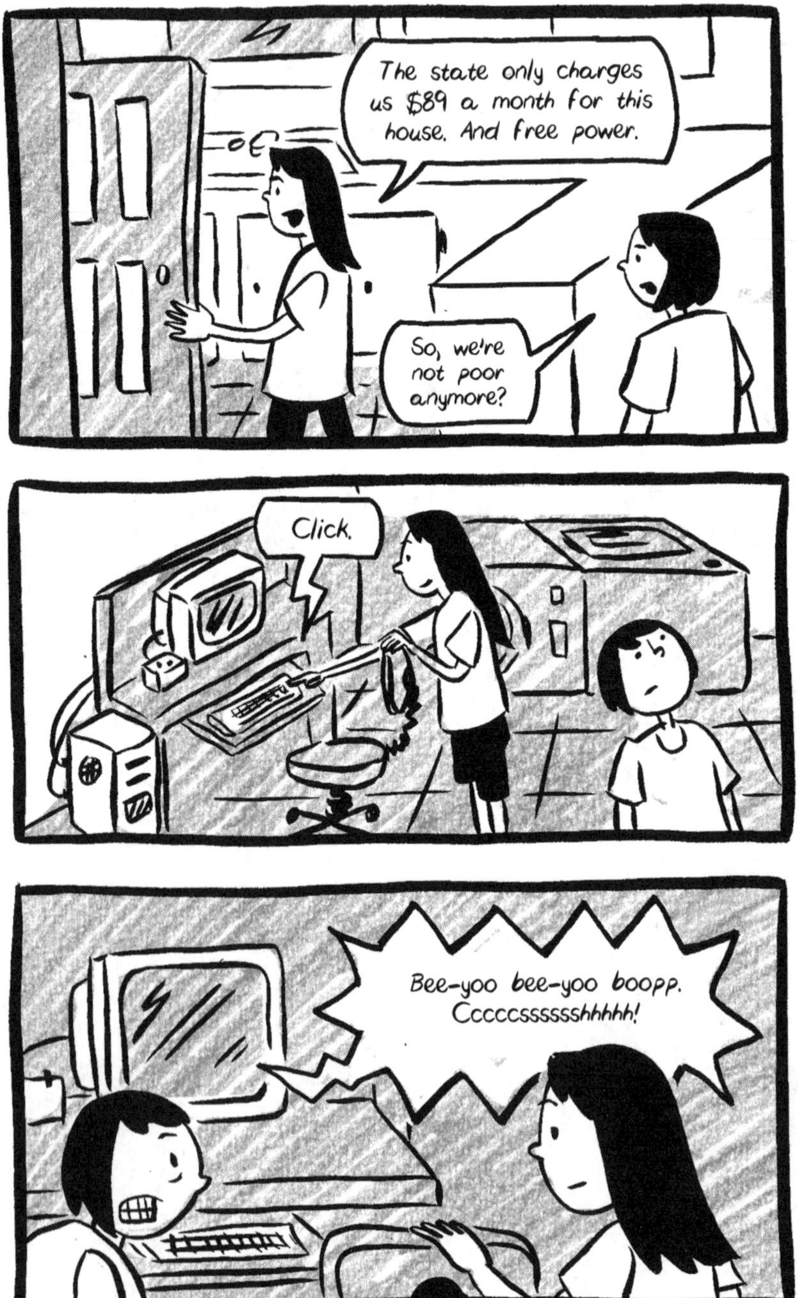
The state only charges us $89 a month for this house. And free power.
So, we're not poor anymore?
Click.
Bee-yoo bee-yoo boopp. Cccccsssssshhhhh!

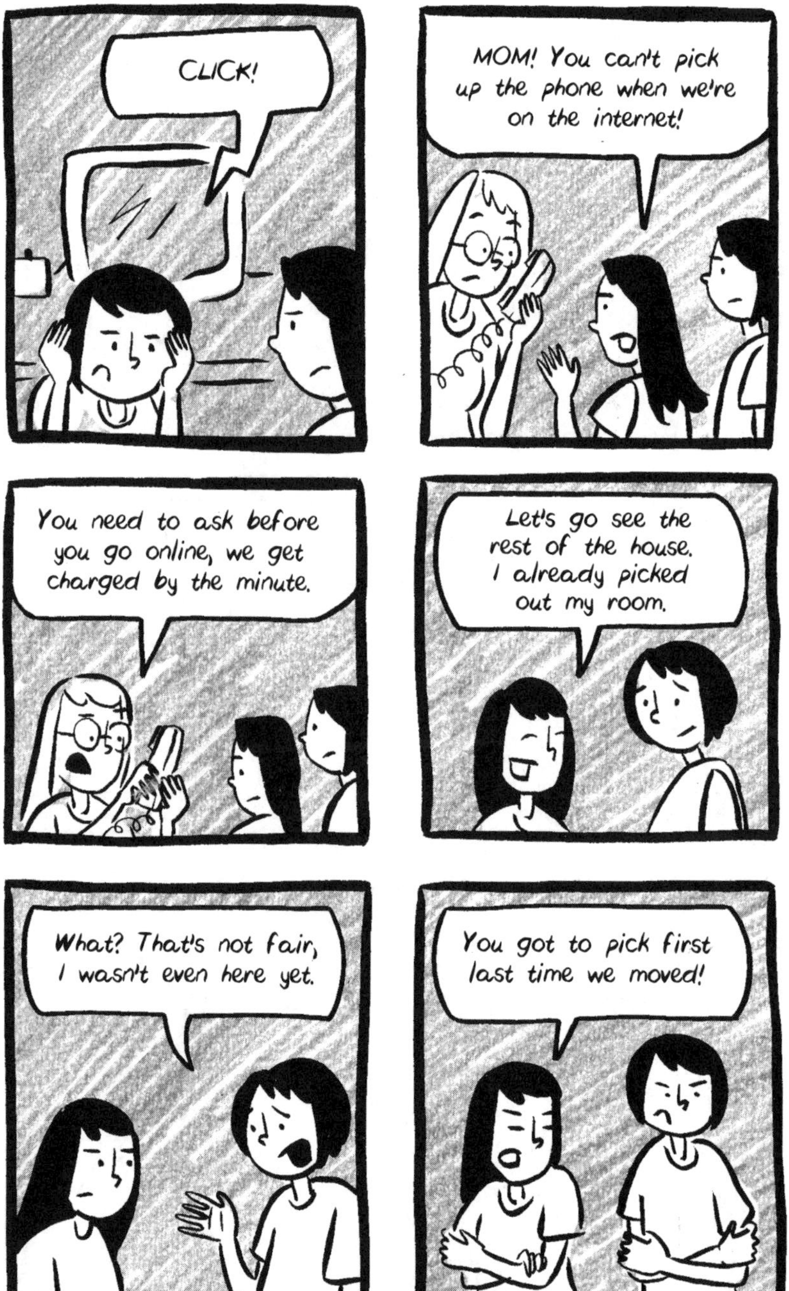
CLICK!
MOM! You can't pick up the phone when we're on the internet!
You need to ask before you go online, we get charged by the minute.
Let's go see the rest of the house. I already picked out my room.
What? That's not fair, I wasn't even here yet.
You got to pick first last time we moved!

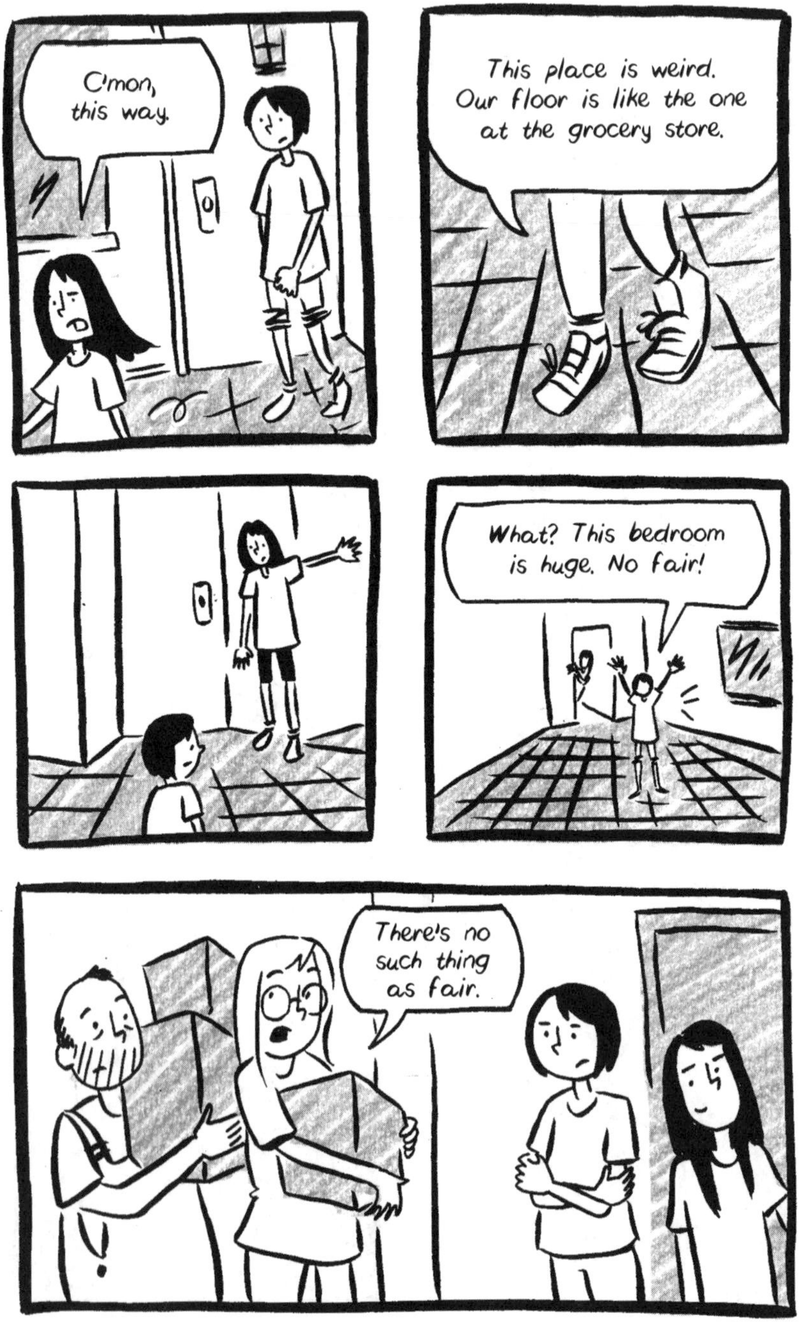
C'mon, this way.
This place is weird. Our floor is like the one at the grocery store.
What? This bedroom is huge. No fair!
There's no such thing as fair.

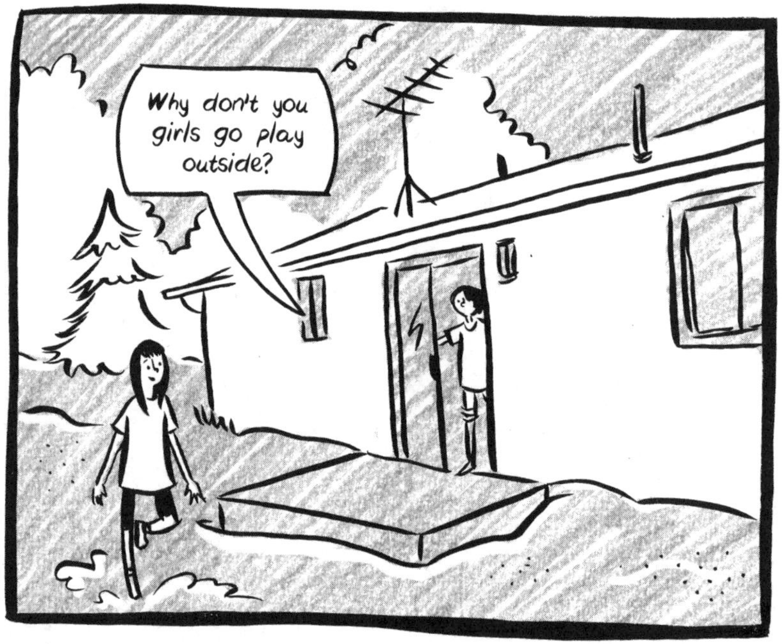
Why don't you girls go play outside?

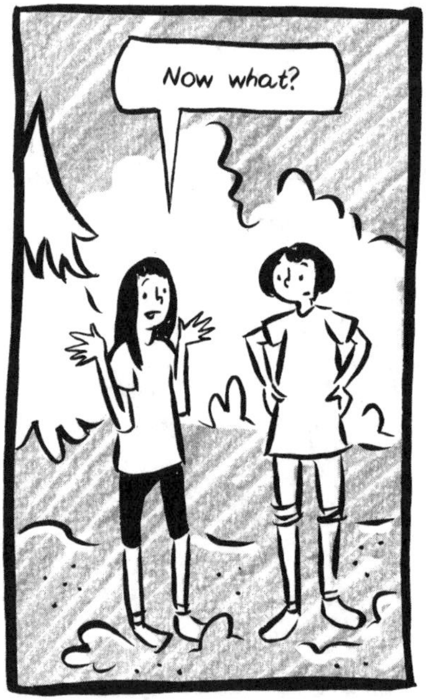
Now what?

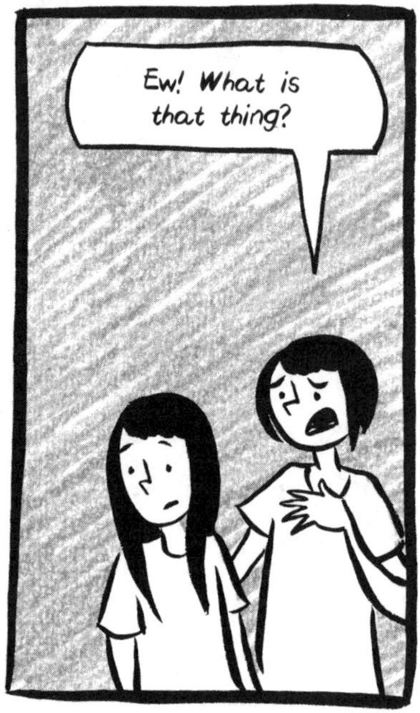
Ew! What is that thing?

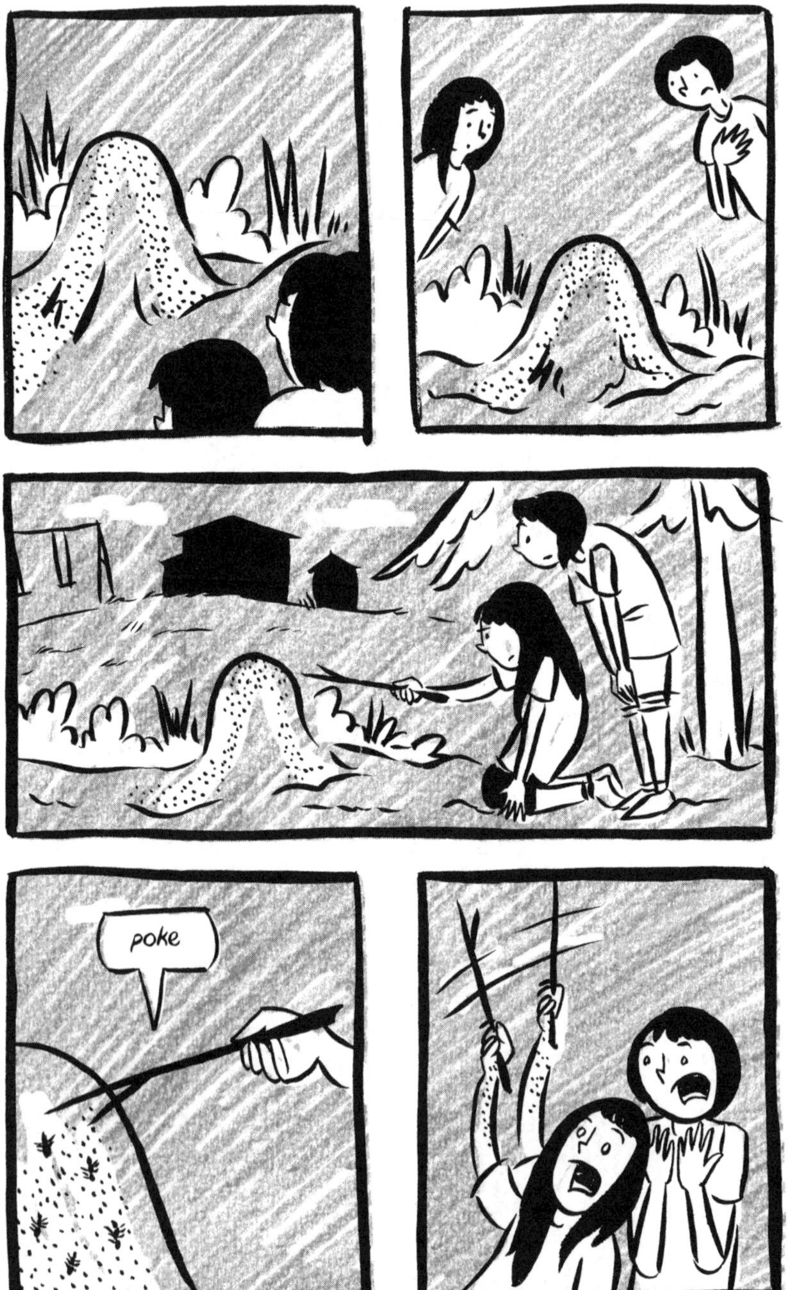
poke

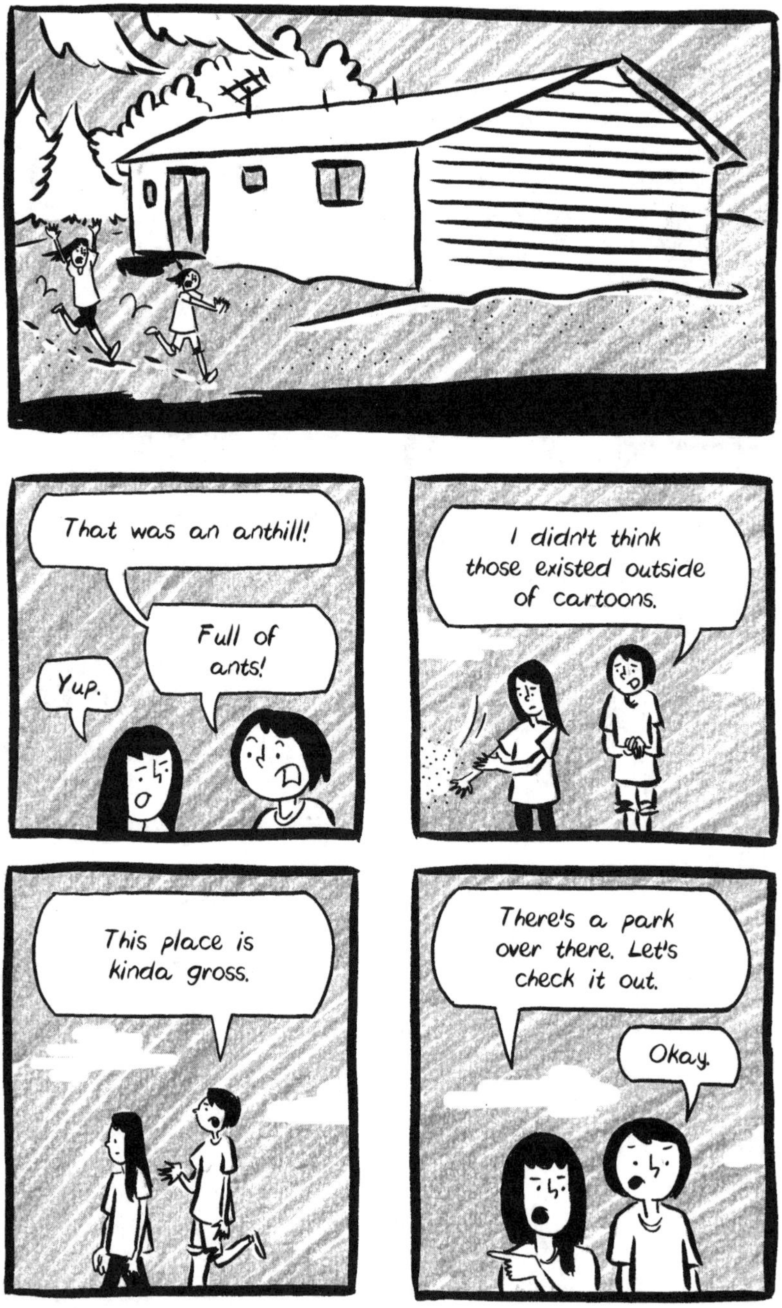
That was an anthill!
Full of ants!
Yup.
I didn't think those existed outside of cartoons.
This place is kinda gross.
There's a park over there. Let's check it out.
Okay.

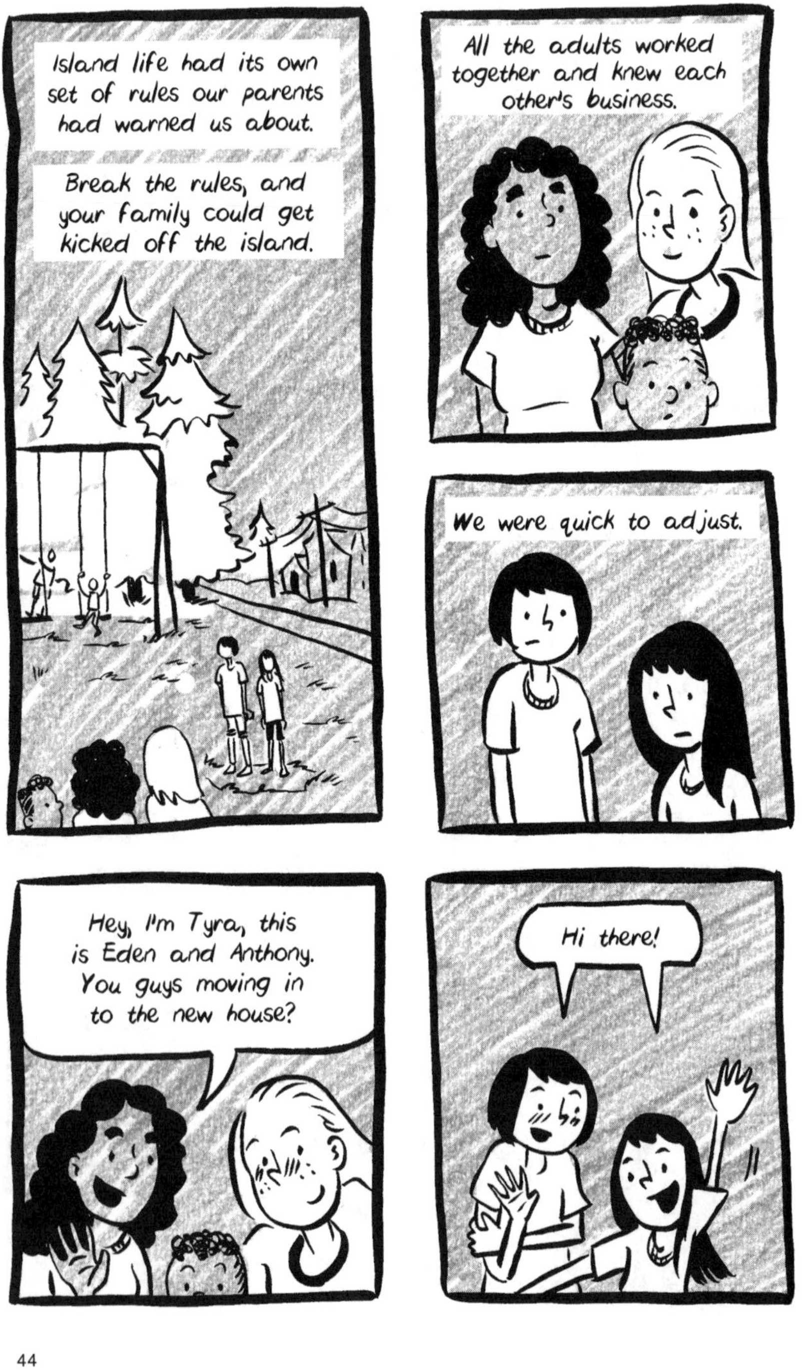
Island life had its own set of rules our parents had warned us about.
Break the rules, and your family could get kicked off the island.
All the adults worked together and knew each other's business.
We were quick to adjust.
Hey, I'm Tyra, this is Eden and Anthony. You guys moving in to the new house?
Hi there!

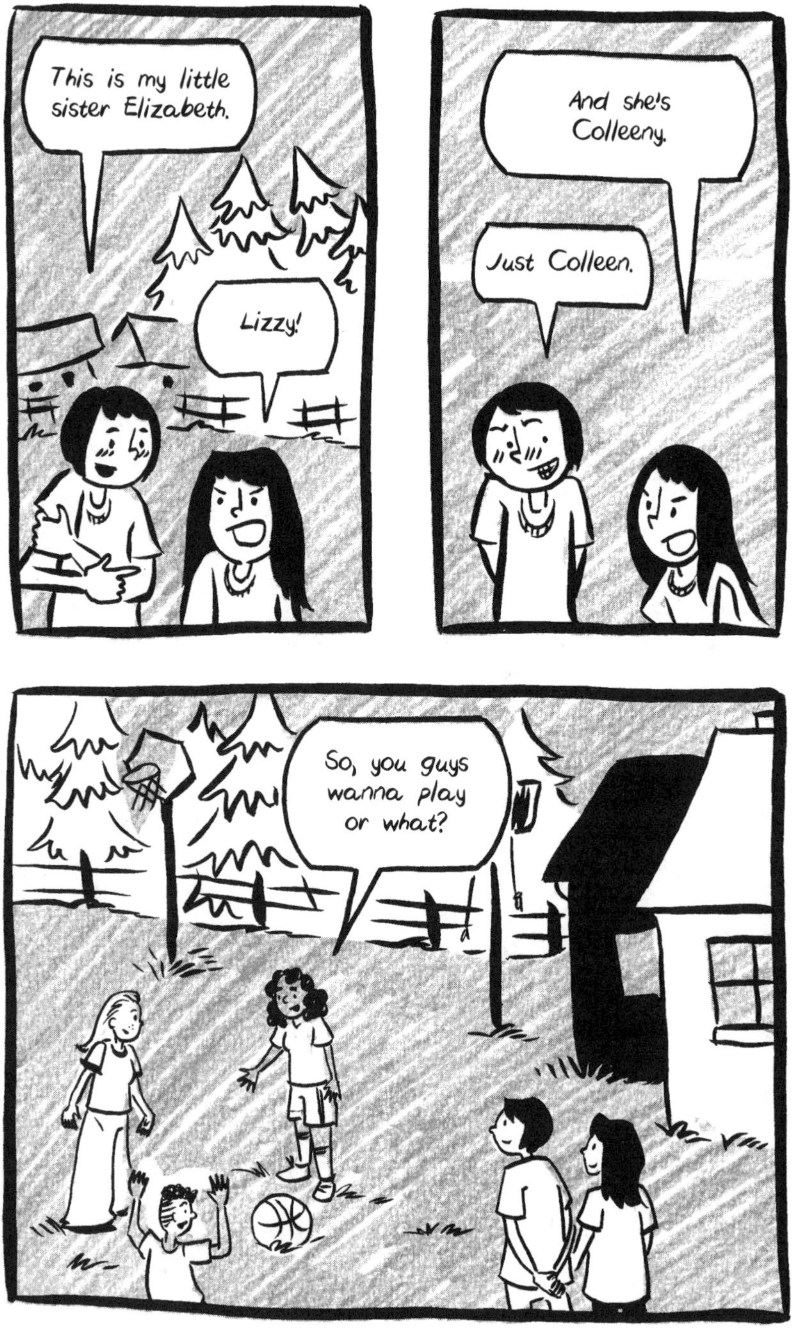
This is my little sister Elizabeth.
Lizzy!
And she's Colleeny.
Just Colleen.
So, you guys wanna play or what?

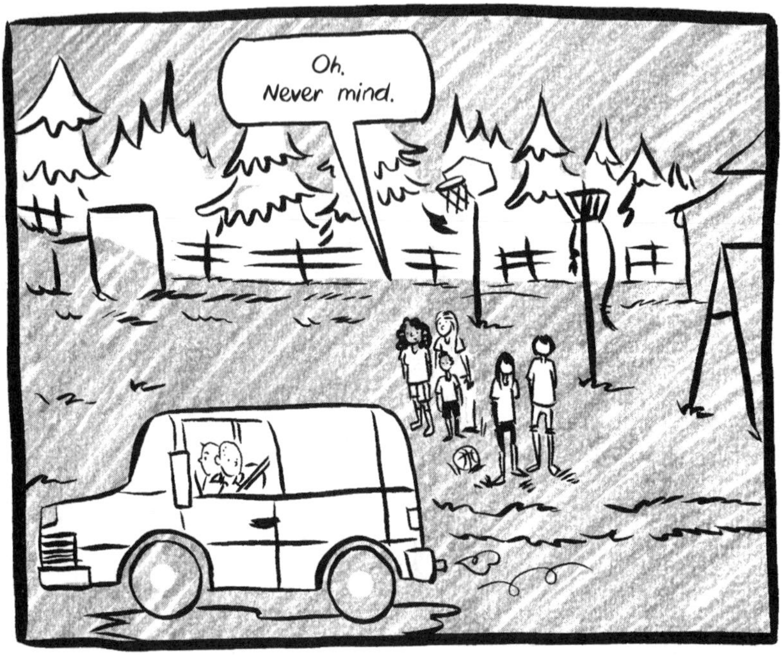
Oh.
Never mind.

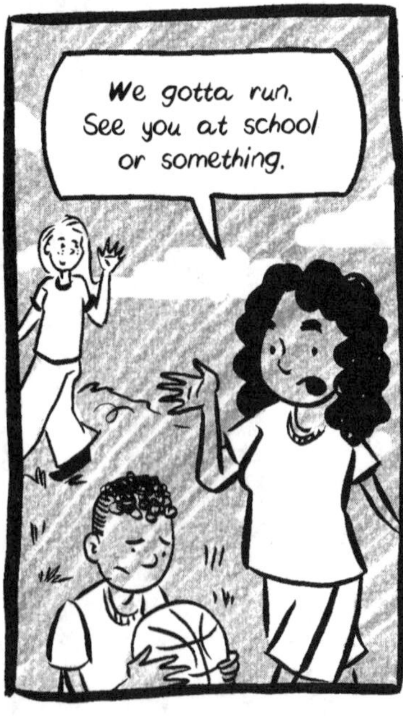
We gotta run.
See you at school
or something.

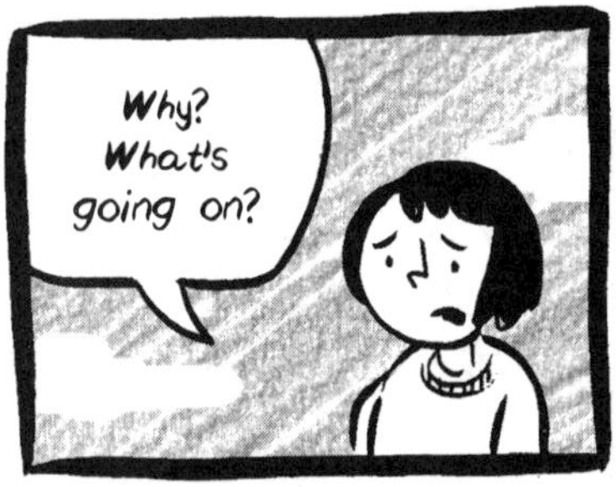
Why?
What's
going on?

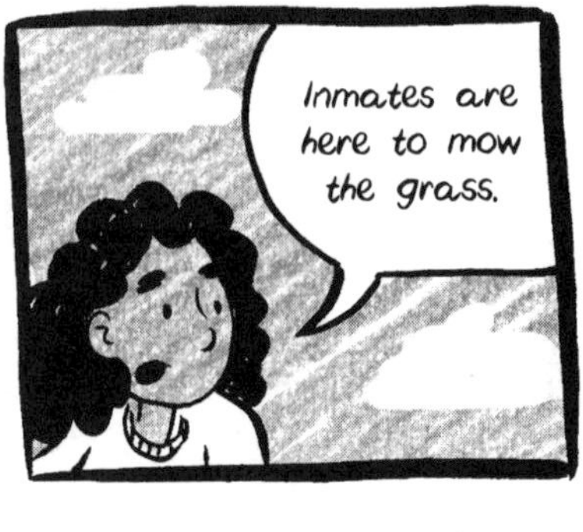
Inmates are
here to mow
the grass.

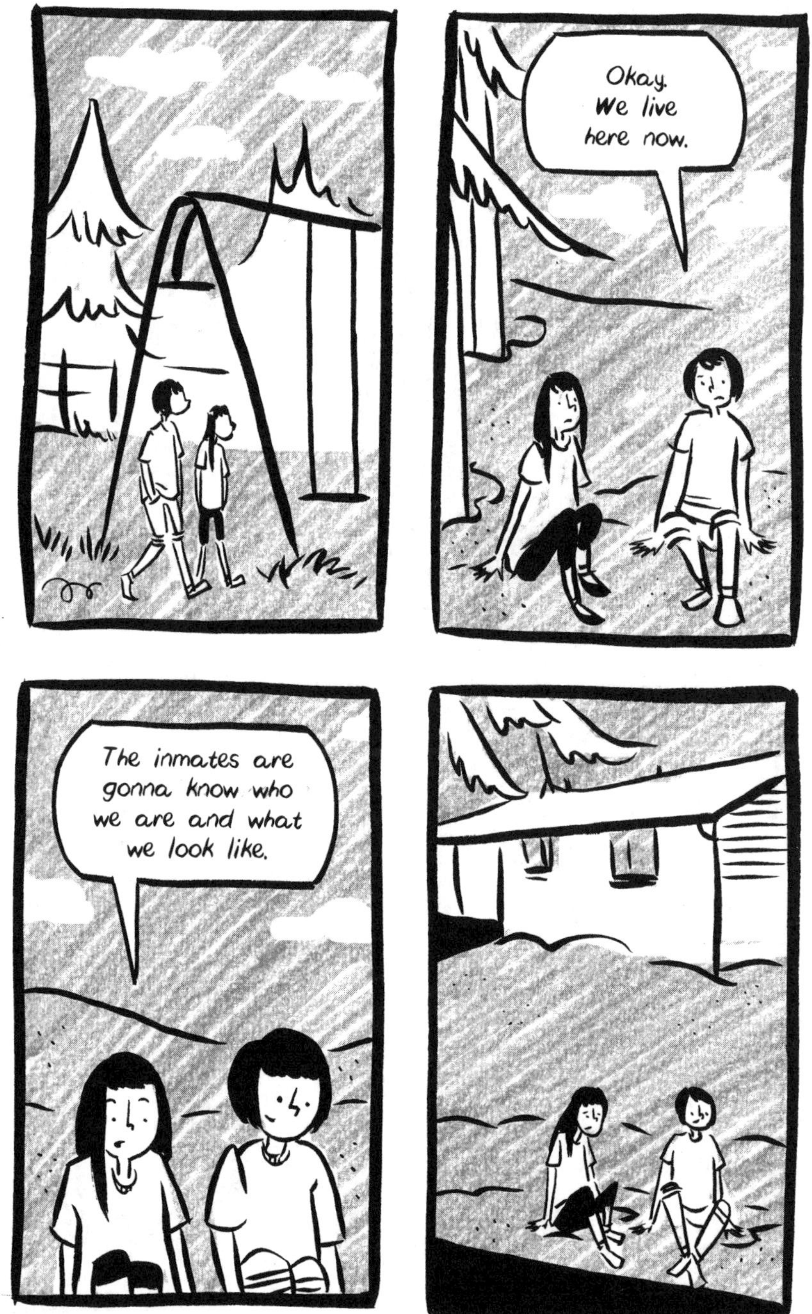
Okay. We live here now.
The inmates are gonna know who we are and what we look like.

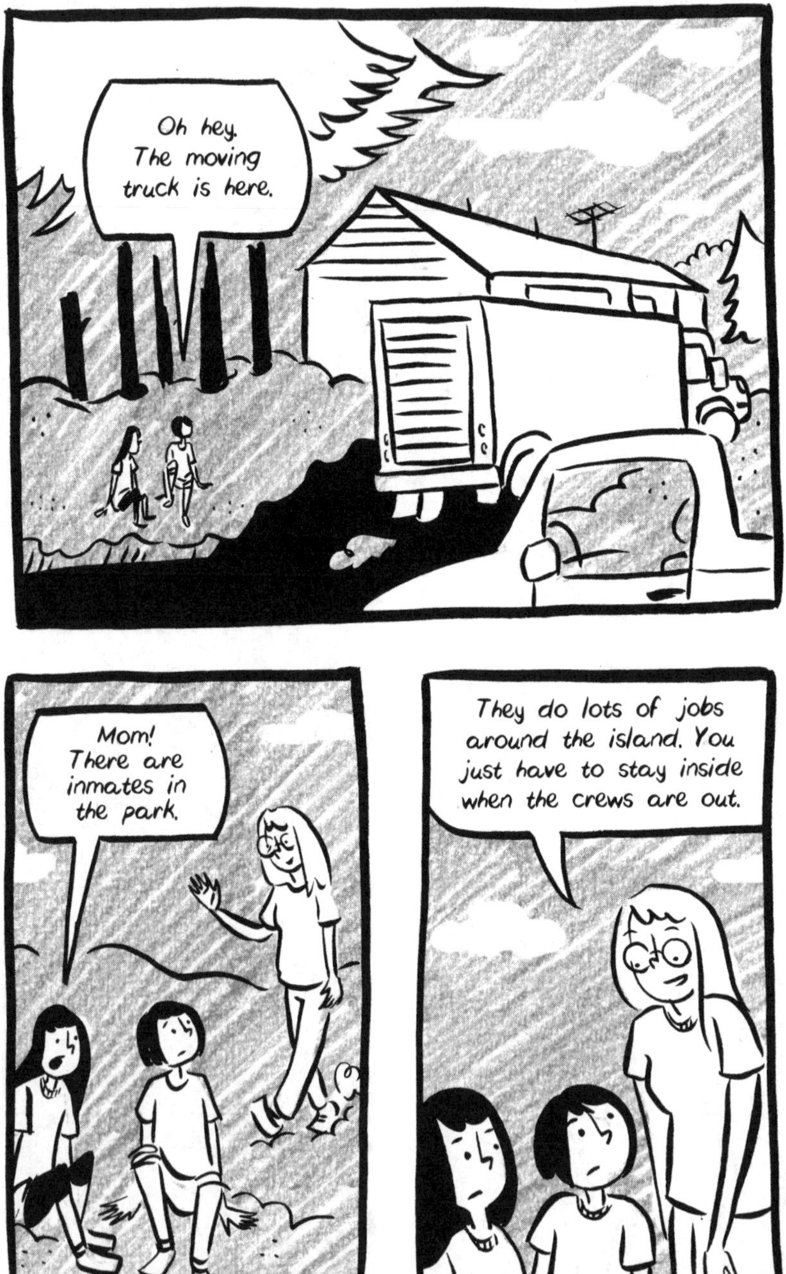
Oh hey. The moving truck is here.
Mom! There are inmates in the park.
They do lots of jobs around the island. You just have to stay inside when the crews are out.

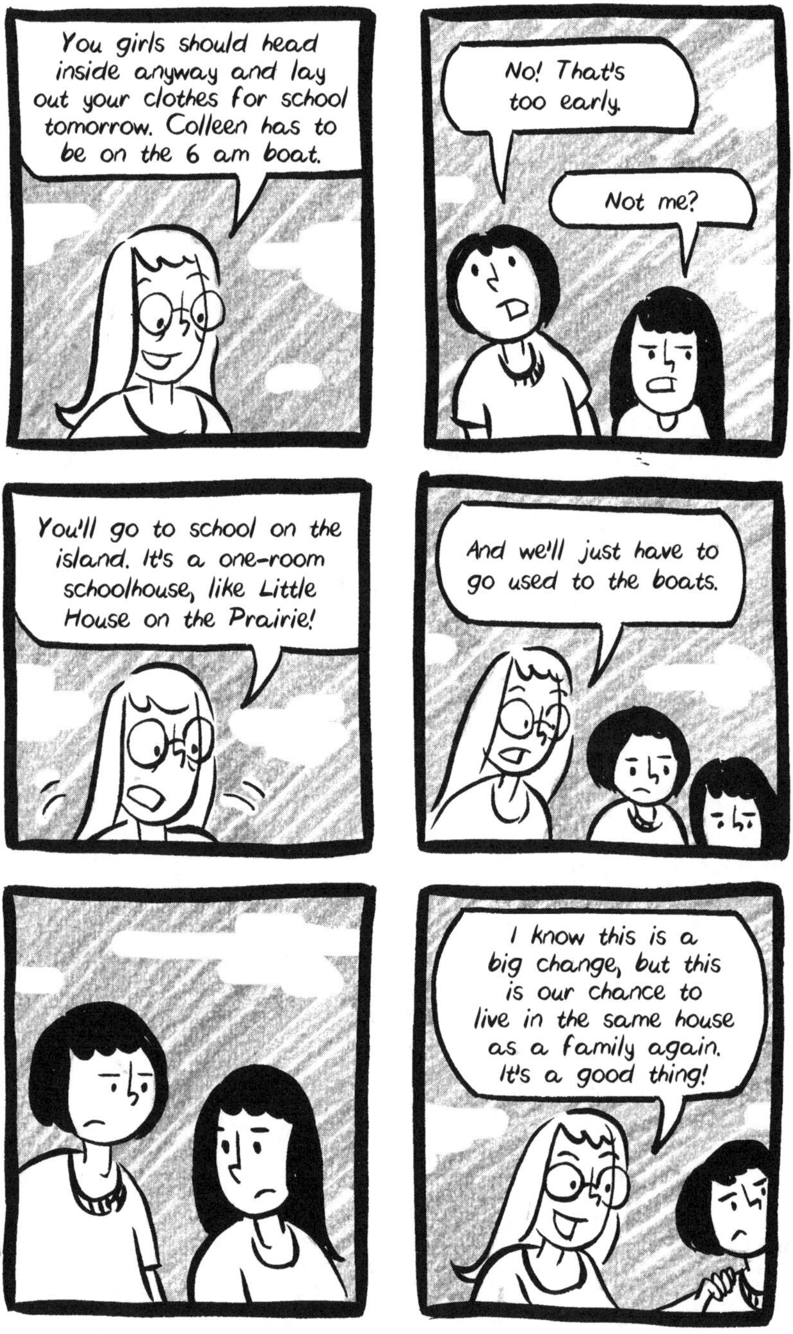
You girls should head inside anyway and lay out your clothes for school tomorrow. Colleen has to be on the 6 am boat.
No! That's too early.
Not me?
You'll go to school on the island. It's a one-room schoolhouse, like Little House on the Prairie!
And we'll just have to go used to the boats.
I know this is a big change, but this is our chance to live in the same house as a family again. It's a good thing!

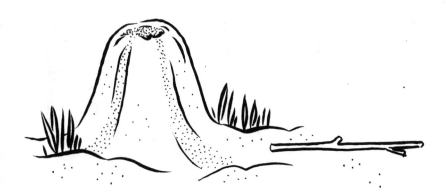

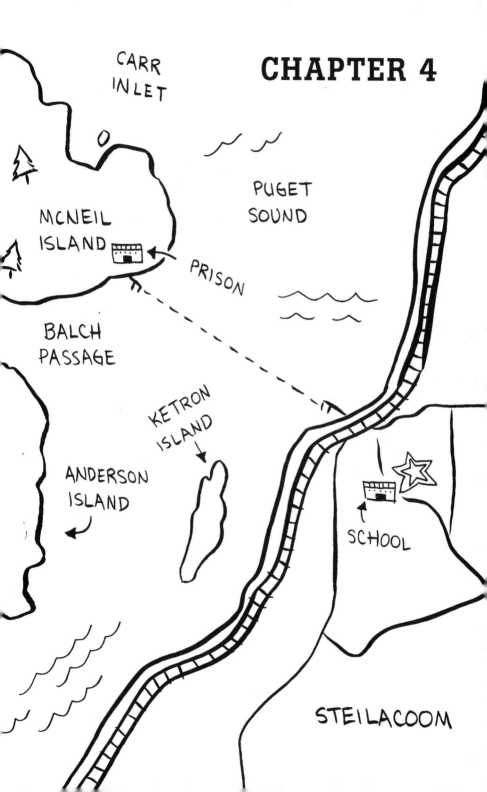

CHAPTER 4

CARR
INLET

PUGET
SOUND

MCNEIL
ISLAND

PRISON

BALCH
PASSAGE

KETRON
ISLAND

ANDERSON
ISLAND

SCHOOL

STEILACOOM

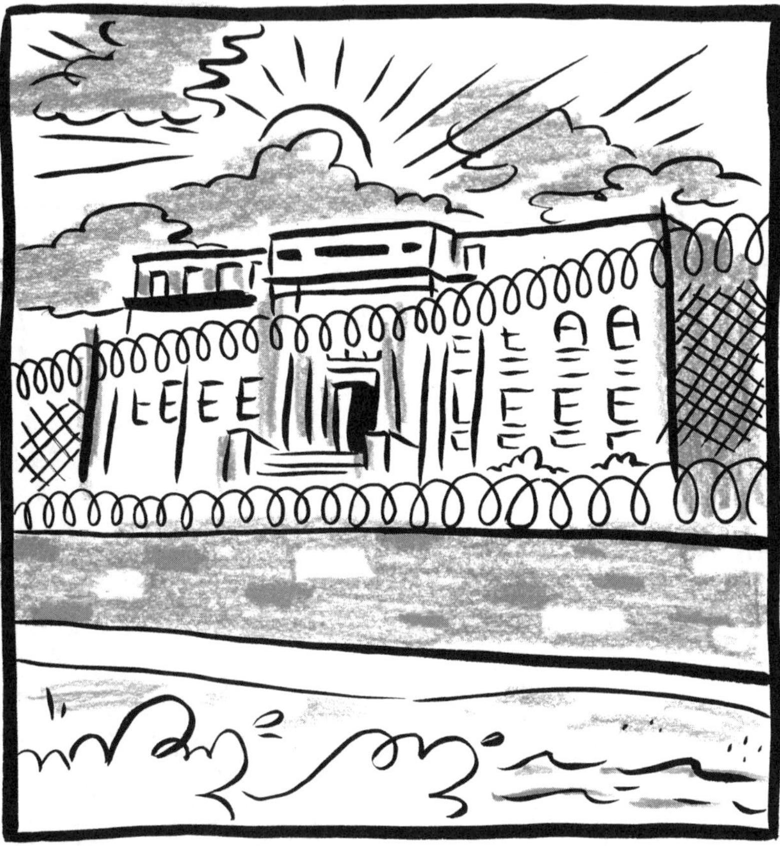

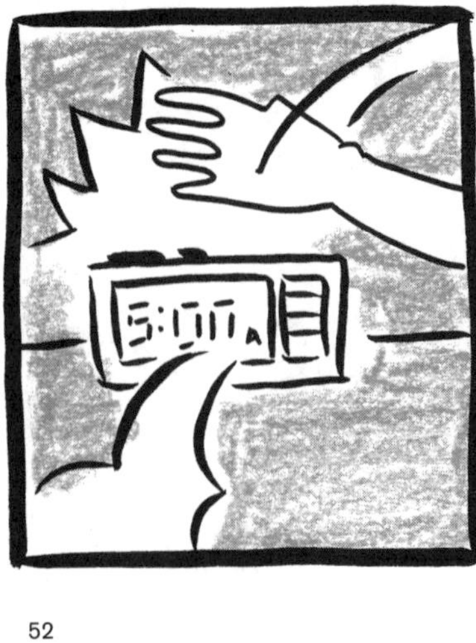

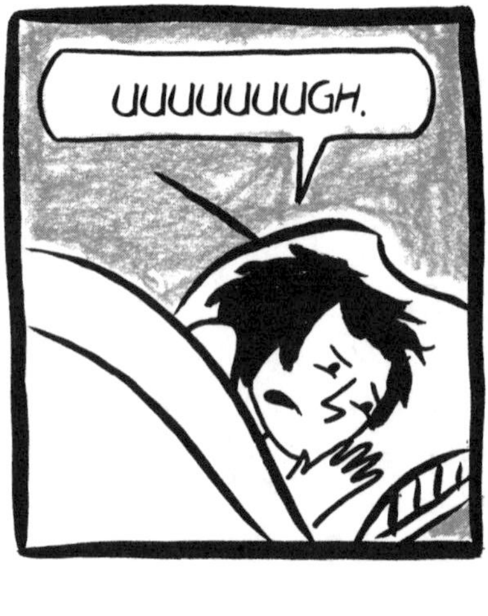
UUUUUUUGH.

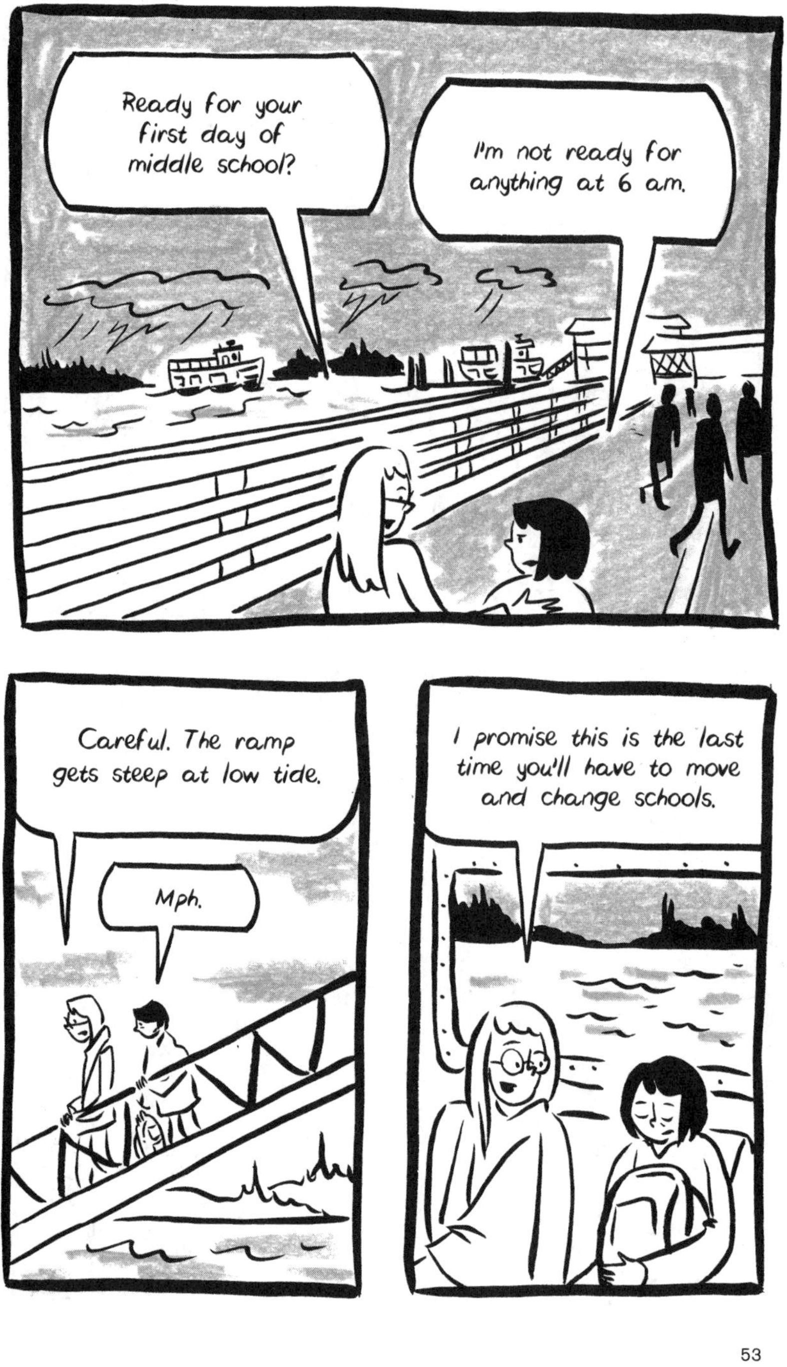
Ready for your first day of middle school?
I'm not ready for anything at 6 am.
Careful. The ramp gets steep at low tide.
Mph.
I promise this is the last time you'll have to move and change schools.

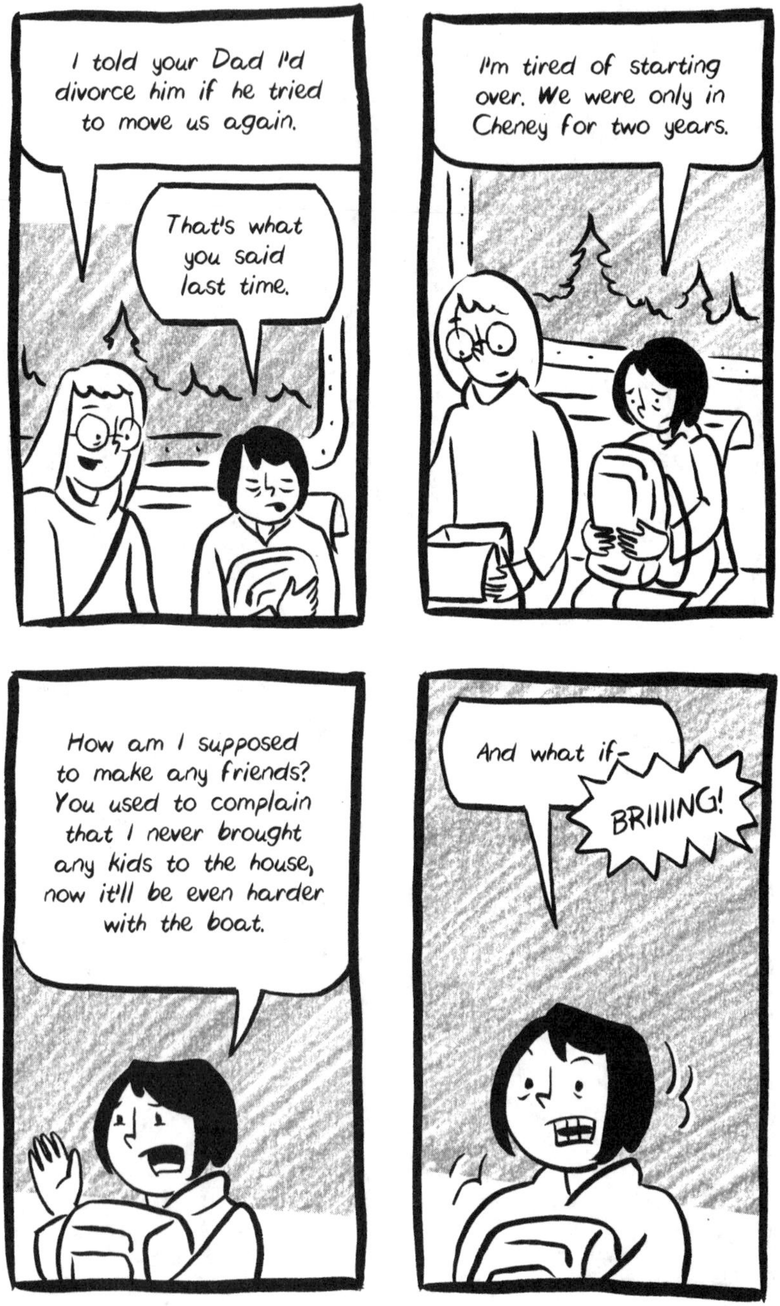
I told your Dad I'd divorce him if he tried to move us again.
That's what you said last time.
I'm tired of starting over. We were only in Cheney for two years.
How am I supposed to make any friends? You used to complain that I never brought any kids to the house, now it'll be even harder with the boat.
And what if-
BRIIIING!

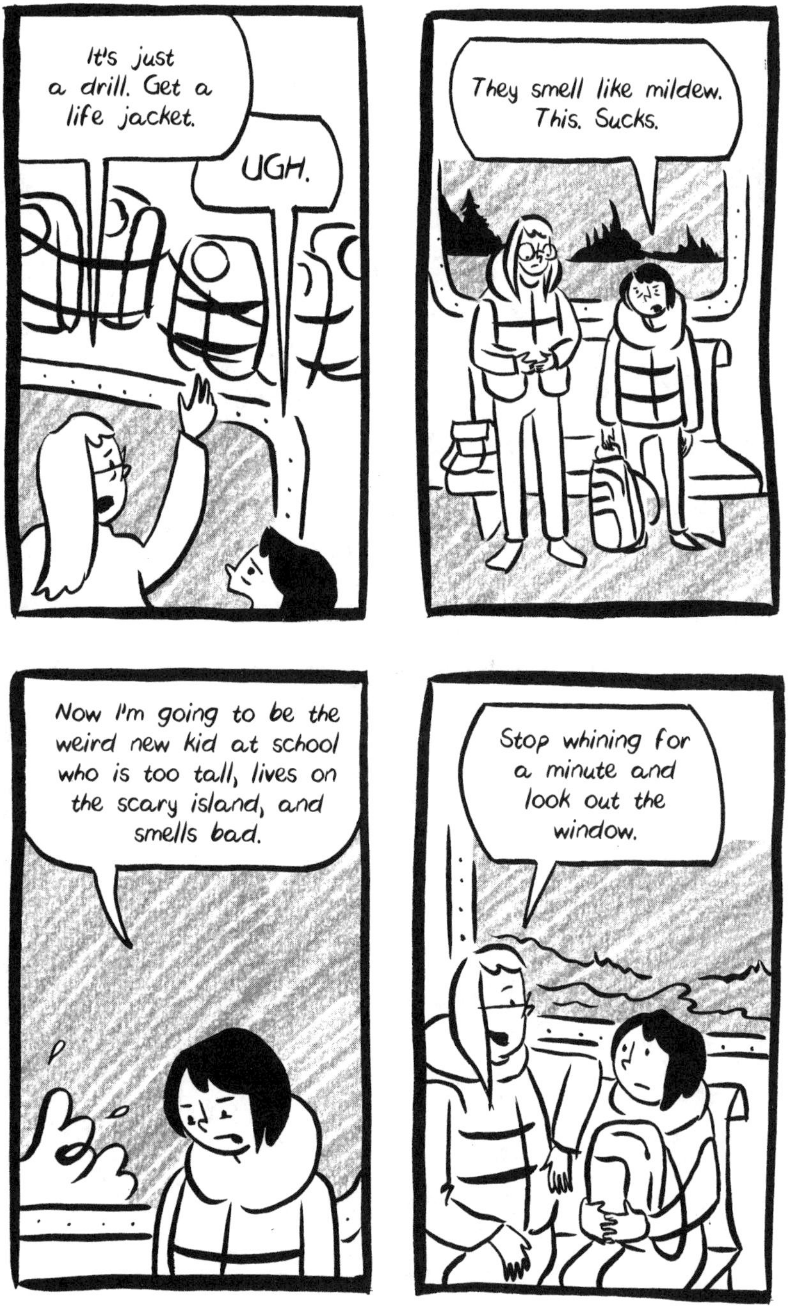
It's just a drill. Get a life jacket.
UGH.
They smell like mildew. This. Sucks.
Now I'm going to be the weird new kid at school who is too tall, lives on the scary island, and smells bad.
Stop whining for a minute and look out the window.

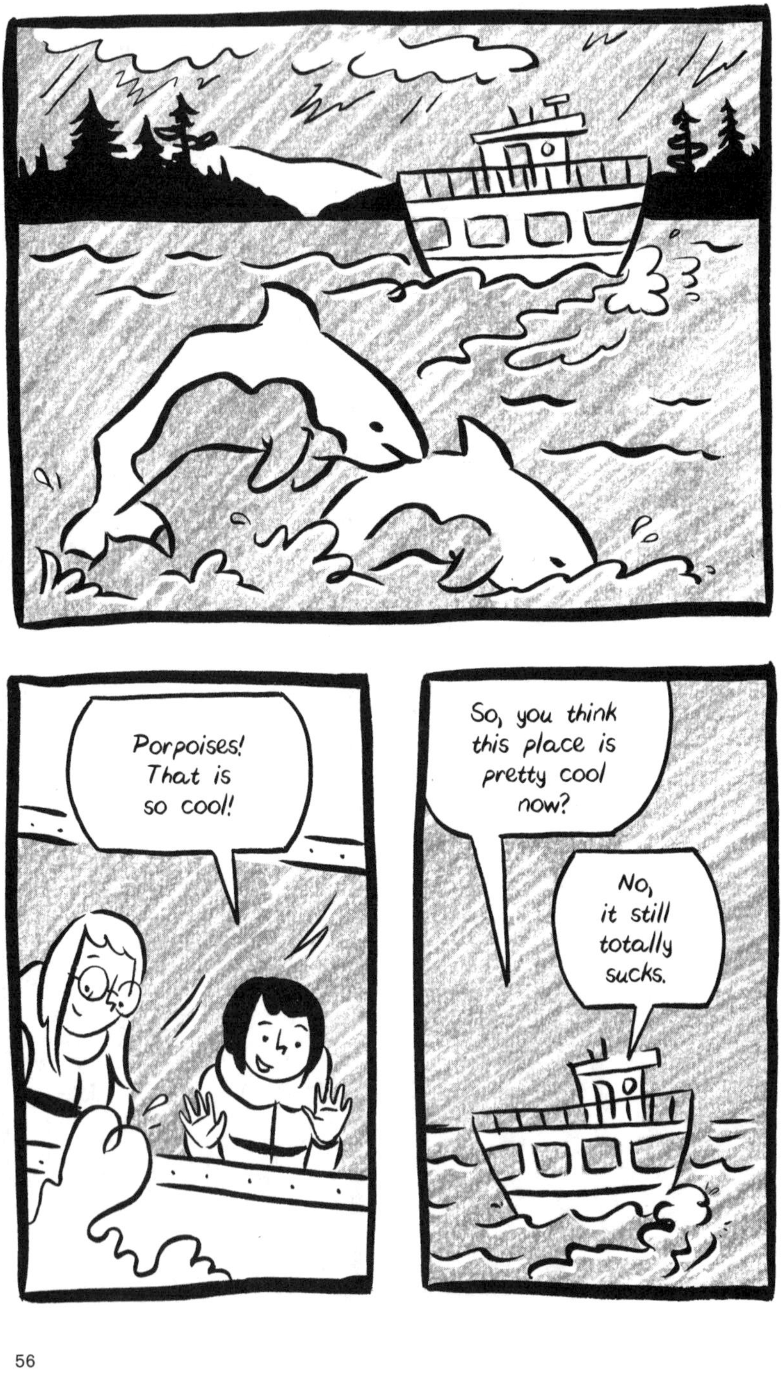
Porpoises!
That is
so cool!
So, you think
this place is
pretty cool
now?
No,
it still
totally
sucks.

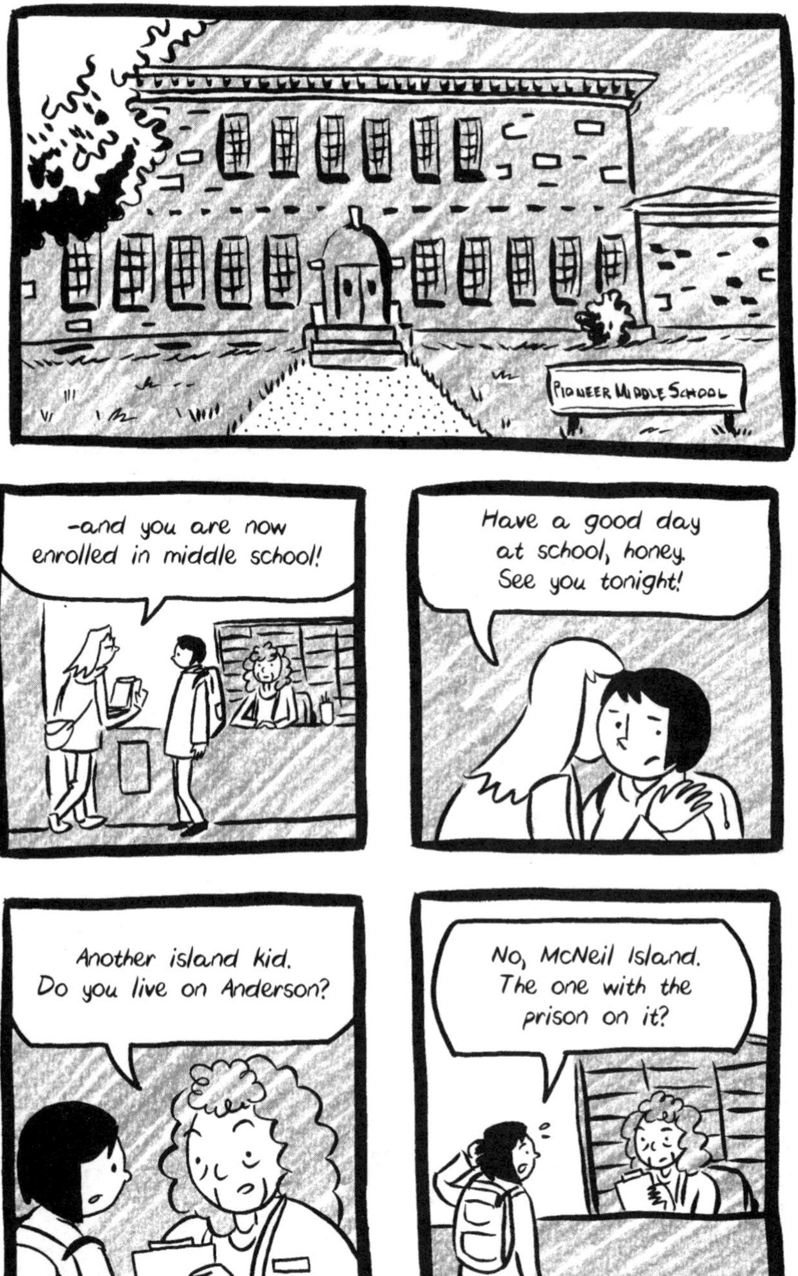
PIONEER MIDDLE SCHOOL
-and you are now enrolled in middle school!
Have a good day at school, honey. See you tonight!
Another island kid. Do you live on Anderson?
No, McNeil Island. The one with the prison on it?

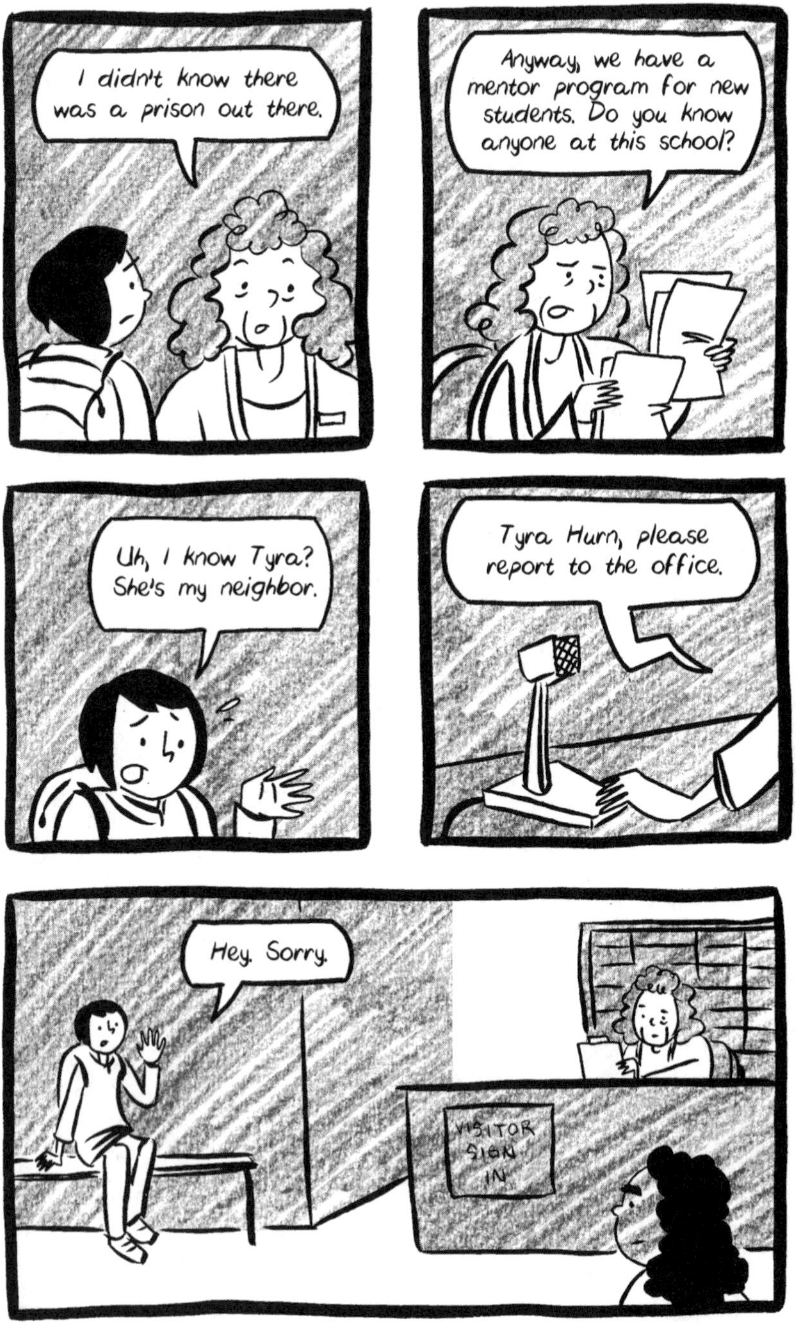
I didn't know there was a prison out there.
Anyway, we have a mentor program for new students. Do you know anyone at this school?
Uh, I know Tyra? She's my neighbor.
Tyra Hurn, please report to the office.
Hey. Sorry.
VISITOR SIGN IN

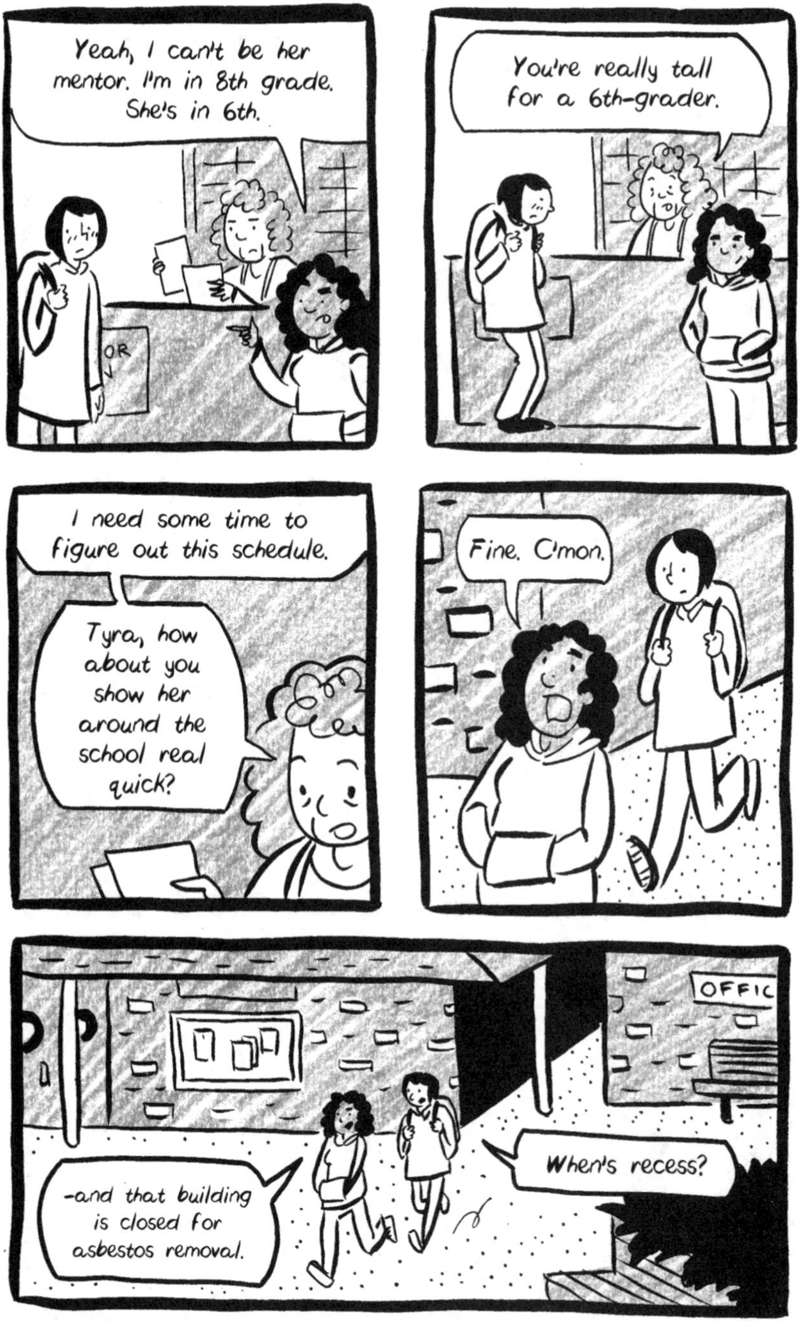
Yeah, I can't be her mentor. I'm in 8th grade. She's in 6th.
You're really tall for a 6th-grader.
I need some time to figure out this schedule.
Tyra, how about you show her around the school real quick?
Fine. C'mon.
OFFIC
-and that building is closed for asbestos removal.
When's recess?

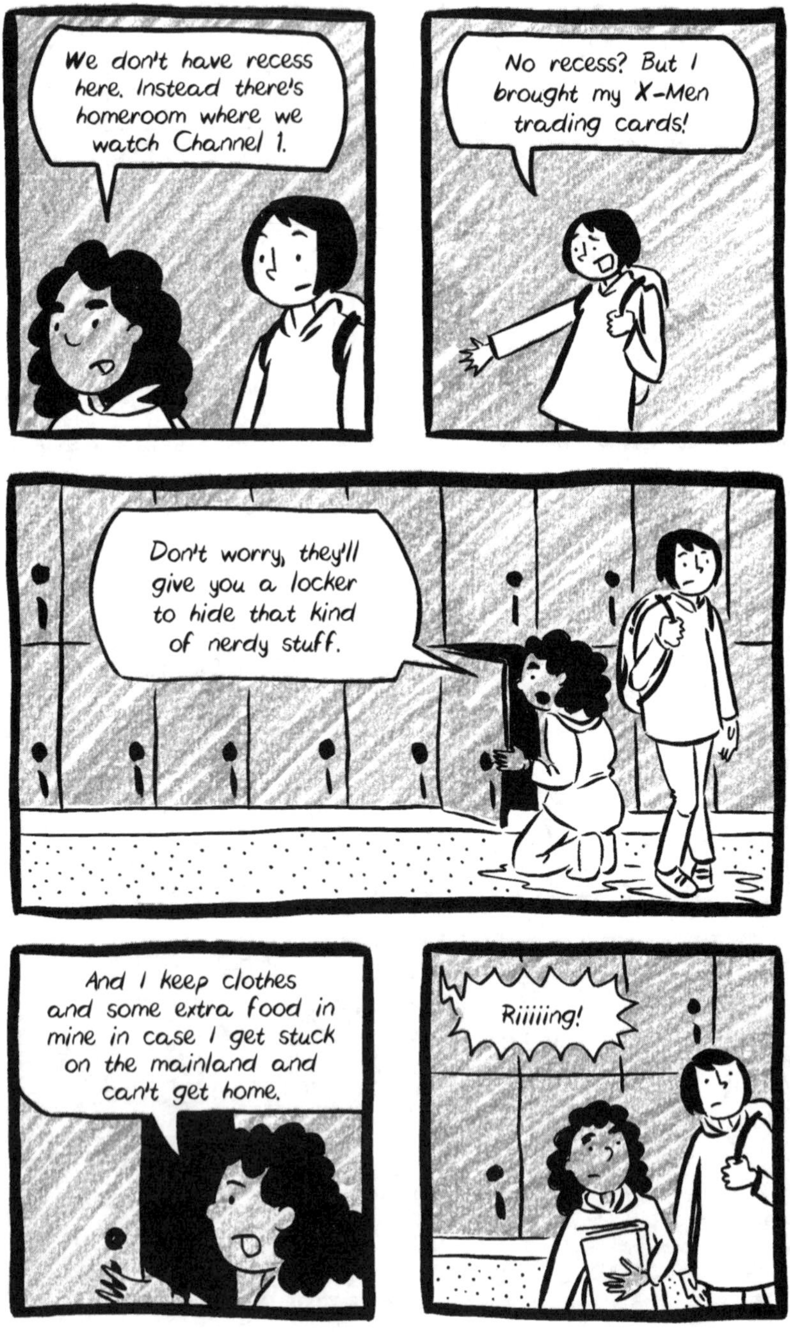
We don't have recess here. Instead there's homeroom where we watch Channel 1.
No recess? But I brought my X-Men trading cards!
Don't worry, they'll give you a locker to hide that kind of nerdy stuff.
And I keep clothes and some extra food in mine in case I get stuck on the mainland and can't get home.
Riiiiing!

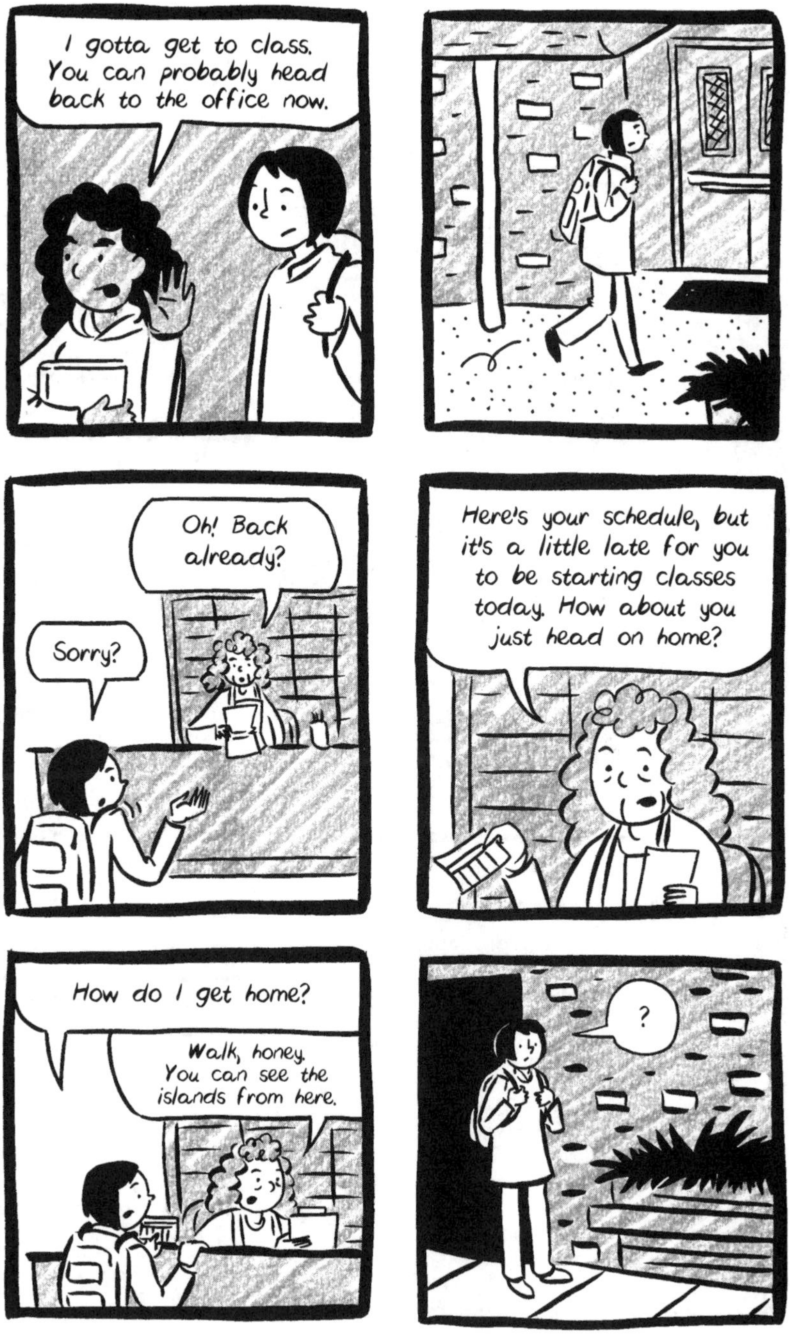
I gotta get to class. You can probably head back to the office now.
Oh! Back already?
Sorry?
Here's your schedule, but it's a little late for you to be starting classes today. How about you just head on home?
How do I get home?
Walk, honey. You can see the islands from here.
?

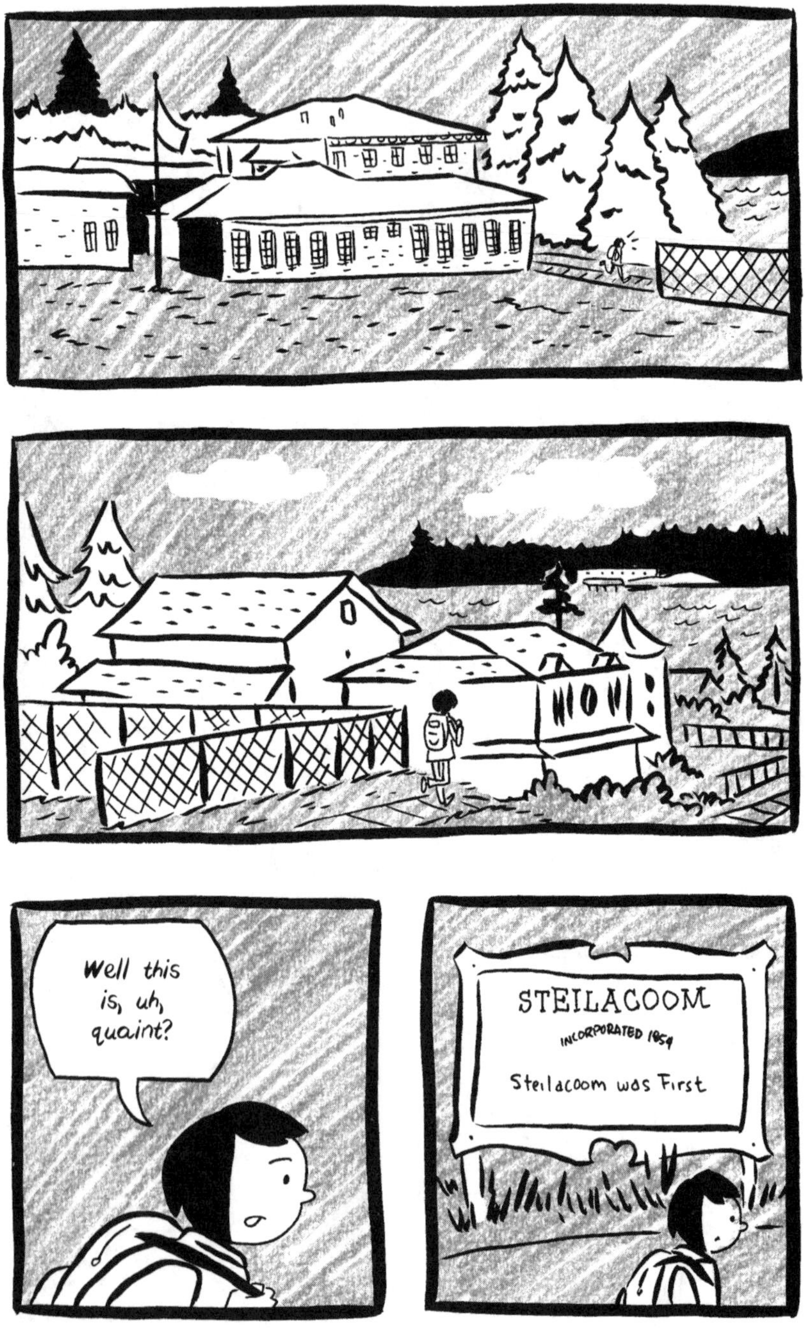
Well this is, uh, quaint?
STEILACOOM
INCORPORATED 1854
Steilacoom was First

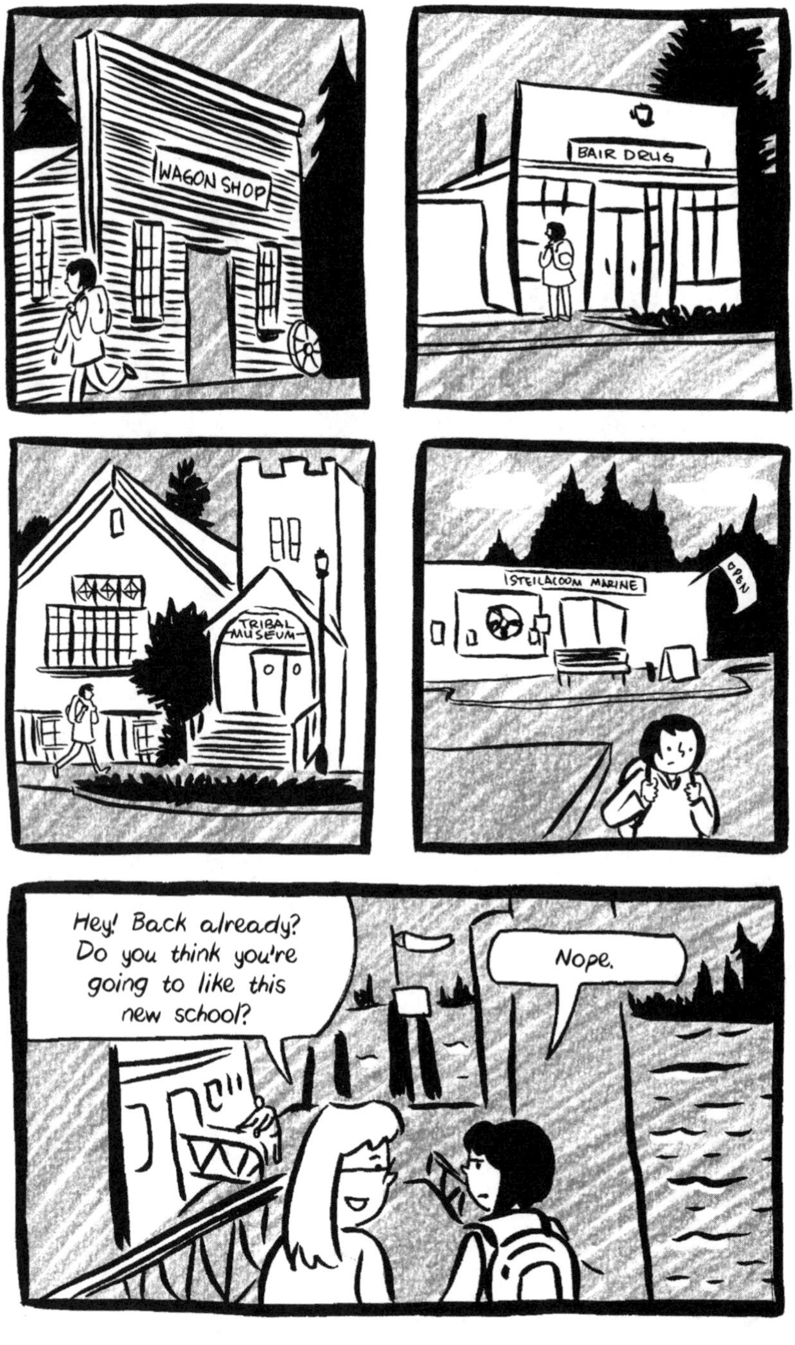
WAGON SHOP
BAIR DRUG
TRIBAL MUSEUM
STEILACOOM MARINE
OPEN
Hey! Back already? Do you think you're going to like this new school?
Nope.

CHAPTER 5

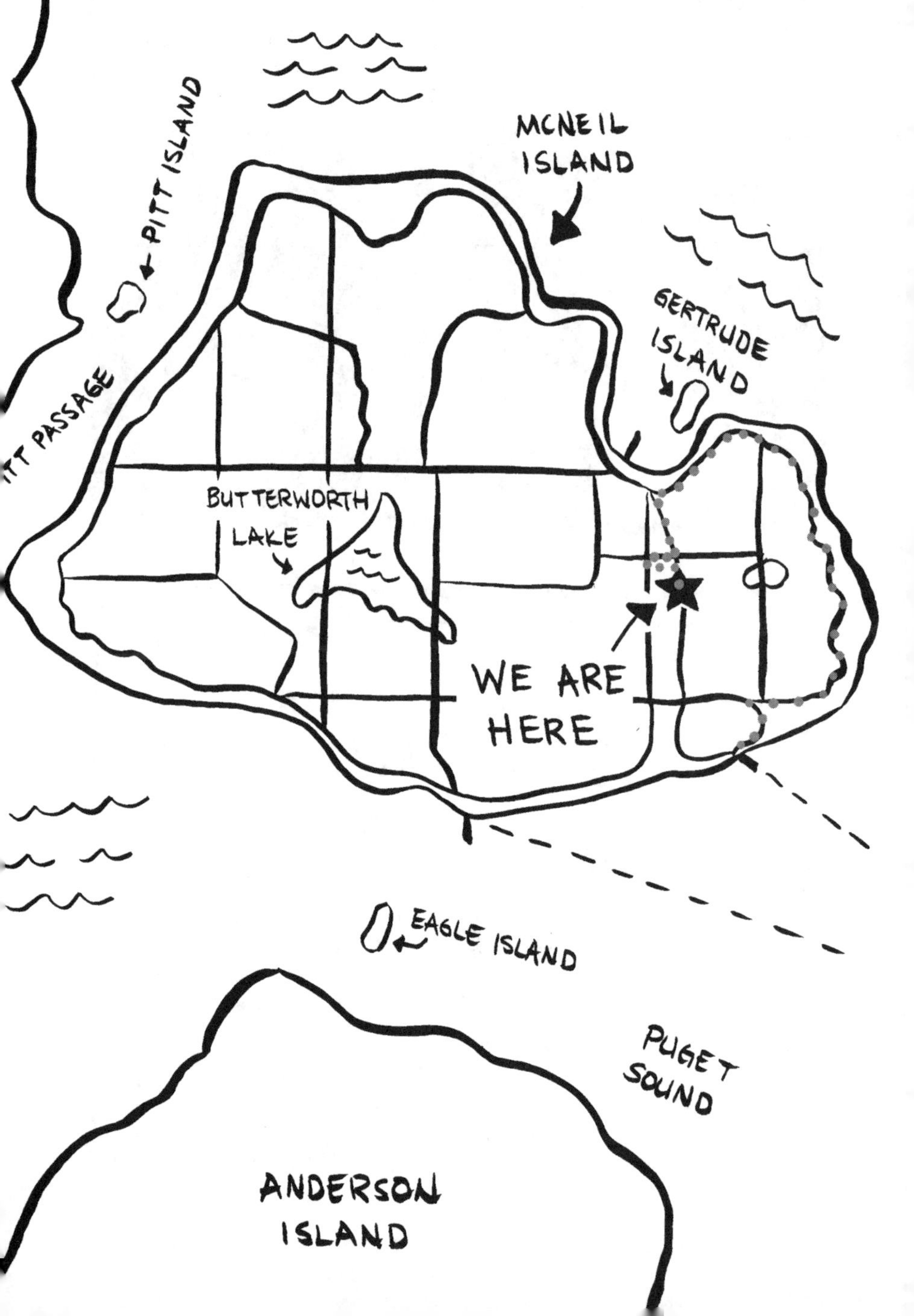

MCNEIL ISLAND
PITT ISLAND
ITT PASSAGE
GERTRUDE ISLAND
BUTTERWORTH LAKE
WE ARE HERE
EAGLE ISLAND
PUGET SOUND
ANDERSON ISLAND

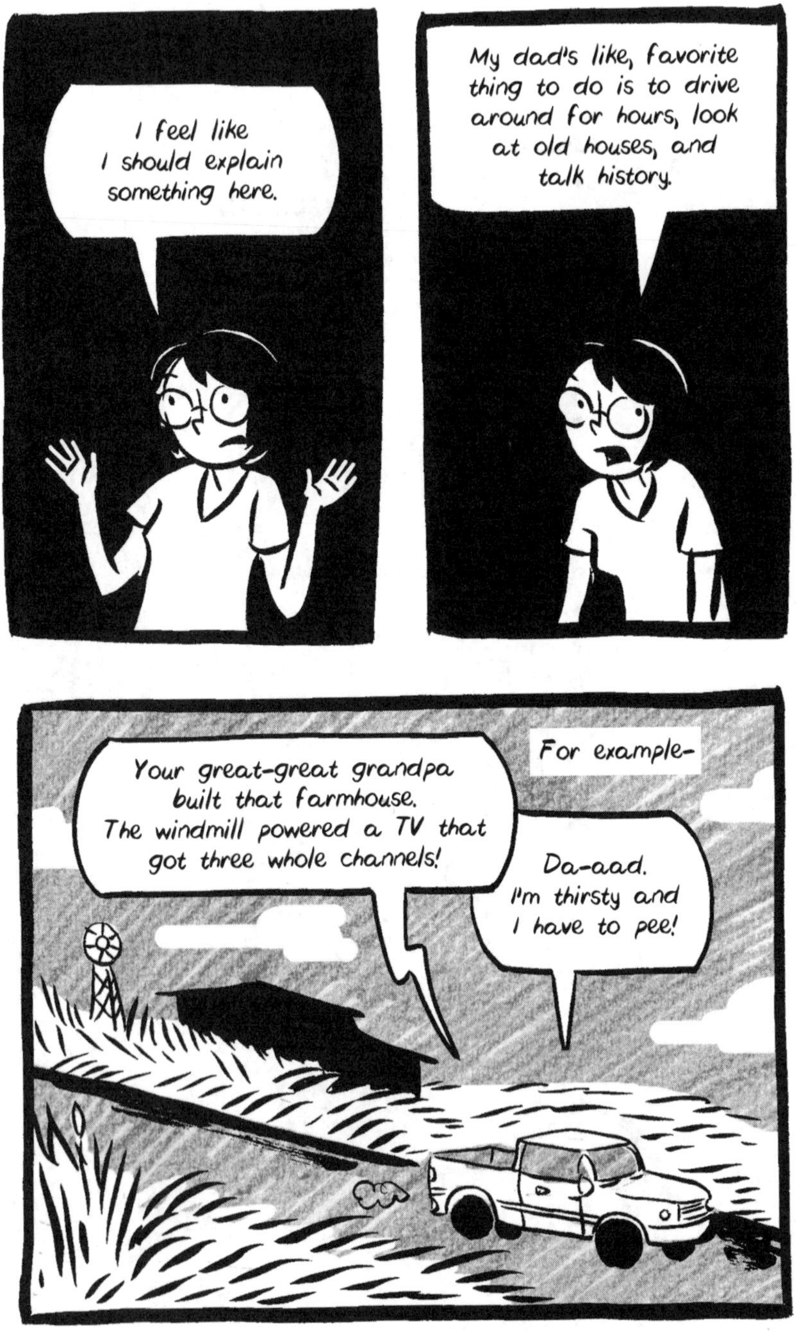
I feel like
I should explain
something here.
My dad's like, favorite thing to do is to drive around for hours, look at old houses, and talk history.
For example-
Your great-great grandpa built that farmhouse. The windmill powered a TV that got three whole channels!
Da-aad. I'm thirsty and I have to pee!

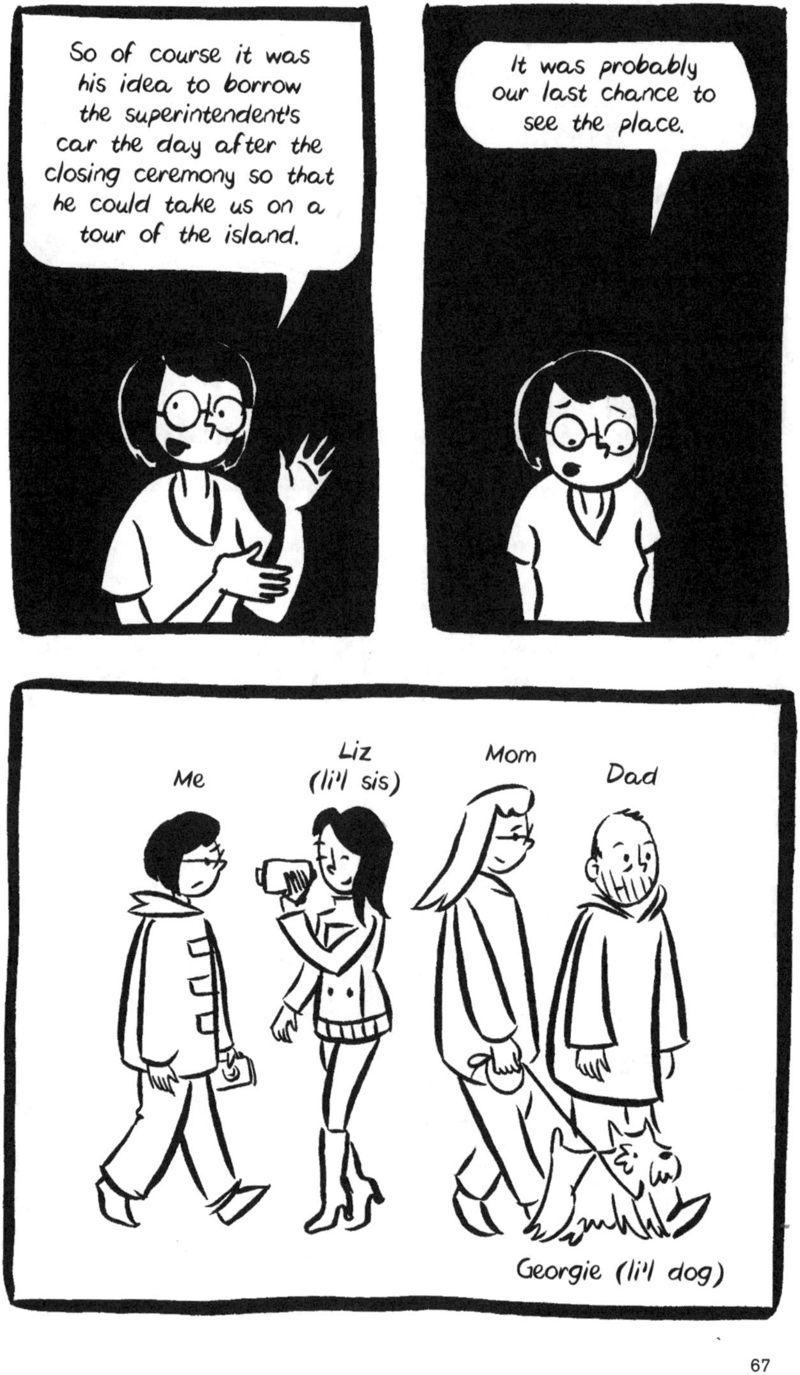
So of course it was his idea to borrow the superintendent's car the day after the closing ceremony so that he could take us on a tour of the island.
It was probably our last chance to see the place.
Me
Liz (li'l sis)
Mom
Dad
Georgie (li'l dog)

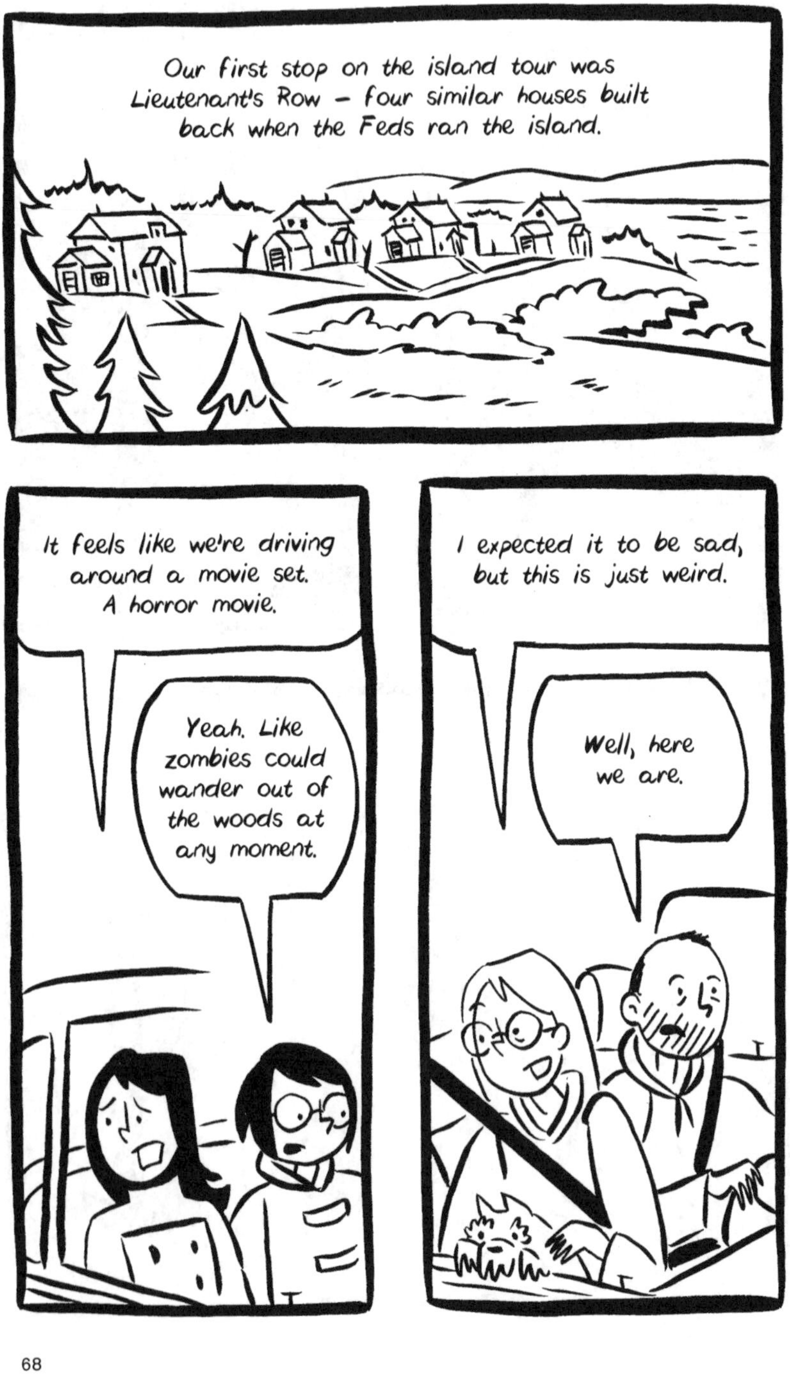
Our first stop on the island tour was Lieutenant's Row – four similar houses built back when the Feds ran the island.
It feels like we're driving around a movie set. A horror movie.
Yeah. Like zombies could wander out of the woods at any moment.
I expected it to be sad, but this is just weird.
Well, here we are.

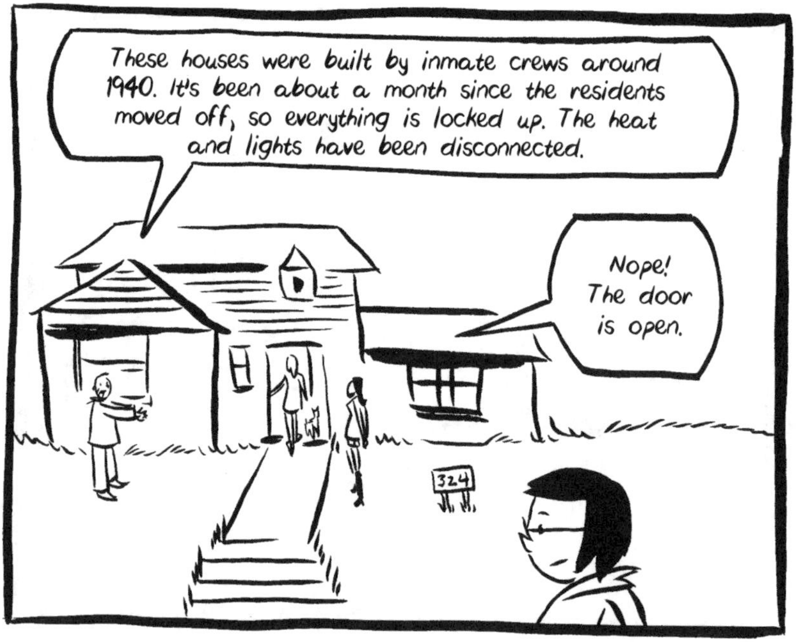
These houses were built by inmate crews around 1940. It's been about a month since the residents moved off, so everything is locked up. The heat and lights have been disconnected.
Nope! The door is open.
324

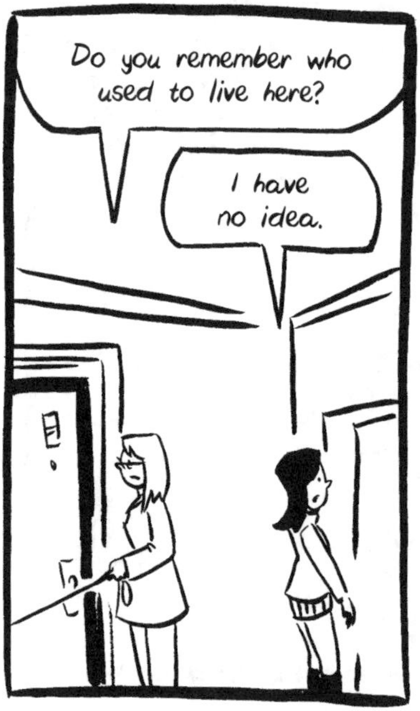
Do you remember who used to live here?
I have no idea.

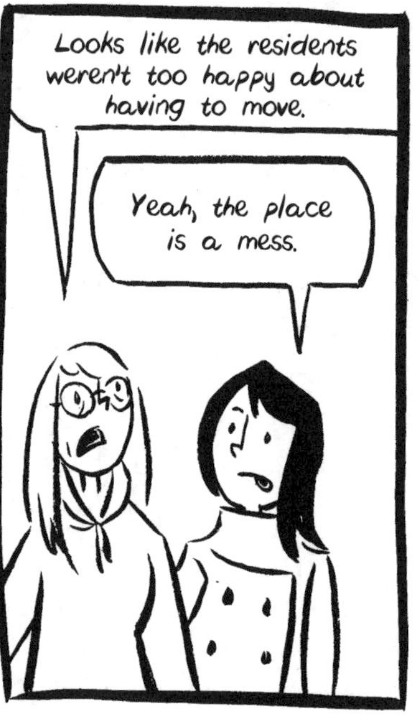
Looks like the residents weren't too happy about having to move.
Yeah, the place is a mess.

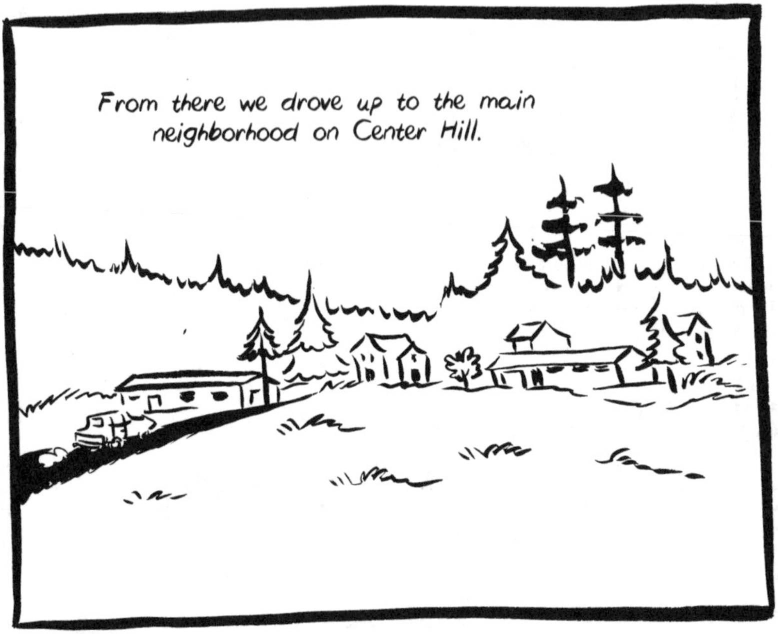
From there we drove up to the main neighborhood on Center Hill.

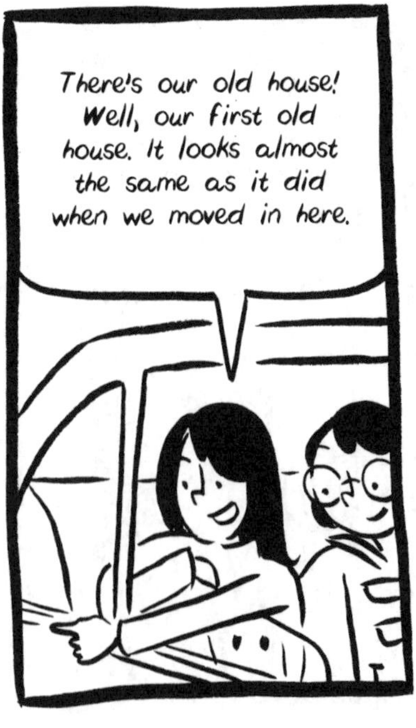
There's our old house! Well, our first old house. It looks almost the same as it did when we moved in here.

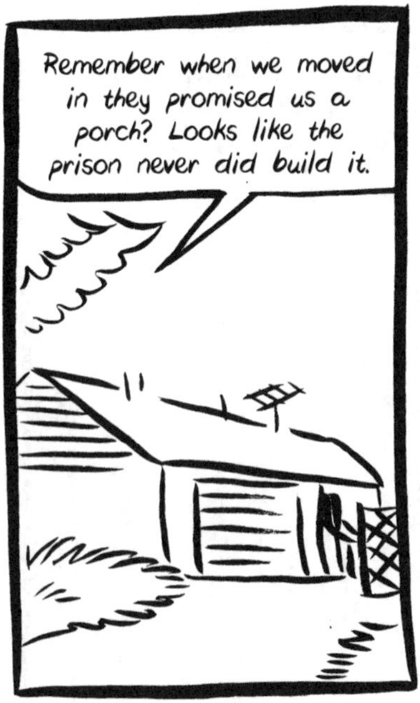
Remember when we moved in they promised us a porch? Looks like the prison never did build it.

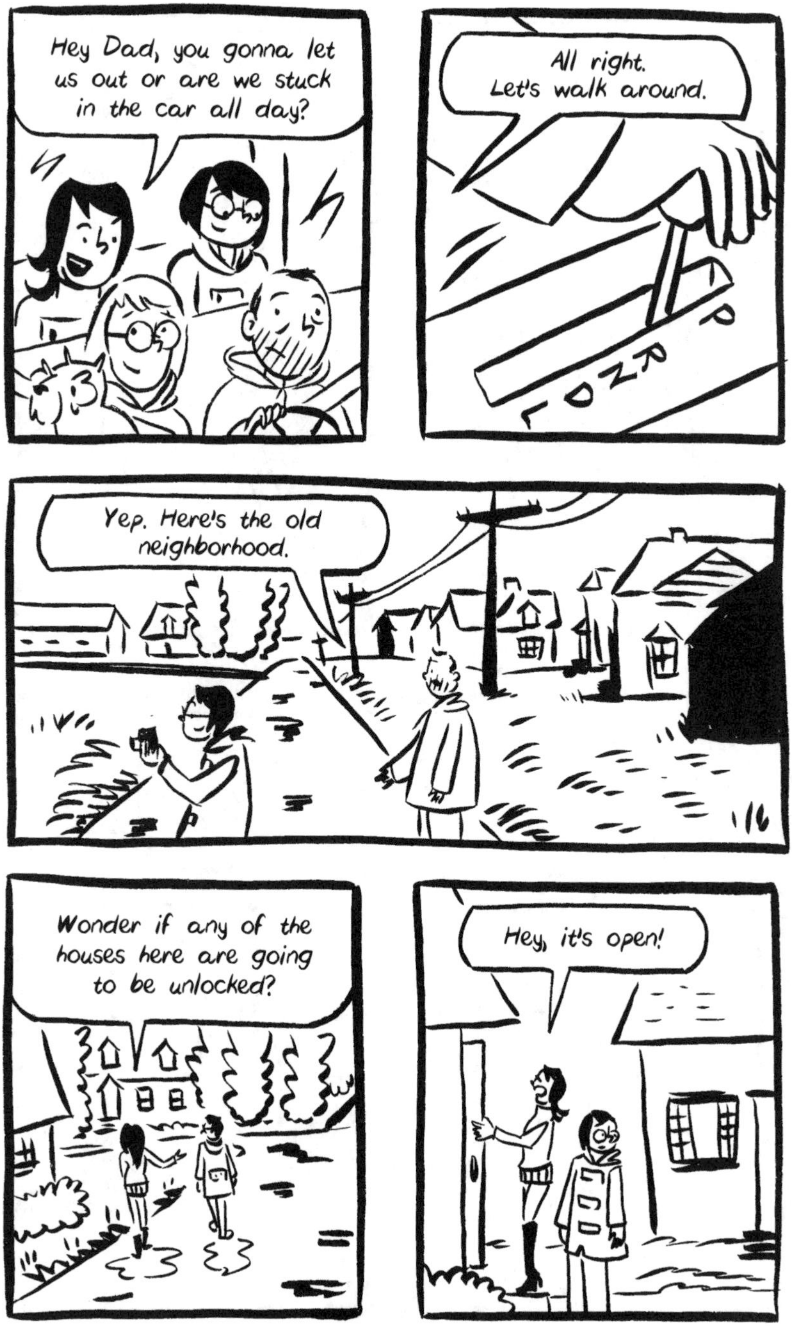
Hey Dad, you gonna let us out or are we stuck in the car all day?
All right. Let's walk around.
Yep. Here's the old neighborhood.
Wonder if any of the houses here are going to be unlocked?
Hey, it's open!

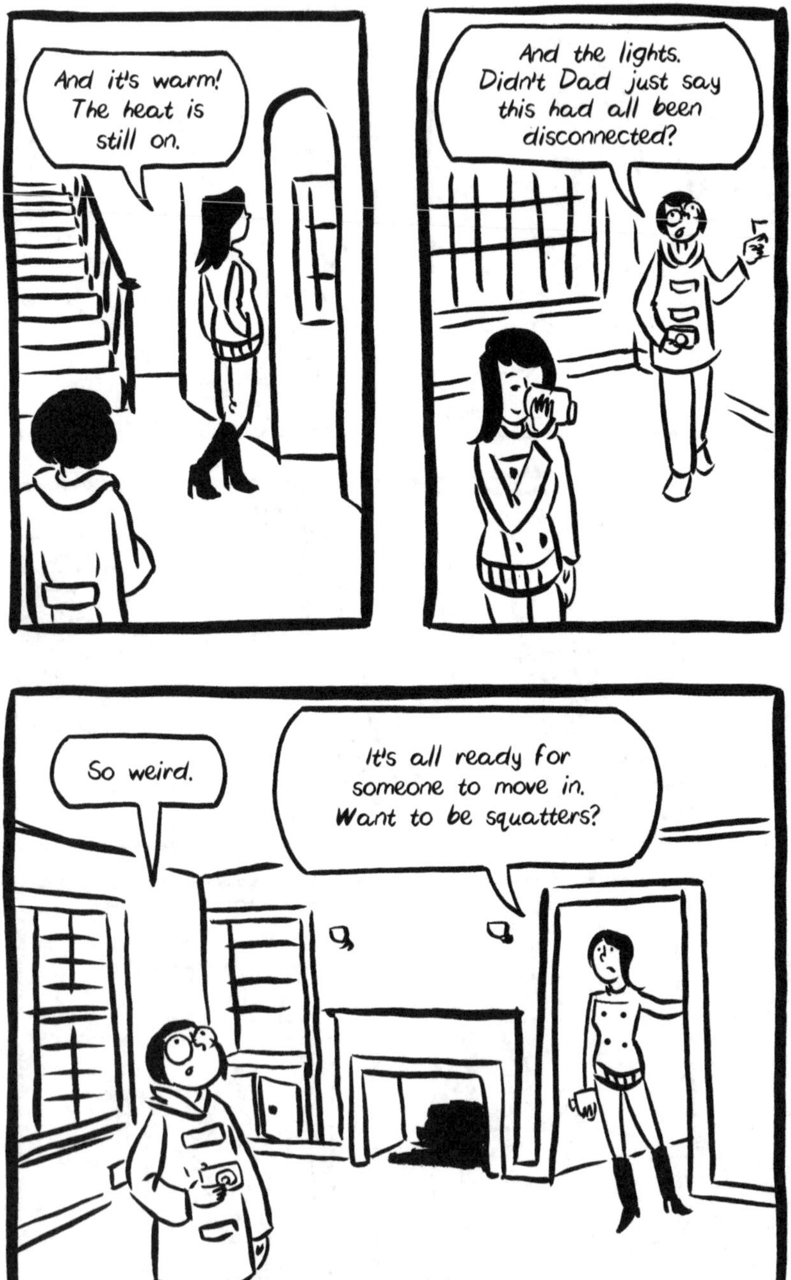
And it's warm! The heat is still on.
And the lights. Didn't Dad just say this had all been disconnected?
So weird.
It's all ready for someone to move in. Want to be squatters?

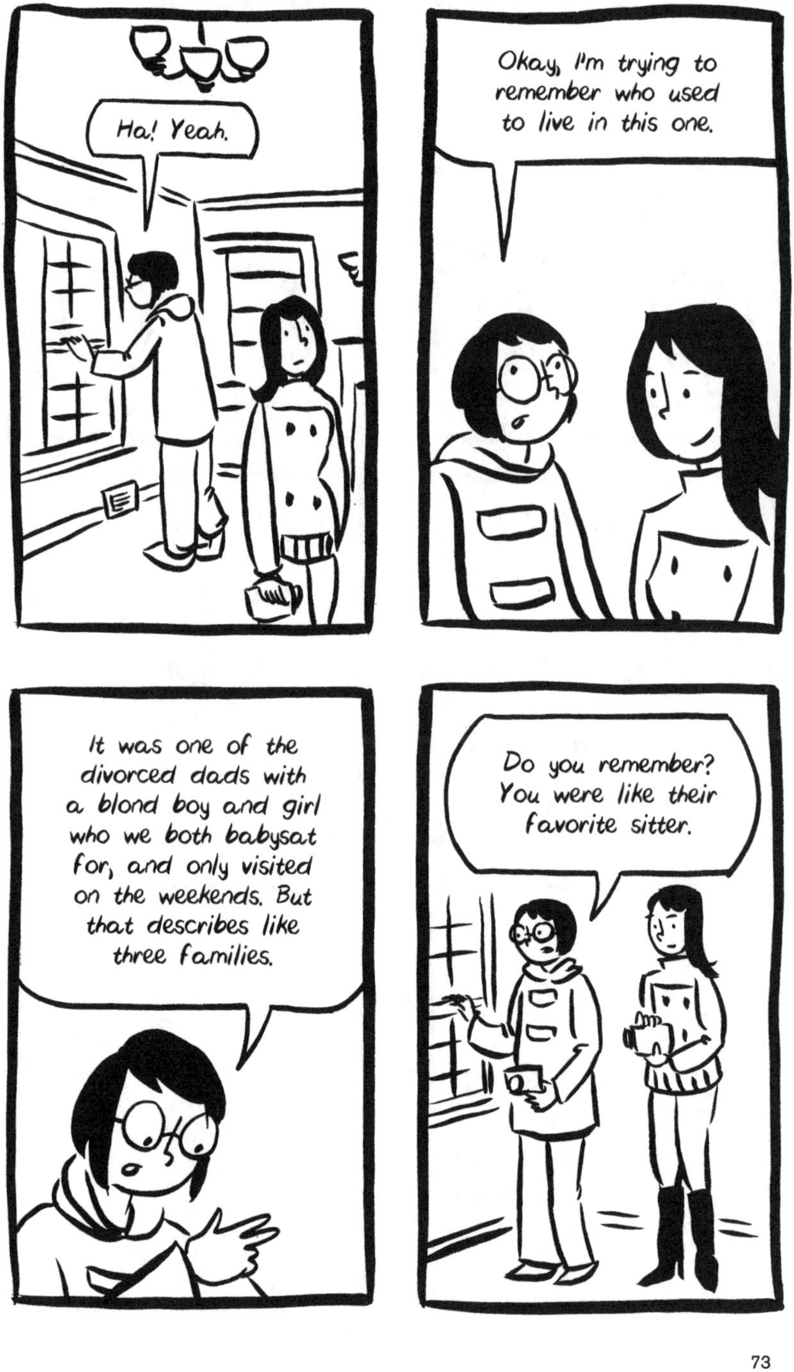
Ha! Yeah.
Okay, I'm trying to remember who used to live in this one.
It was one of the divorced dads with a blond boy and girl who we both babysat for, and only visited on the weekends. But that describes like three families.
Do you remember? You were like their favorite sitter.

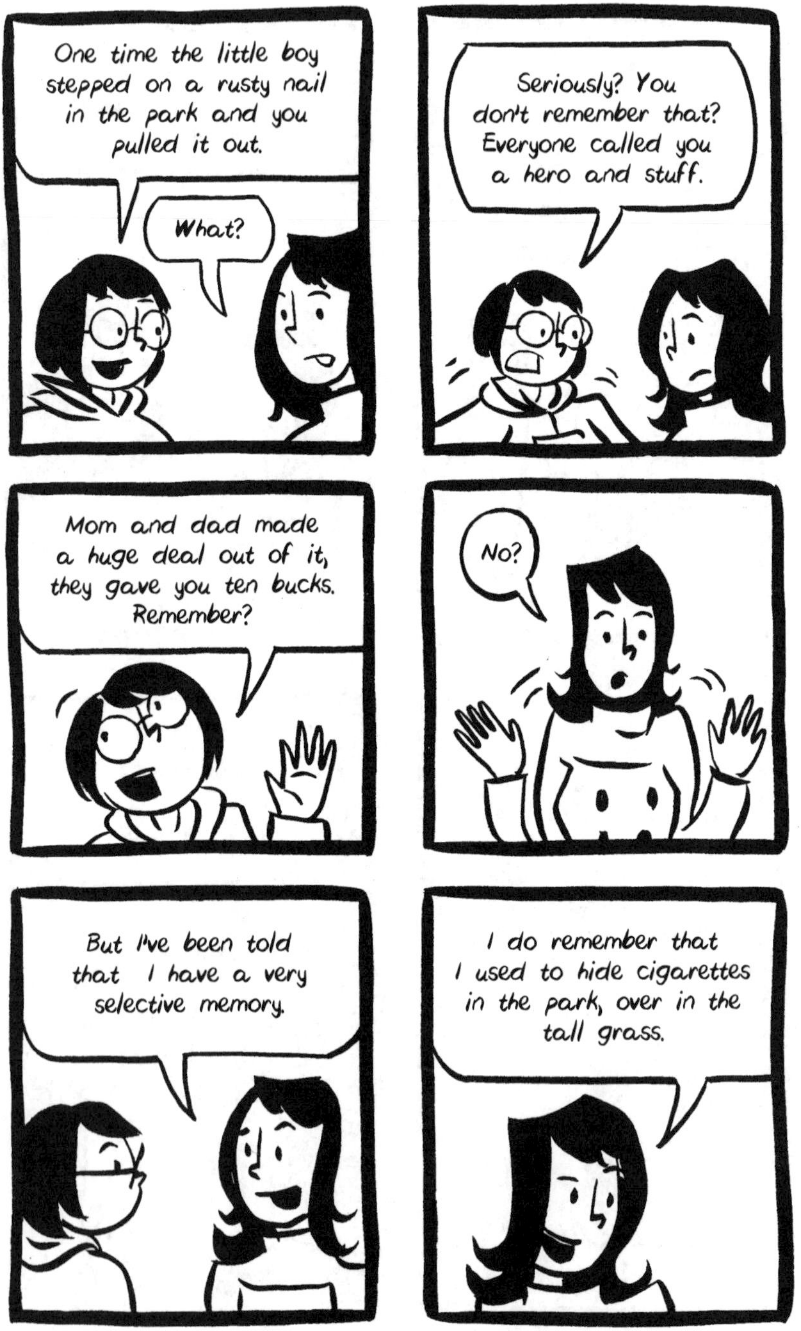
One time the little boy stepped on a rusty nail in the park and you pulled it out.
What?
Seriously? You don't remember that? Everyone called you a hero and stuff.
Mom and dad made a huge deal out of it, they gave you ten bucks. Remember?
No?
But I've been told that I have a very selective memory.
I do remember that I used to hide cigarettes in the park, over in the tall grass.

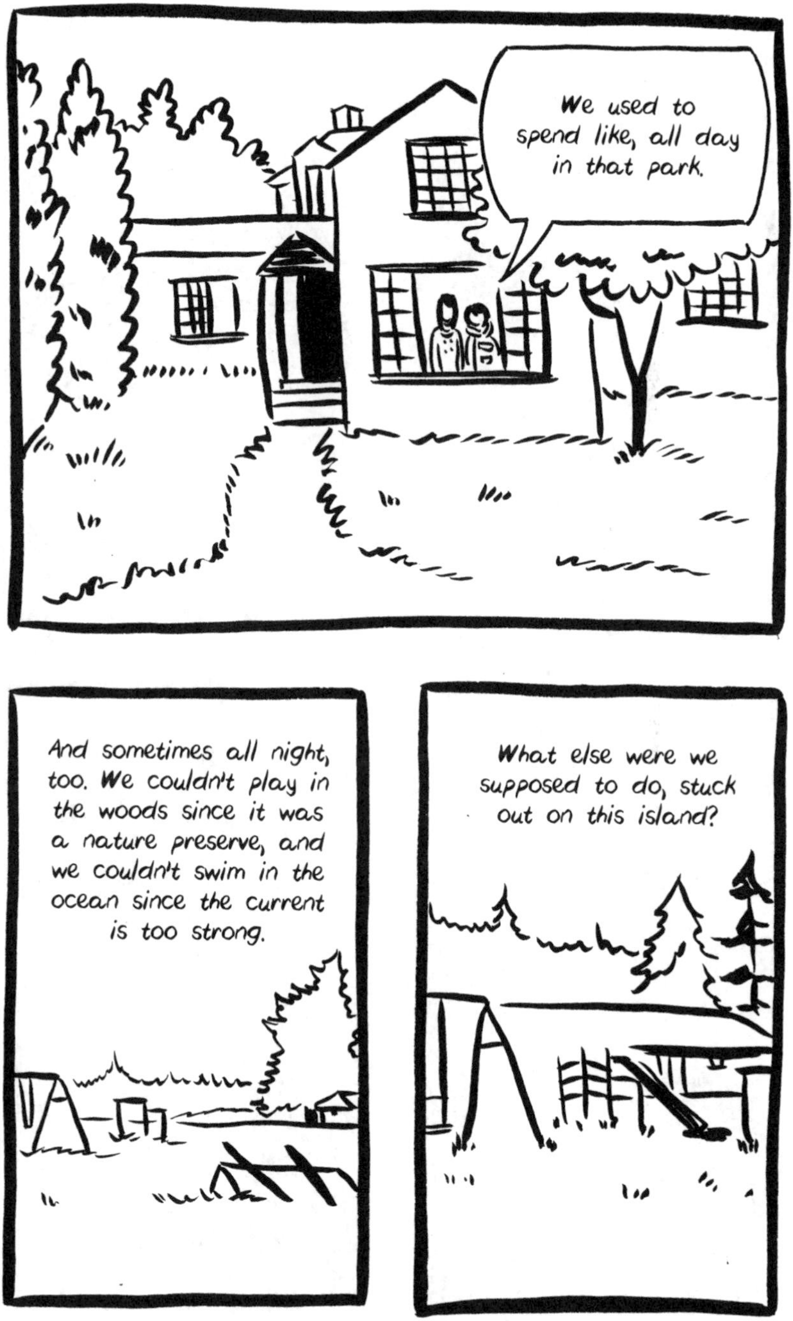
We used to spend like, all day in that park.
And sometimes all night, too. We couldn't play in the woods since it was a nature preserve, and we couldn't swim in the ocean since the current is too strong.
What else were we supposed to do, stuck out on this island?

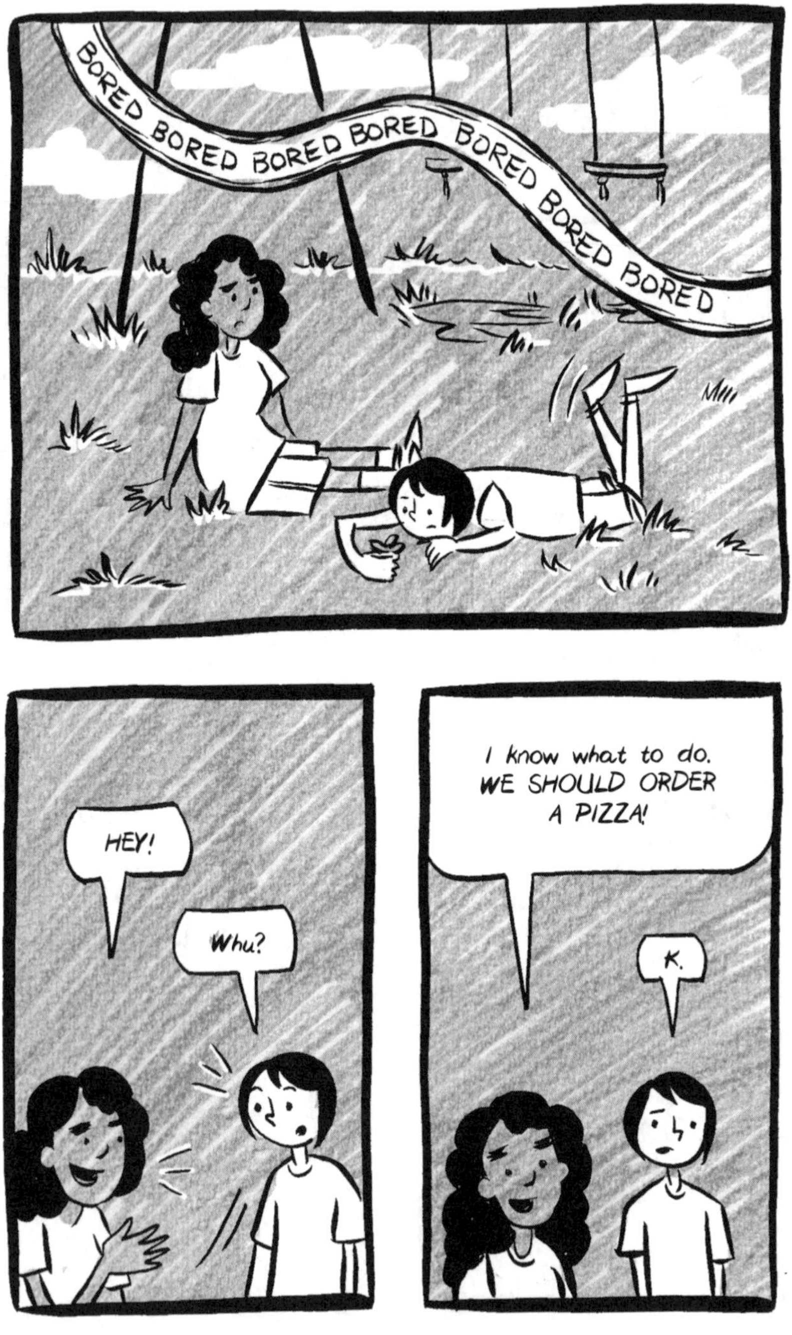
BORED BORED BORED BORED BORED BORED BORED BORED
HEY!
Whu?
I know what to do. WE SHOULD ORDER A PIZZA!
K.

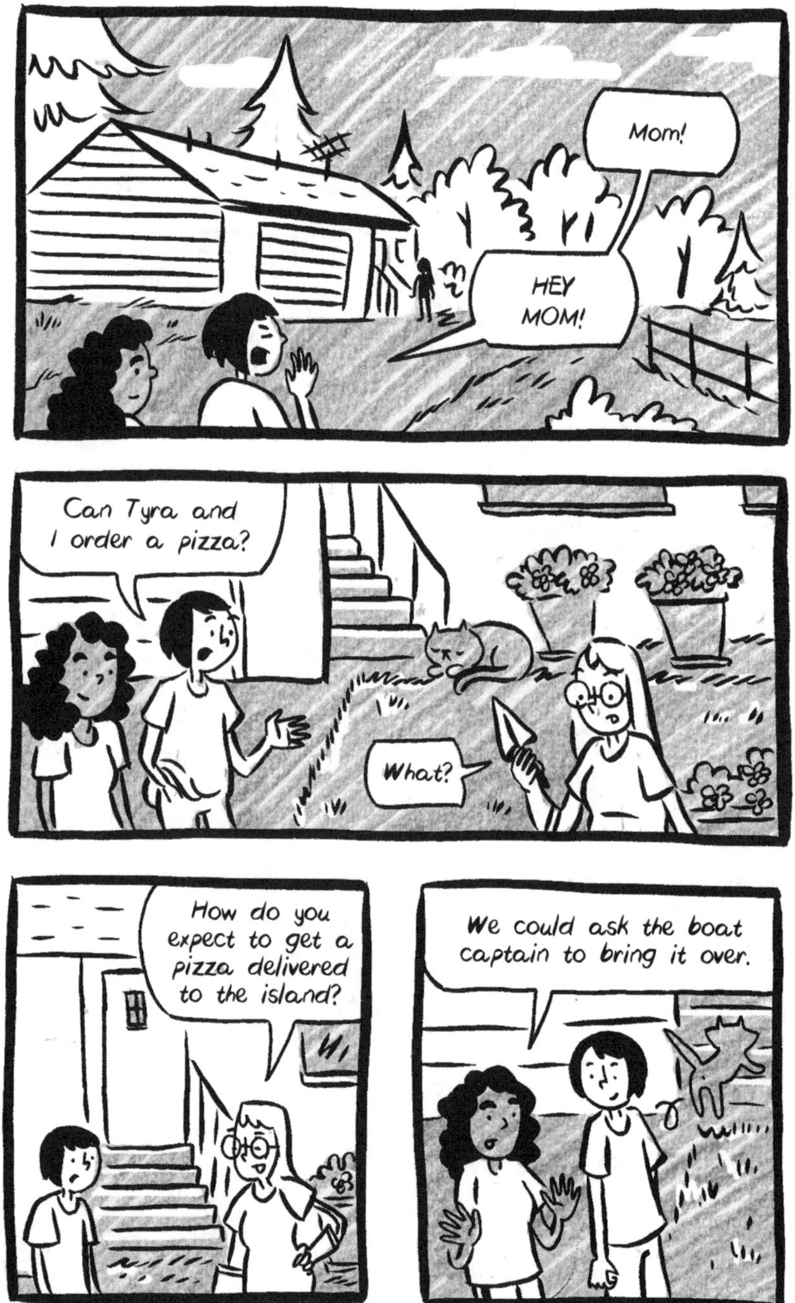
Mom!
HEY MOM!
Can Tyra and I order a pizza?
What?
How do you expect to get a pizza delivered to the island?
We could ask the boat captain to bring it over.

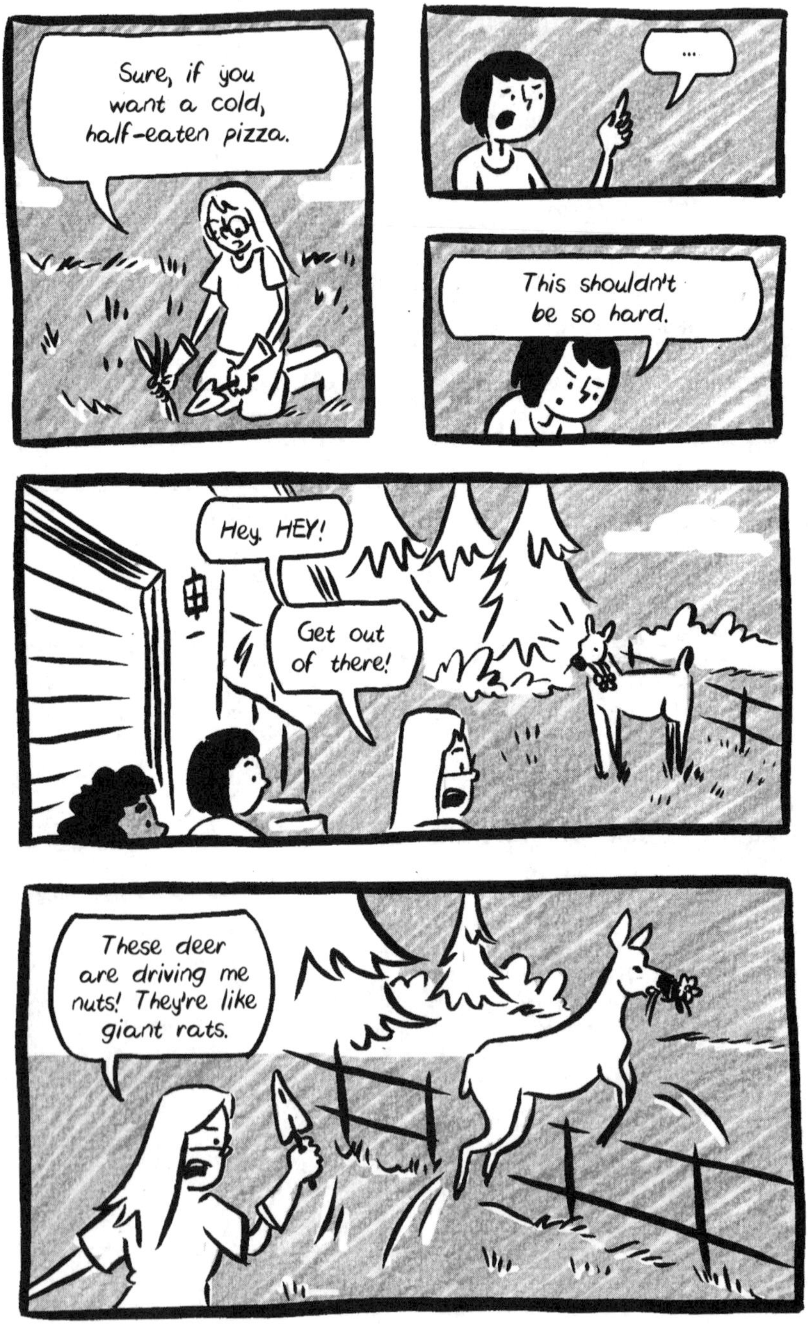
Sure, if you want a cold, half-eaten pizza.
...
This shouldn't be so hard.
Hey. HEY!
Get out of there!
These deer are driving me nuts! They're like giant rats.

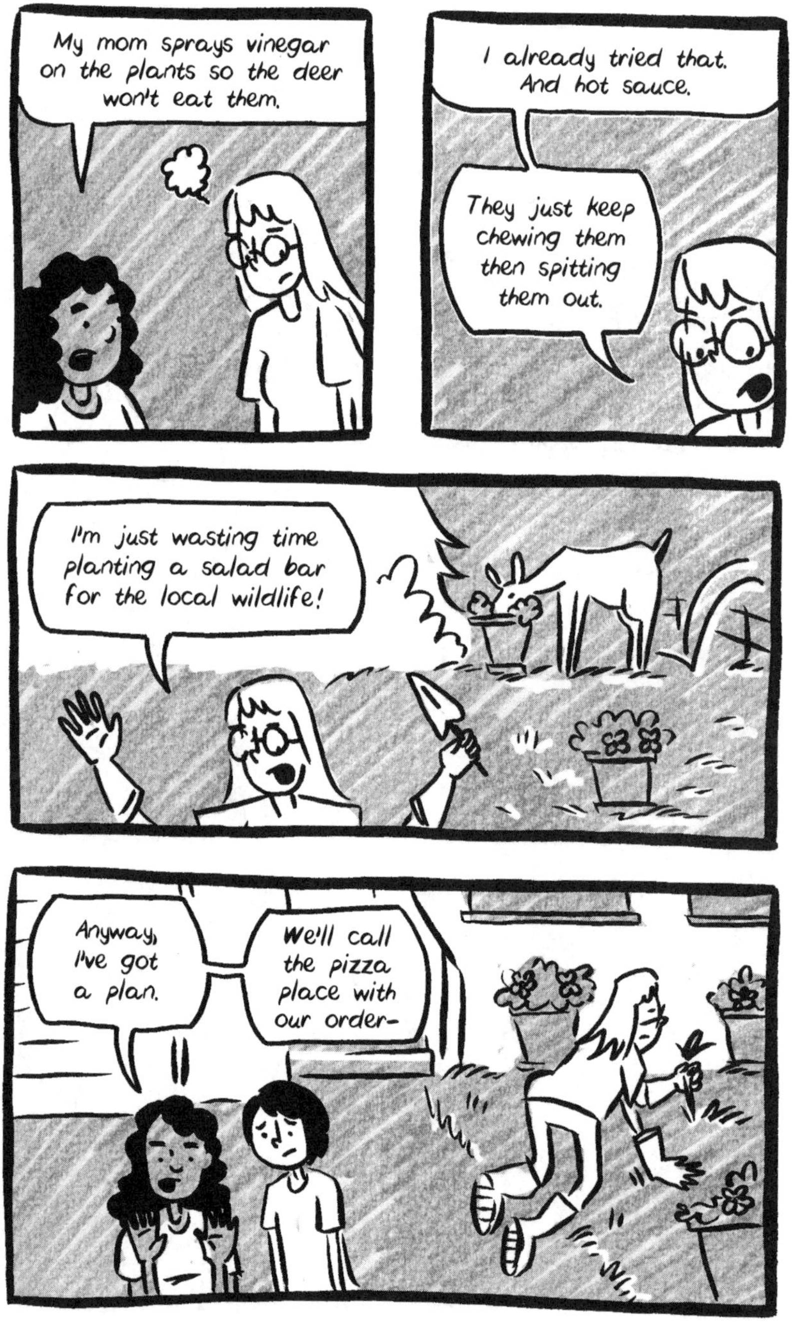
My mom sprays vinegar on the plants so the deer won't eat them.
I already tried that. And hot sauce.
They just keep chewing them then spitting them out.
I'm just wasting time planting a salad bar for the local wildlife!
Anyway, I've got a plan.
We'll call the pizza place with our order-

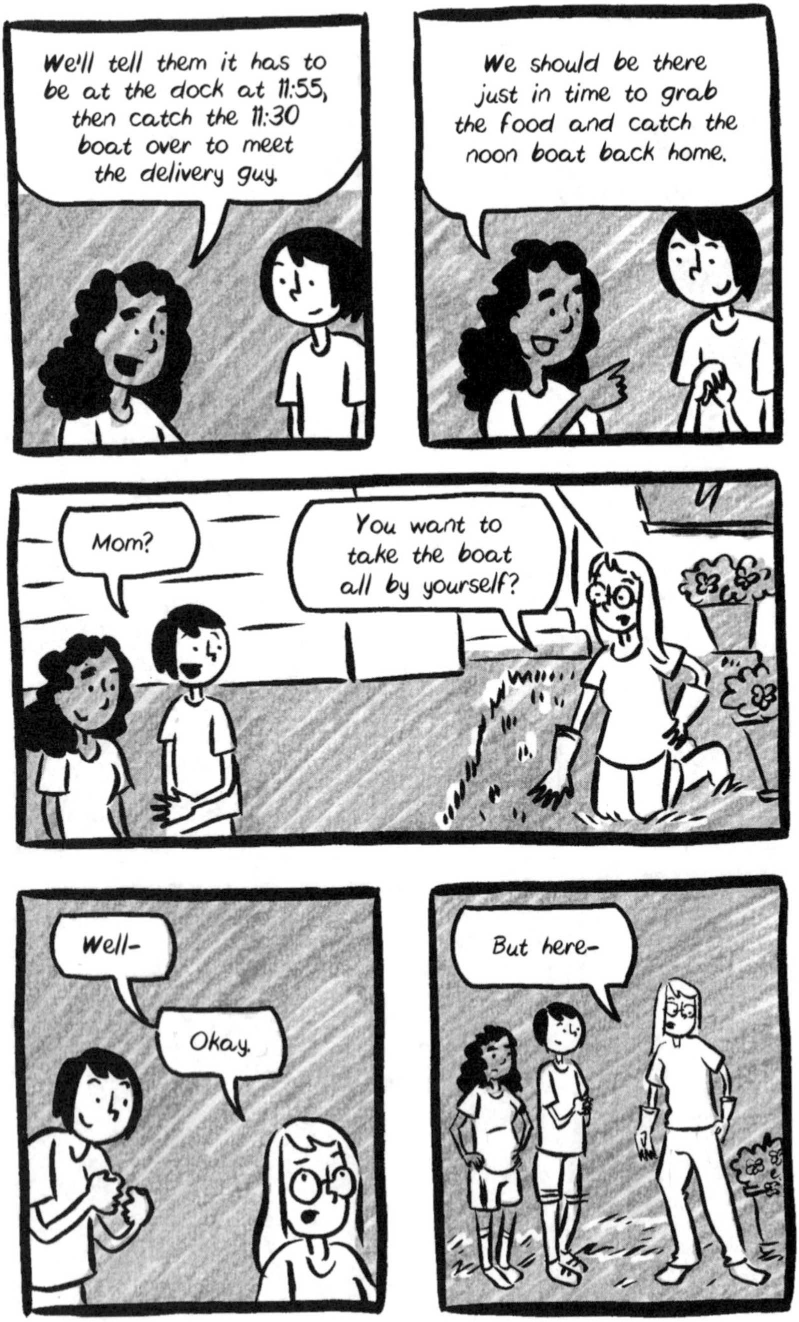
We'll tell them it has to be at the dock at 11:55, then catch the 11:30 boat over to meet the delivery guy.
We should be there just in time to grab the food and catch the noon boat back home.
Mom?
You want to take the boat all by yourself?
Well-
Okay.
But here-

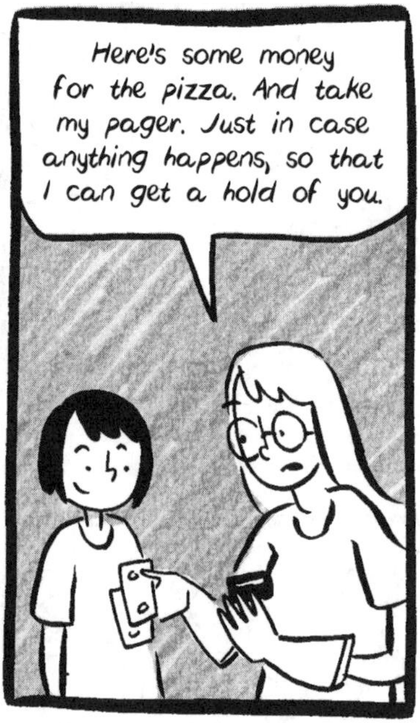
Here's some money for the pizza. And take my pager. Just in case anything happens, so that I can get a hold of you.

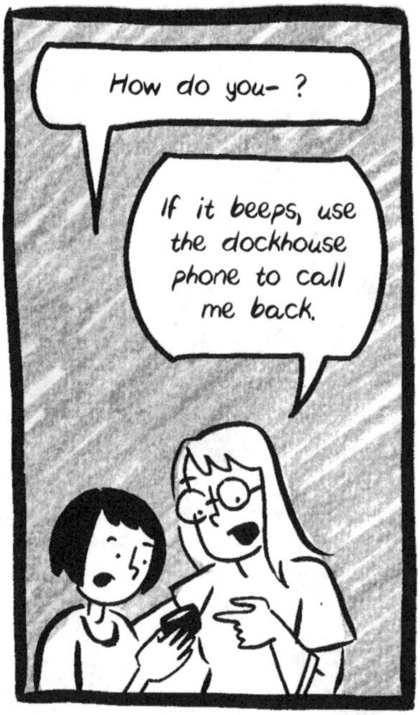
How do you- ?
If it beeps, use the dockhouse phone to call me back.

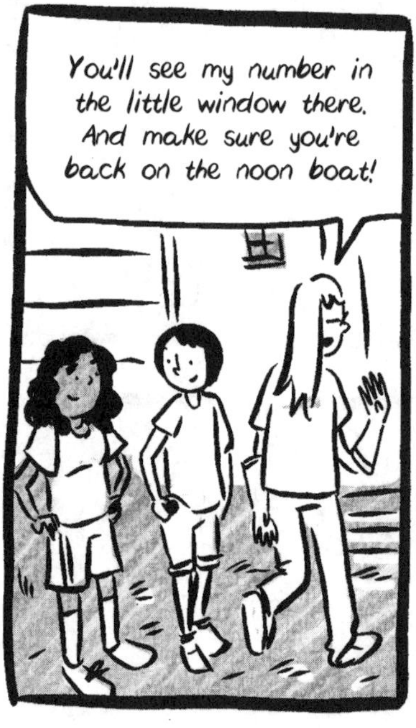
You'll see my number in the little window there. And make sure you're back on the noon boat!

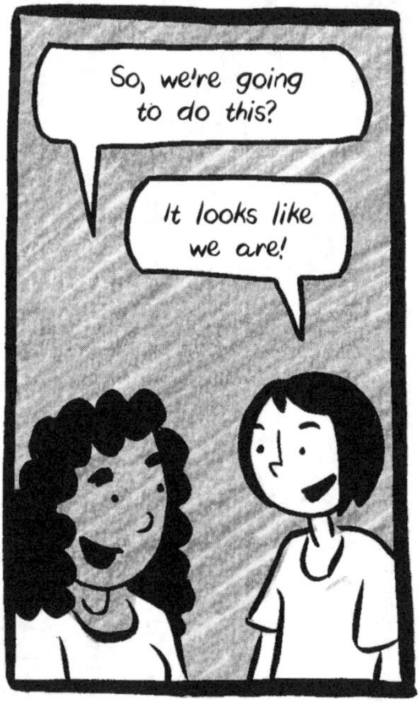
So, we're going to do this?
It looks like we are!

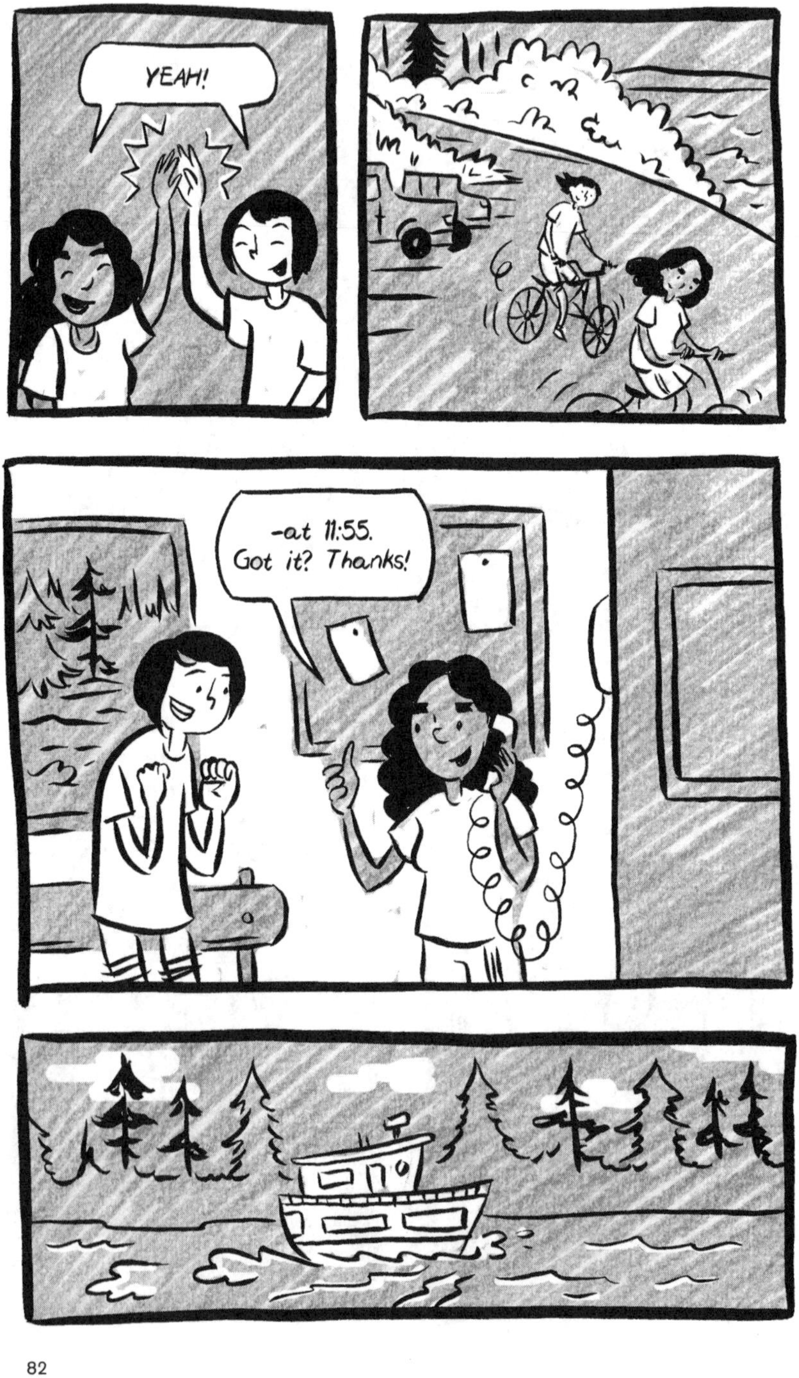
YEAH!
-at 11:55. Got it? Thanks!

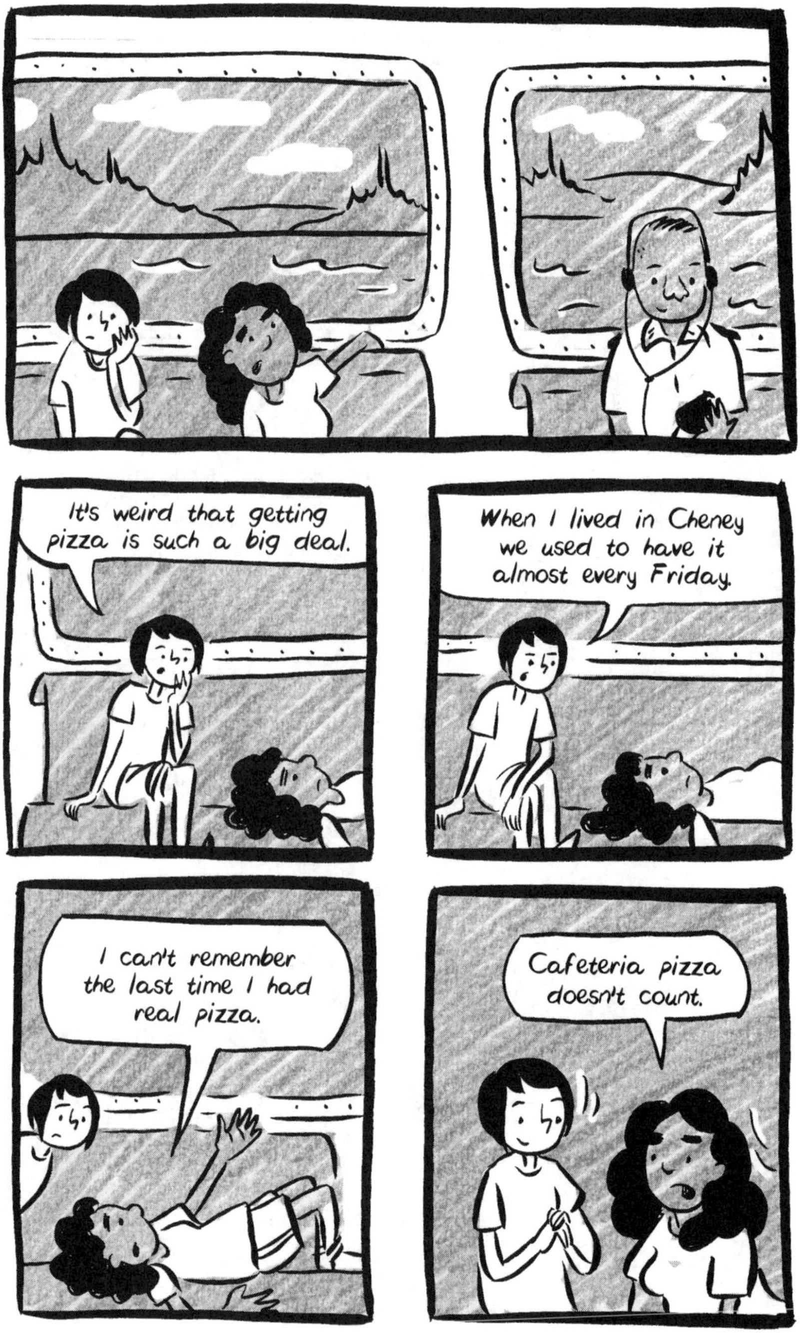
It's weird that getting pizza is such a big deal.
When I lived in Cheney we used to have it almost every Friday.
I can't remember the last time I had real pizza.
Cafeteria pizza doesn't count.

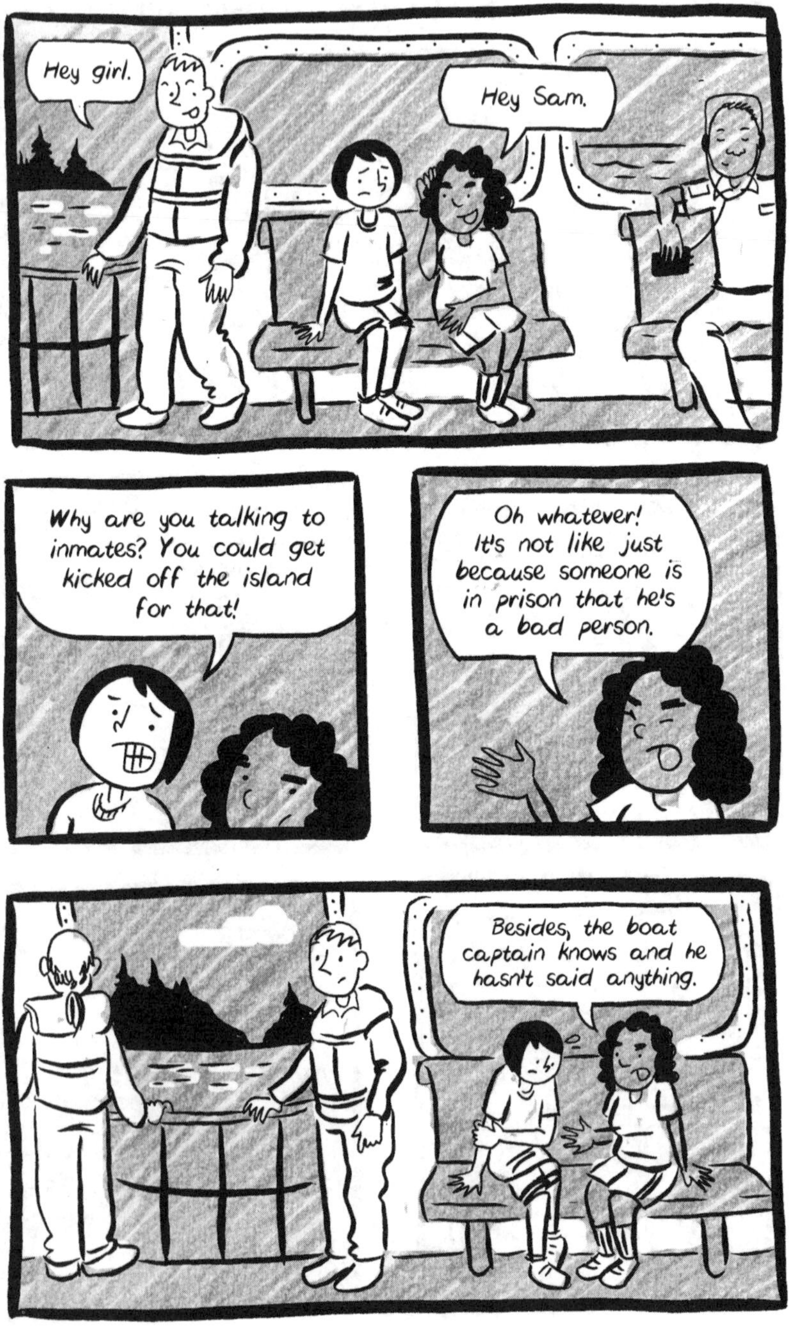
Hey girl.
Hey Sam.
Why are you talking to inmates? You could get kicked off the island for that!
Oh whatever! It's not like just because someone is in prison that he's a bad person.
Besides, the boat captain knows and he hasn't said anything.

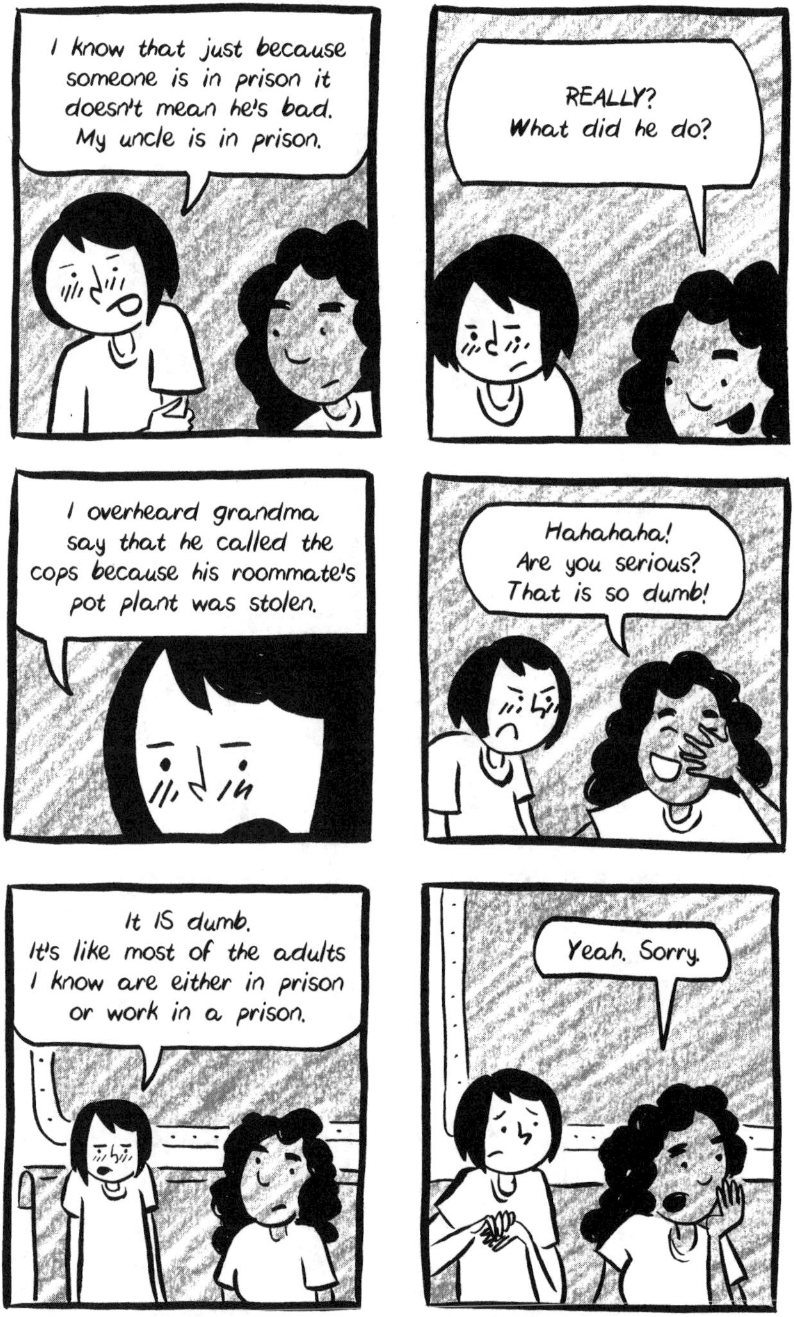
I know that just because someone is in prison it doesn't mean he's bad. My uncle is in prison.
REALLY? What did he do?
I overheard grandma say that he called the cops because his roommate's pot plant was stolen.
Hahahaha! Are you serious? That is so dumb!
It IS dumb. It's like most of the adults I know are either in prison or work in a prison.
Yeah. Sorry.

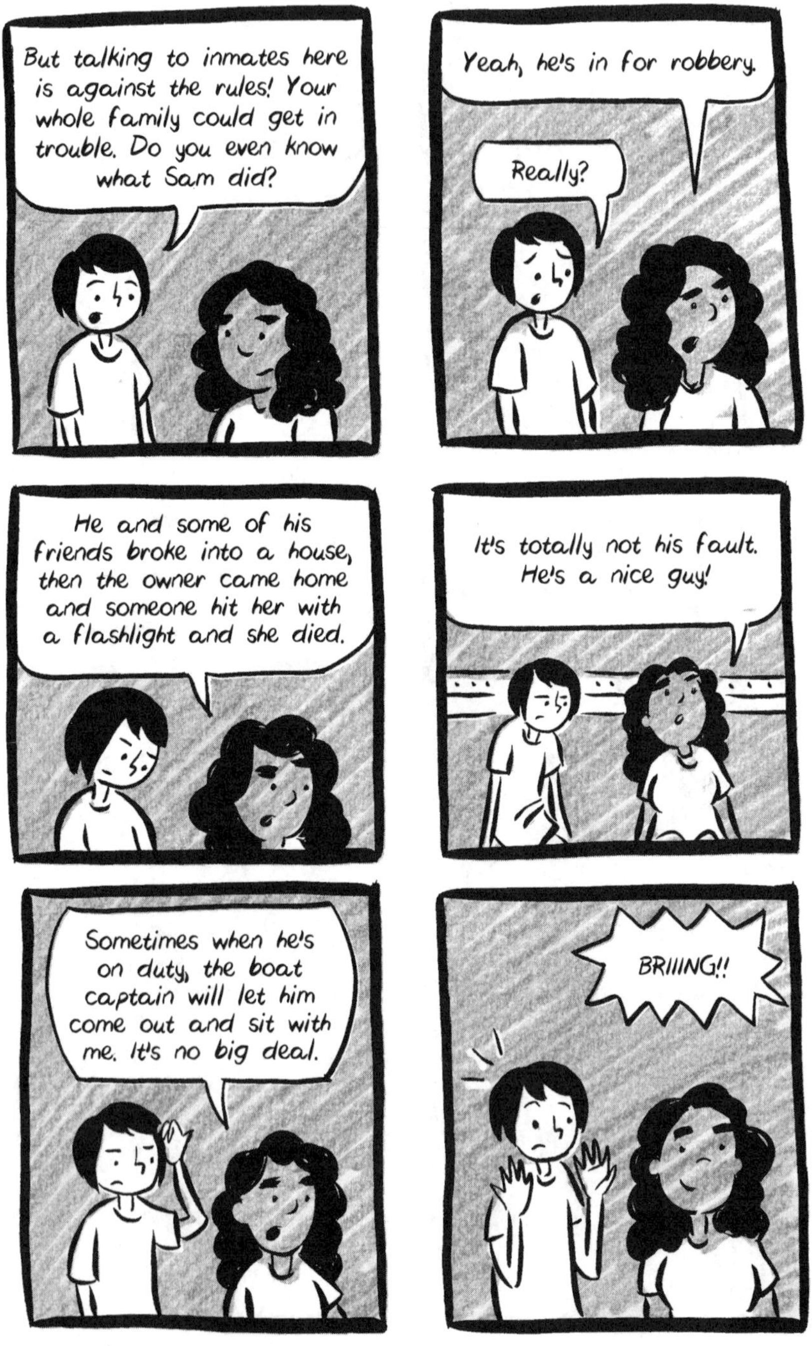
But talking to inmates here is against the rules! Your whole family could get in trouble. Do you even know what Sam did?
Yeah, he's in for robbery.
Really?
He and some of his friends broke into a house, then the owner came home and someone hit her with a flashlight and she died.
It's totally not his fault. He's a nice guy!
Sometimes when he's on duty, the boat captain will let him come out and sit with me. It's no big deal.
BRIIING!!

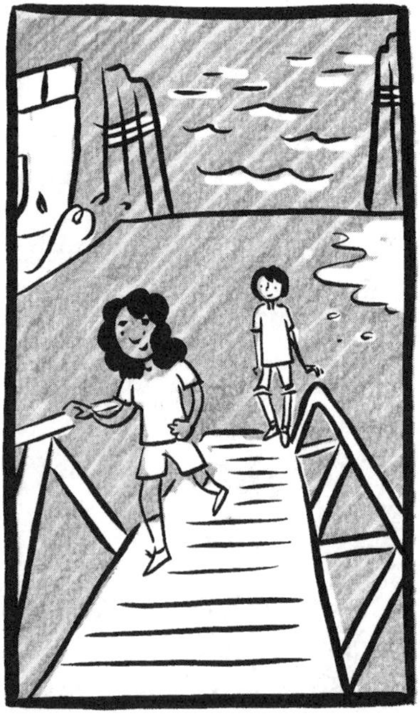

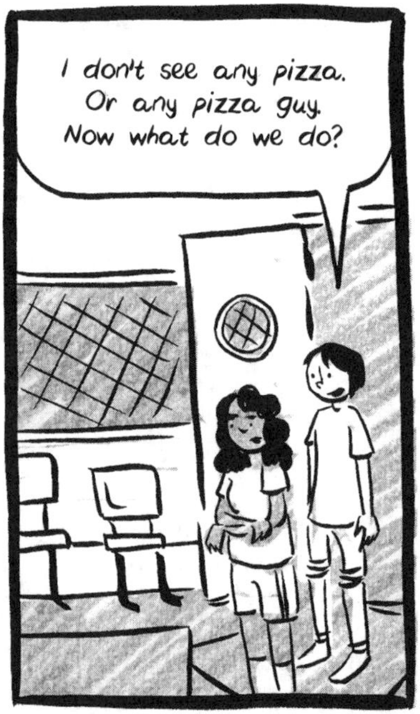
I don't see any pizza.
Or any pizza guy.
Now what do we do?

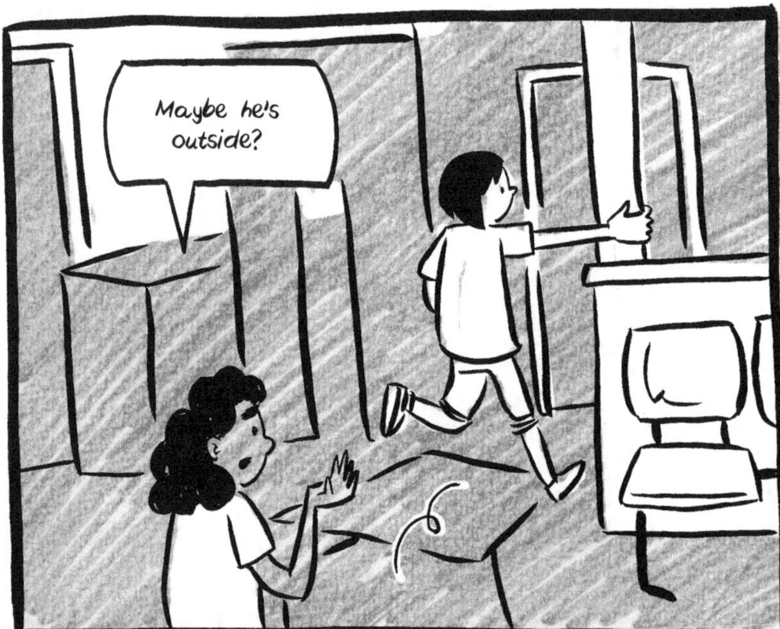
Maybe he's outside?

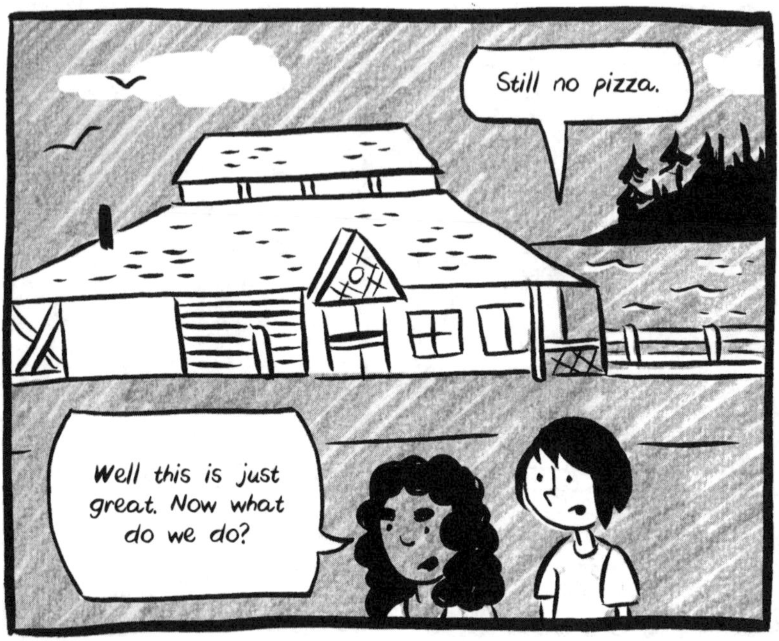
Still no pizza.
Well this is just great. Now what do we do?

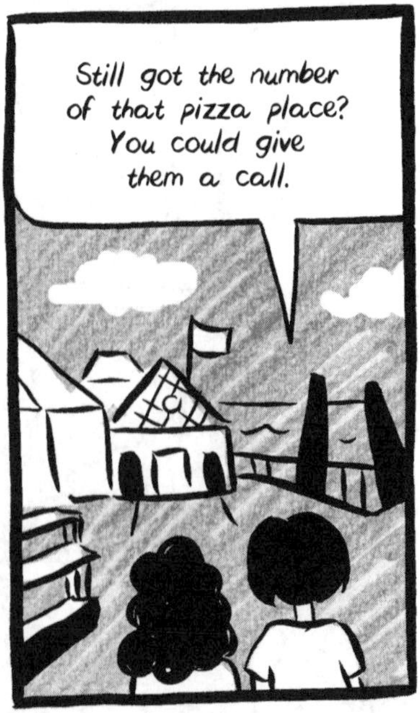
Still got the number of that pizza place? You could give them a call.

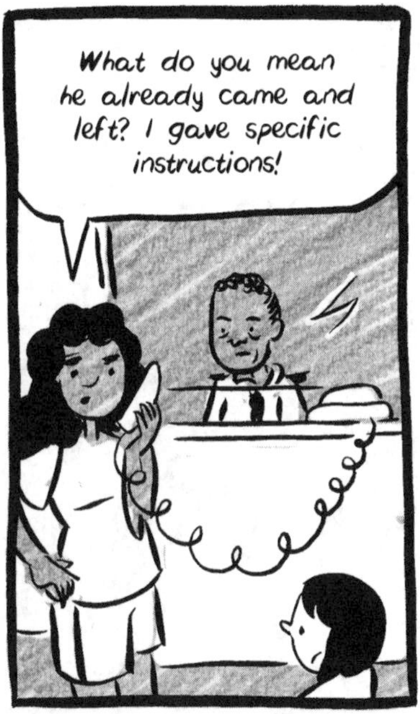
What do you mean he already came and left? I gave specific instructions!

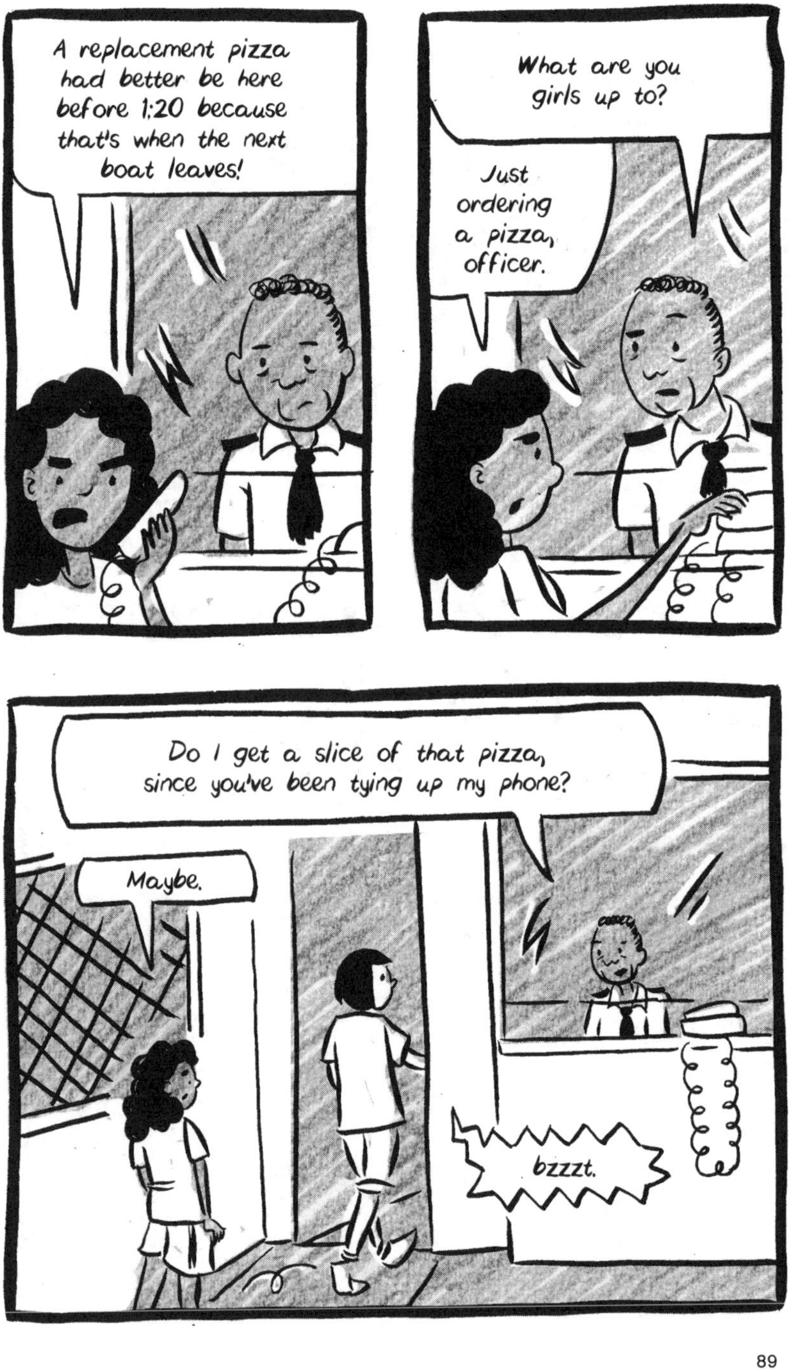
A replacement pizza had better be here before 1:20 because that's when the next boat leaves!
What are you girls up to?
Just ordering a pizza, officer.
Do I get a slice of that pizza, since you've been tying up my phone?
Maybe.
bzzzt.

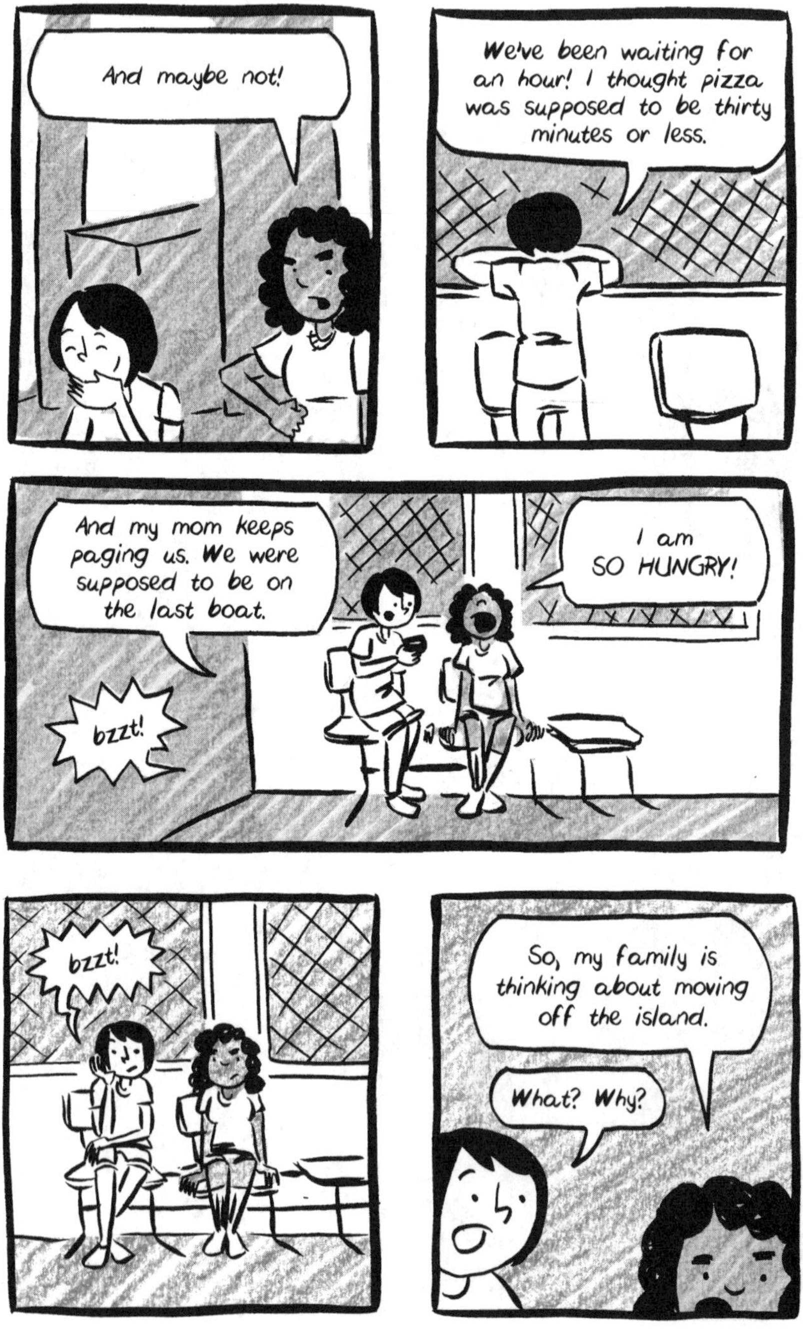
And maybe not!
We've been waiting for an hour! I thought pizza was supposed to be thirty minutes or less.
And my mom keeps paging us. We were supposed to be on the last boat.
bzzt!
I am SO HUNGRY!
bzzt!
So, my family is thinking about moving off the island.
What? Why?

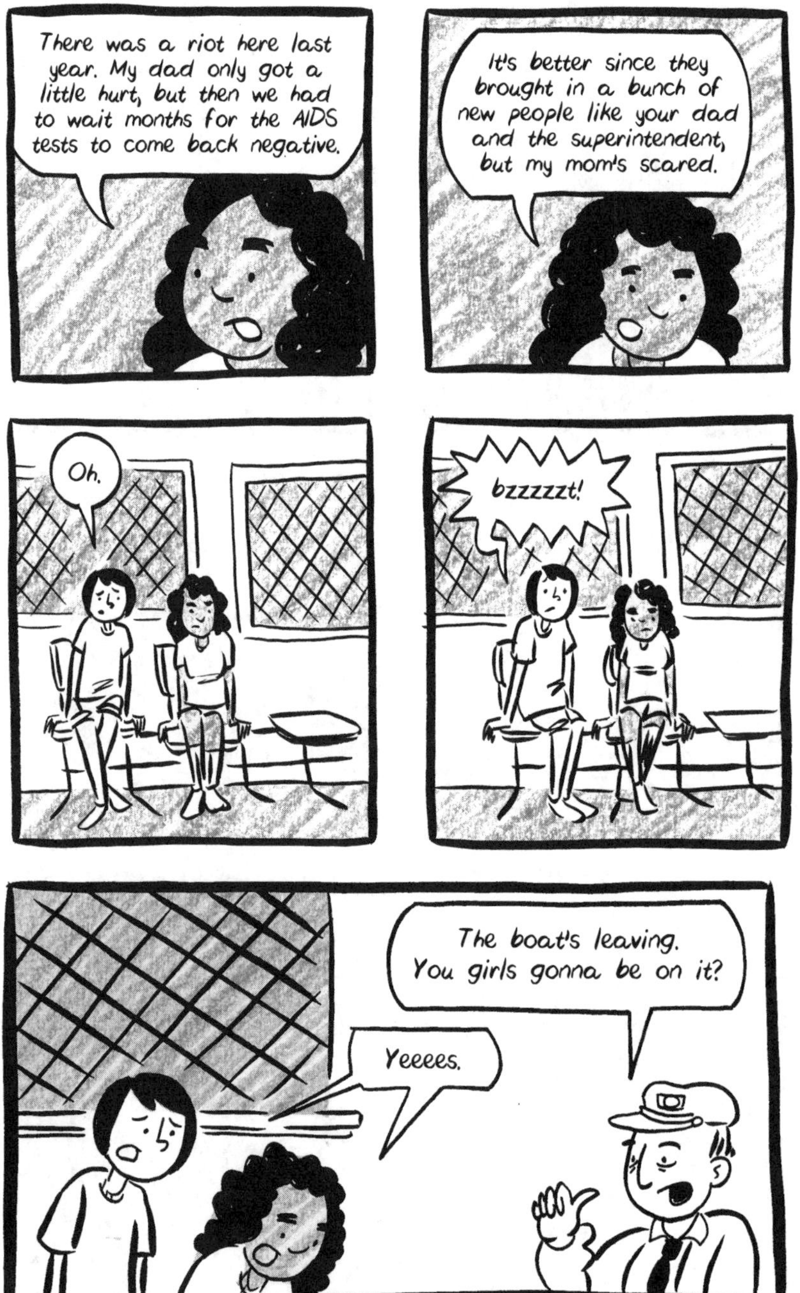
There was a riot here last year. My dad only got a little hurt, but then we had to wait months for the AIDS tests to come back negative.
It's better since they brought in a bunch of new people like your dad and the superintendent, but my mom's scared.
Oh.
bzzzzzt!
The boat's leaving. You girls gonna be on it?
Yeeees.

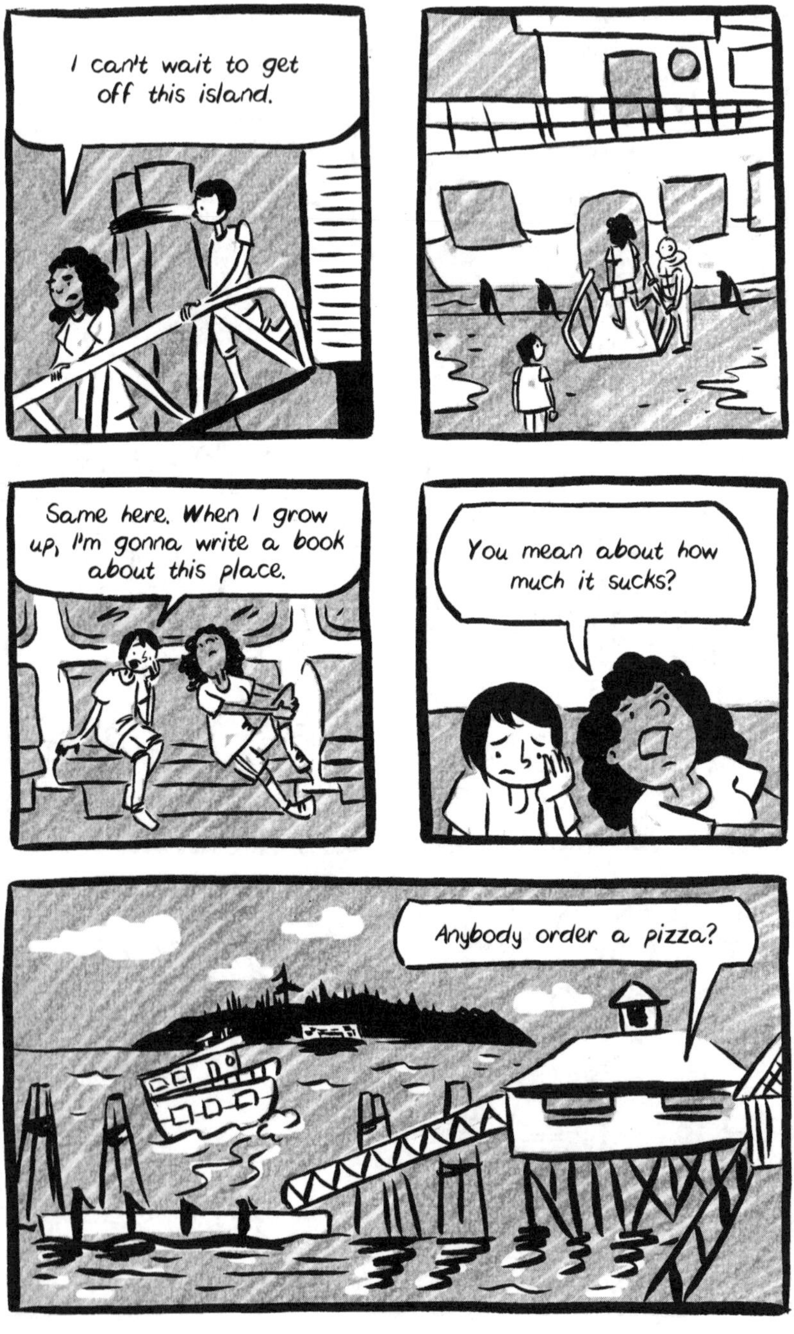
I can't wait to get off this island.
Same here. When I grow up, I'm gonna write a book about this place.
You mean about how much it sucks?
Anybody order a pizza?

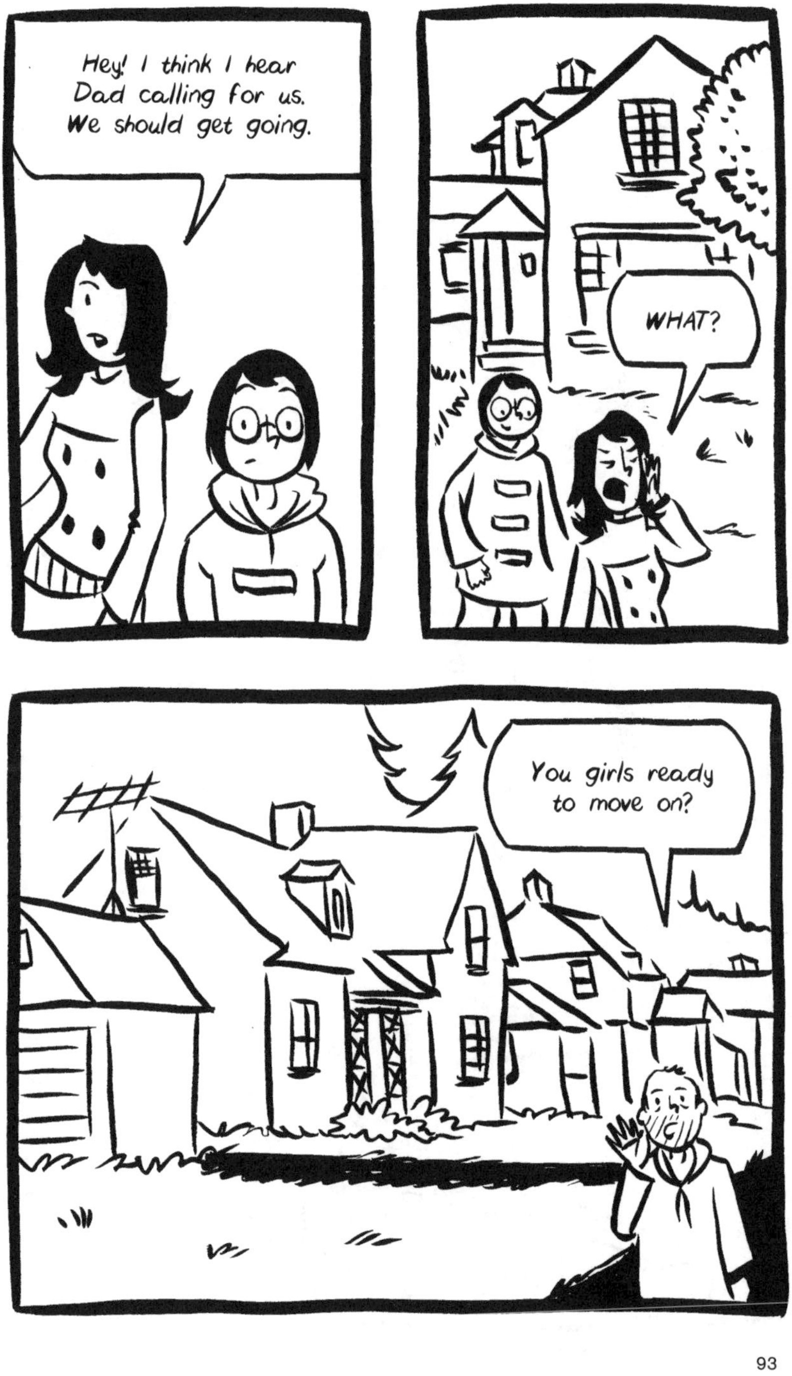
Hey! I think I hear Dad calling for us. We should get going.
WHAT?
You girls ready to move on?

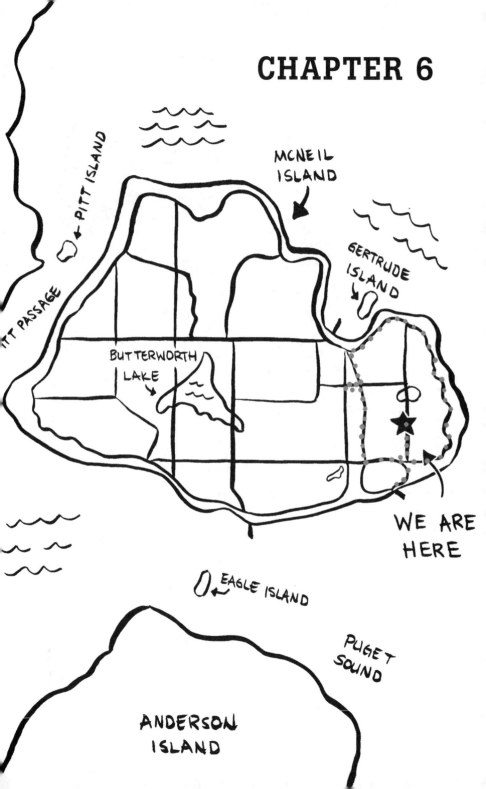

CHAPTER 6

MCNEIL
ISLAND

PITT ISLAND

PITT PASSAGE

GERTRUDE
ISLAND

BUTTERWORTH
LAKE

WE ARE
HERE

EAGLE ISLAND

PUGET
SOUND

ANDERSON
ISLAND

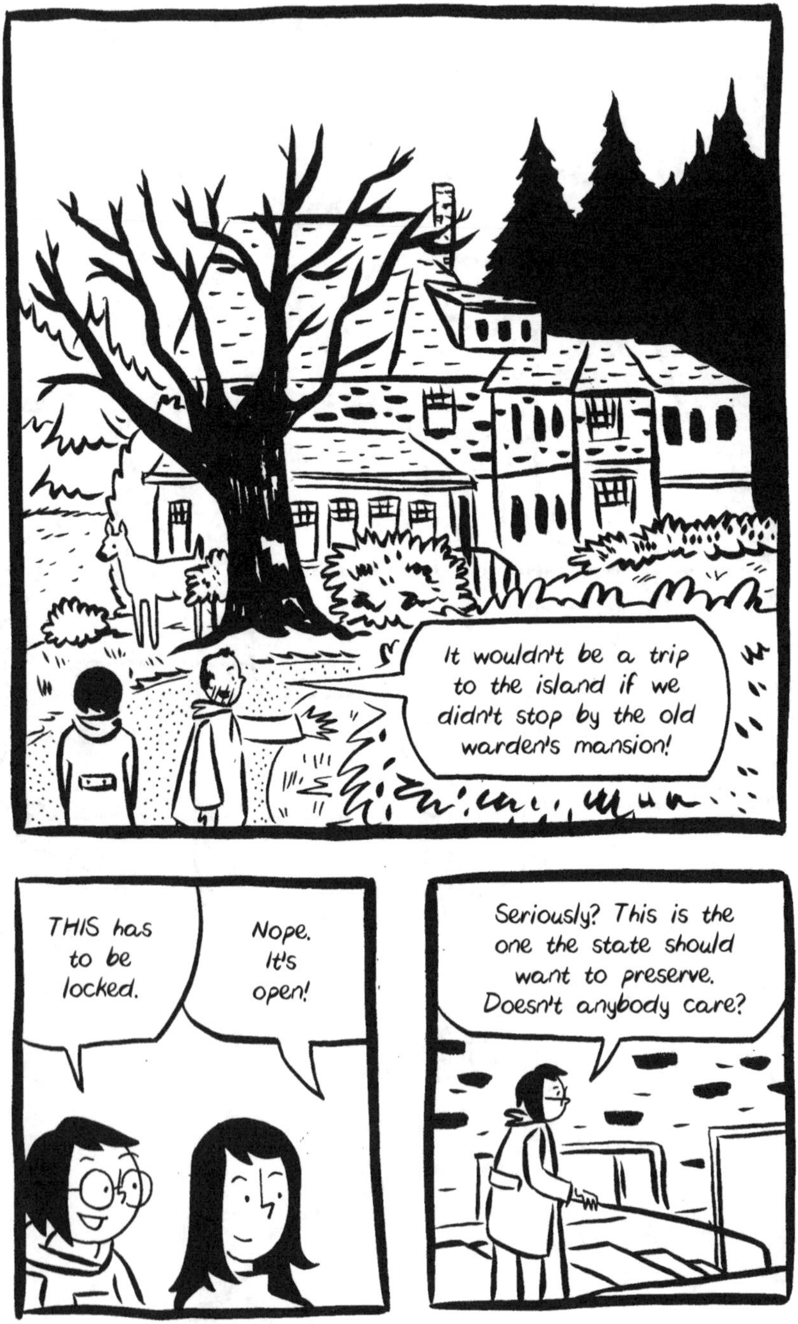
It wouldn't be a trip to the island if we didn't stop by the old warden's mansion!
THIS has to be locked.
Nope. It's open!
Seriously? This is the one the state should want to preserve. Doesn't anybody care?

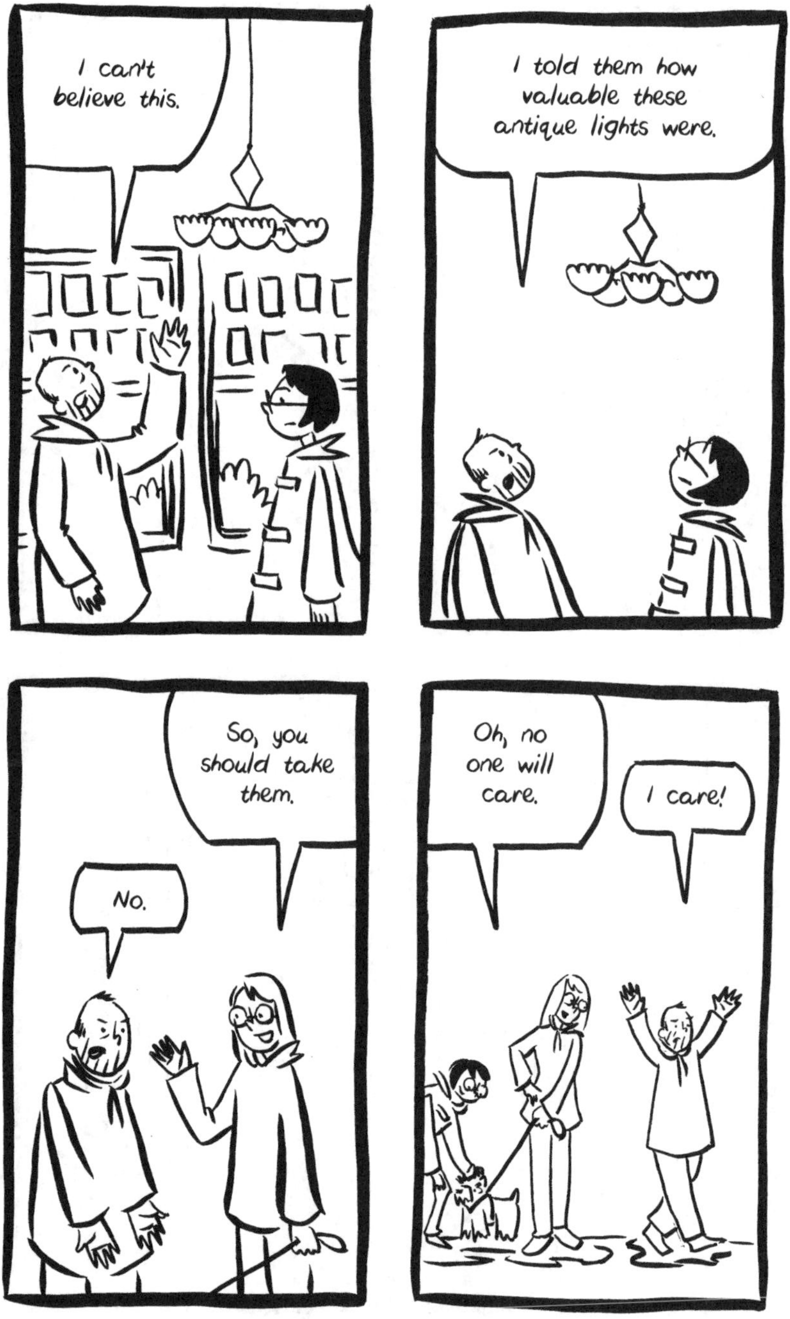
I can't believe this.
I told them how valuable these antique lights were.
So, you should take them.
No.
Oh, no one will care.
I care!

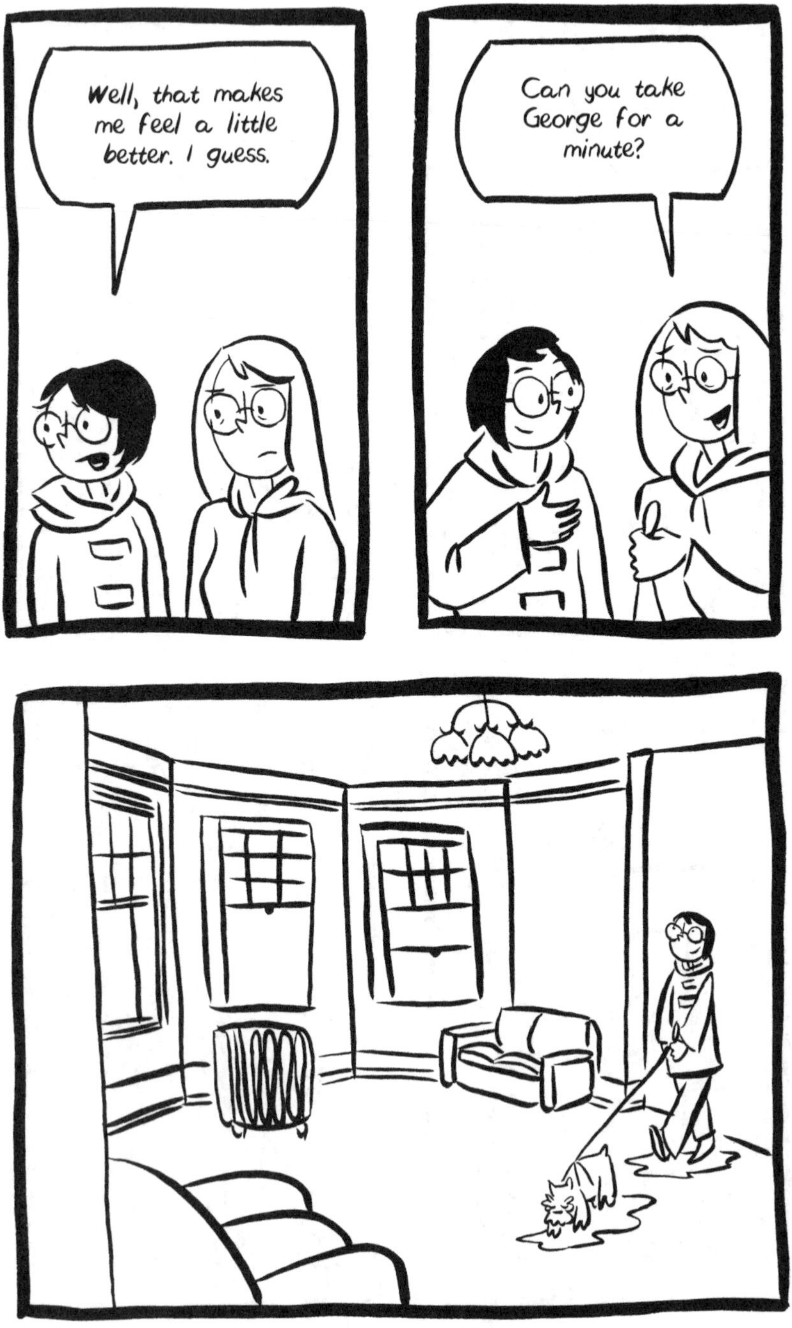
Well, that makes me feel a little better. I guess.
Can you take George for a minute?

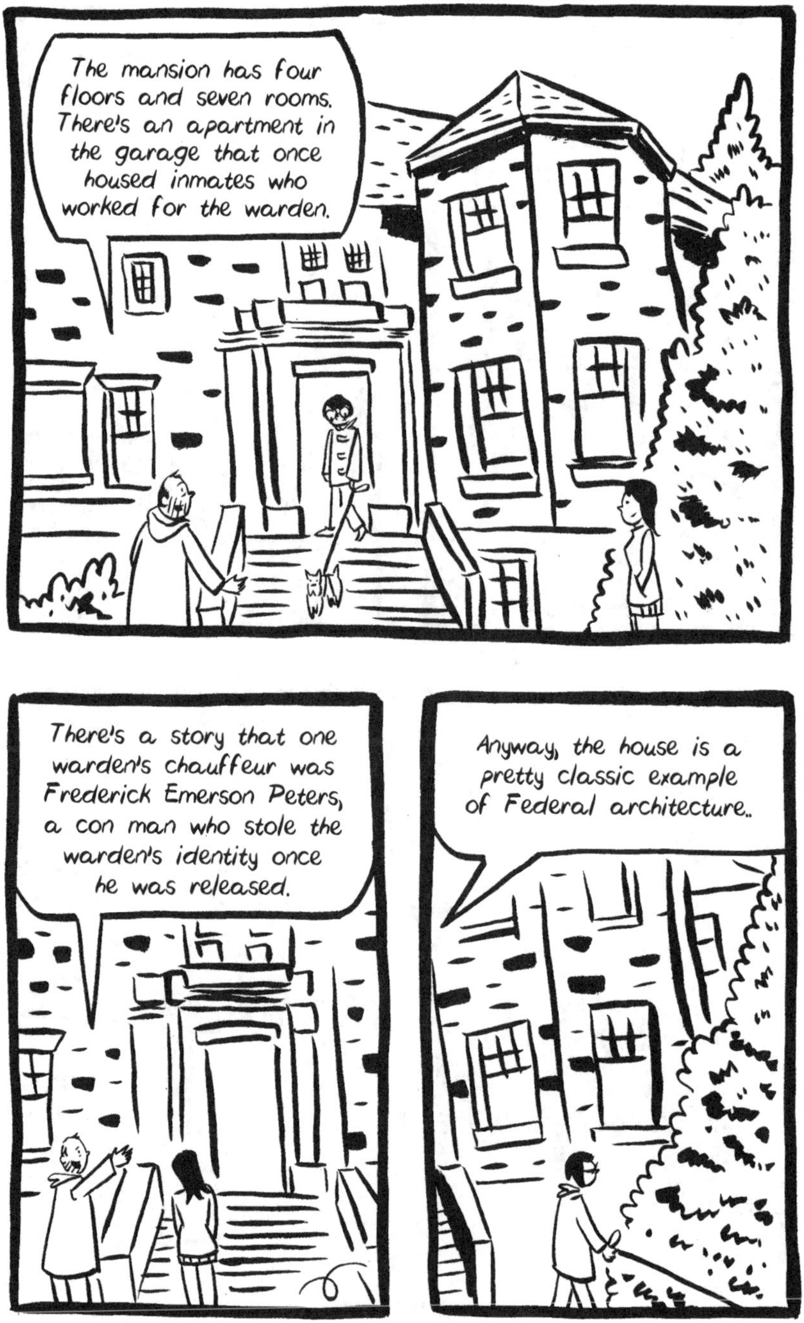
The mansion has four floors and seven rooms. There's an apartment in the garage that once housed inmates who worked for the warden.
There's a story that one warden's chauffeur was Frederick Emerson Peters, a con man who stole the warden's identity once he was released.
Anyway, the house is a pretty classic example of Federal architecture..

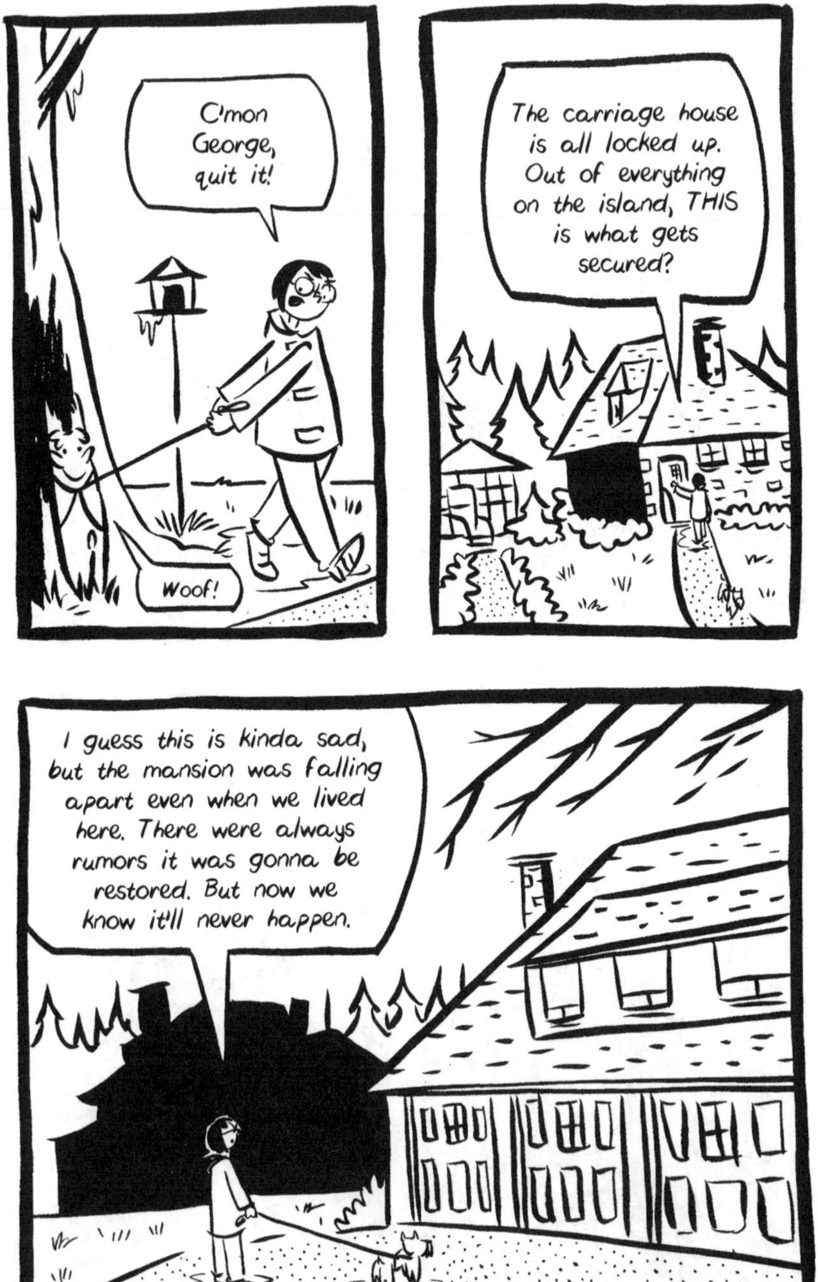
C'mon George, quit it!
Woof!
The carriage house is all locked up. Out of everything on the island, THIS is what gets secured?
I guess this is kinda sad, but the mansion was falling apart even when we lived here. There were always rumors it was gonna be restored. But now we know it'll never happen.

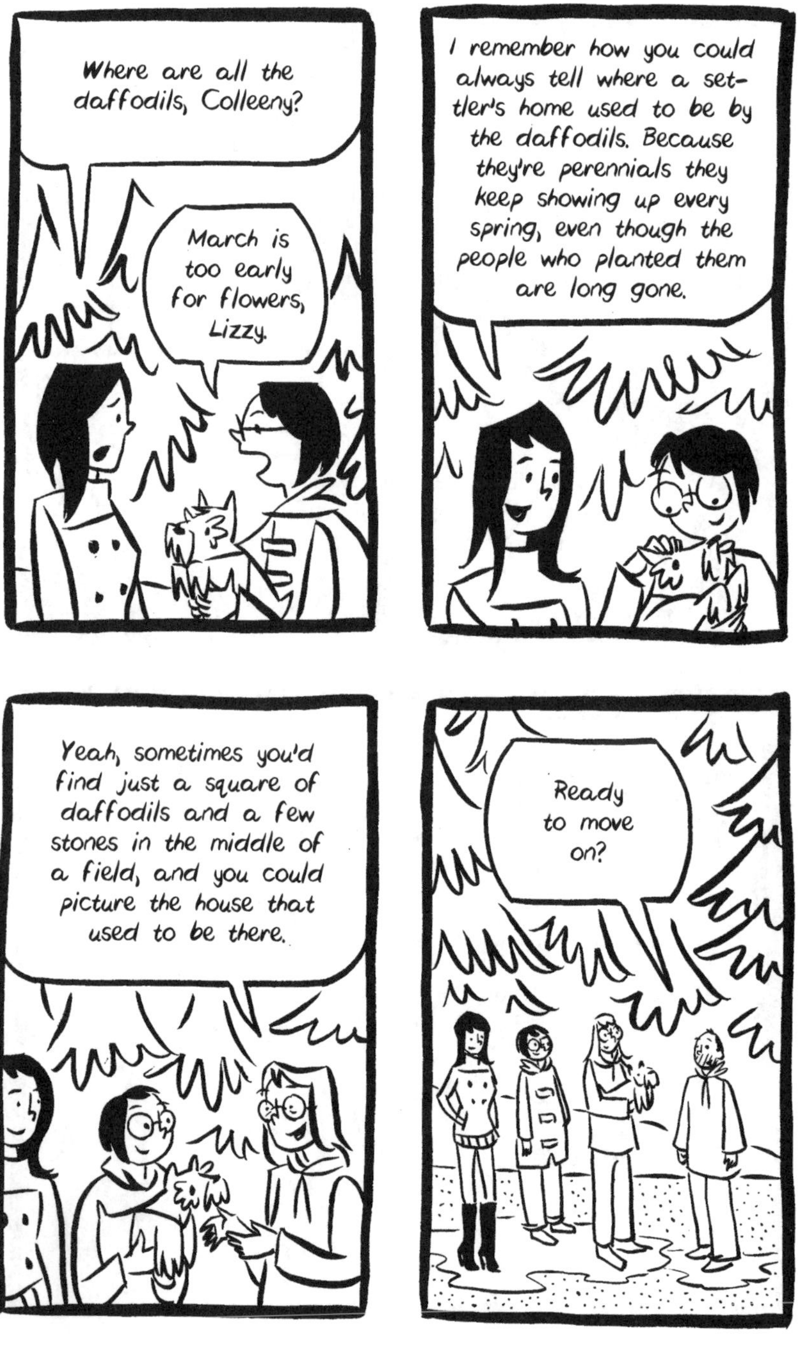
Where are all the daffodils, Colleeny?
March is too early for flowers, Lizzy.
I remember how you could always tell where a settler's home used to be by the daffodils. Because they're perennials they keep showing up every spring, even though the people who planted them are long gone.
Yeah, sometimes you'd find just a square of daffodils and a few stones in the middle of a field, and you could picture the house that used to be there.
Ready to move on?

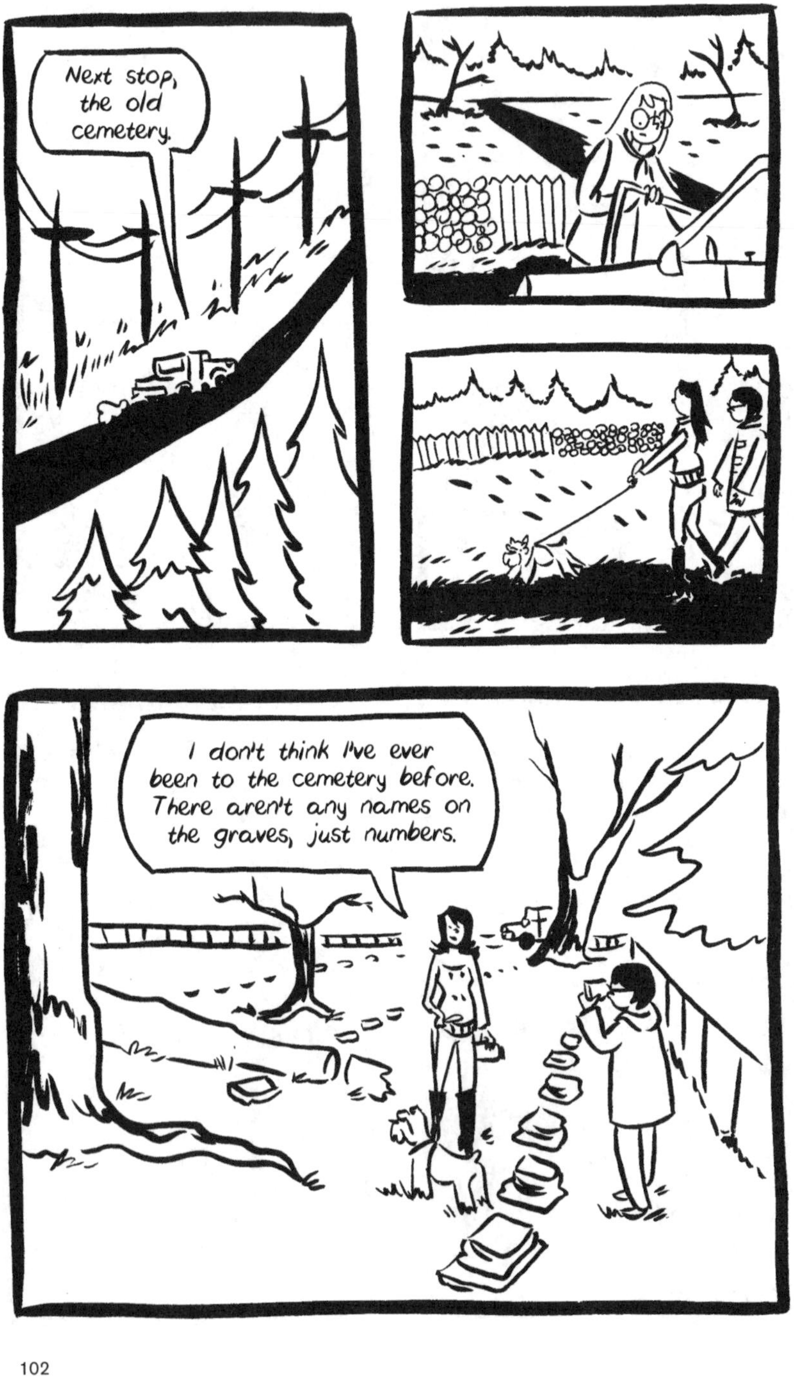
Next stop, the old cemetery.
I don't think I've ever been to the cemetery before. There aren't any names on the graves, just numbers.

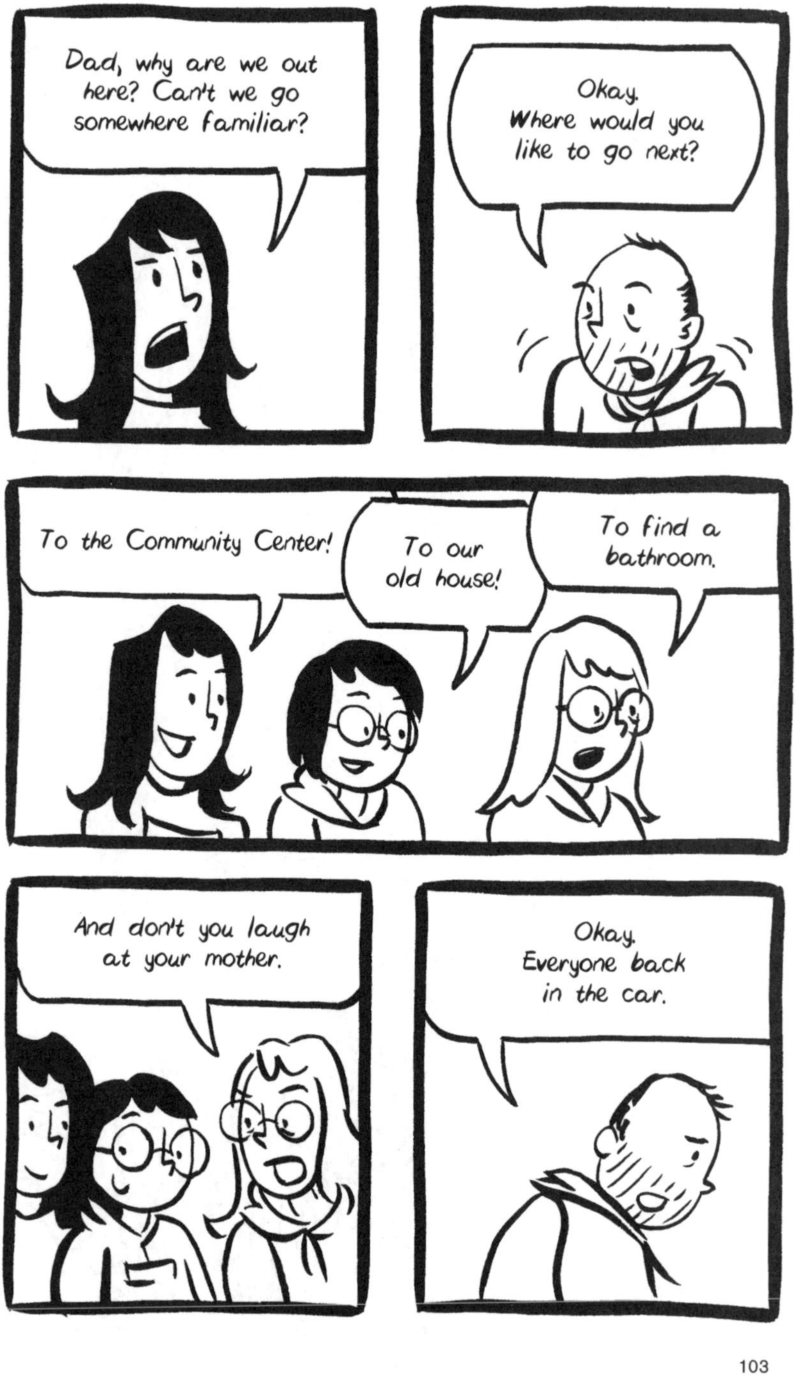
Dad, why are we out here? Can't we go somewhere familiar?
Okay. Where would you like to go next?
To the Community Center!
To our old house!
To find a bathroom.
And don't you laugh at your mother.
Okay. Everyone back in the car.

CHAPTER 7

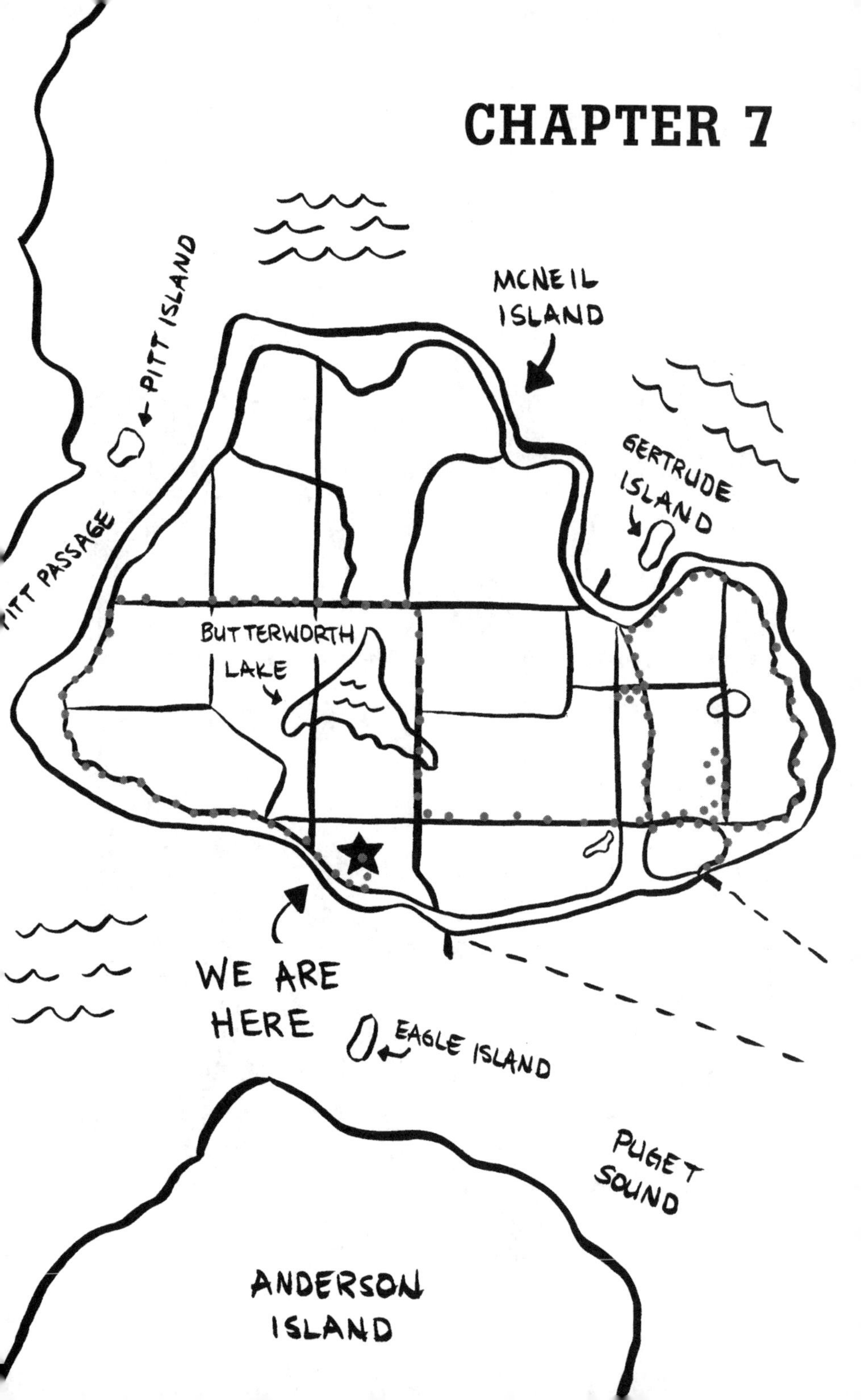

PITT ISLAND
PITT PASSAGE
MCNEIL ISLAND
GERTRUDE ISLAND
BUTTERWORTH LAKE
WE ARE HERE
EAGLE ISLAND
PUGET SOUND
ANDERSON ISLAND

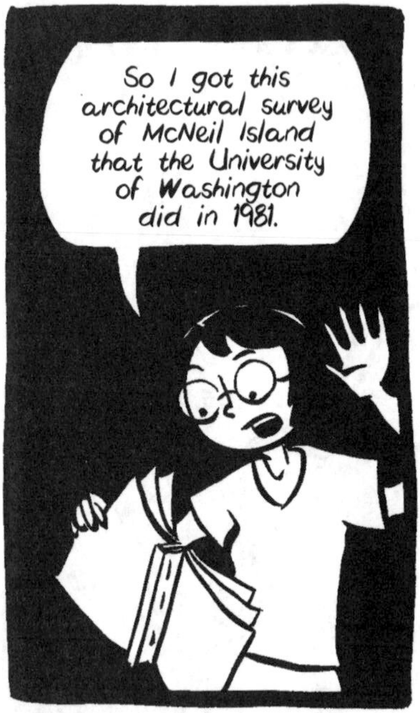
So I got this architectural survey of McNeil Island that the University of Washington did in 1981.

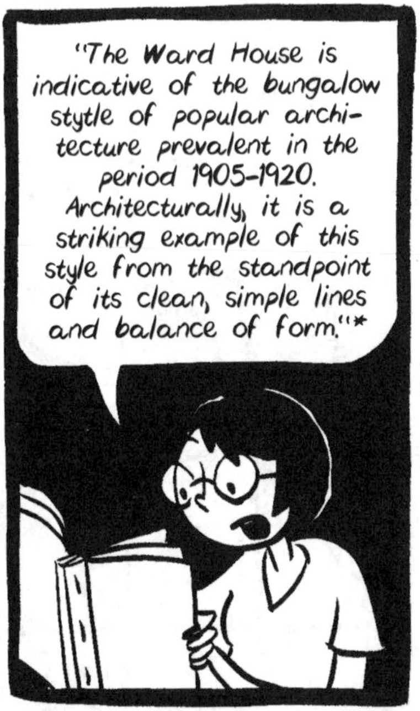
"The Ward House is indicative of the bungalow stytle of popular architecture prevalent in the period 1905-1920. Architecturally, it is a striking example of this style from the standpoint of its clean, simple lines and balance of form."*

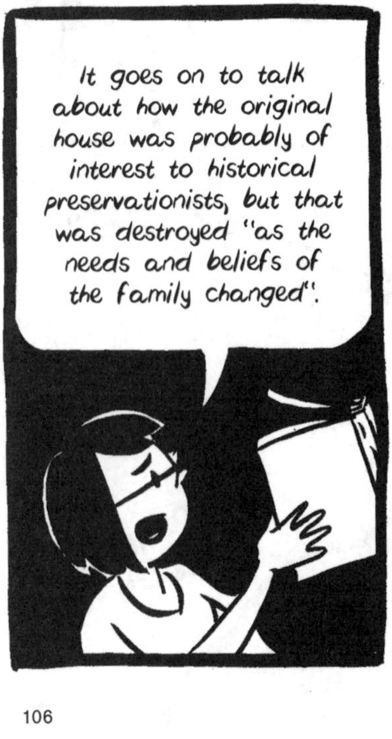
It goes on to talk about how the original house was probably of interest to historical preservationists, but that was destroyed "as the needs and beliefs of the family changed".

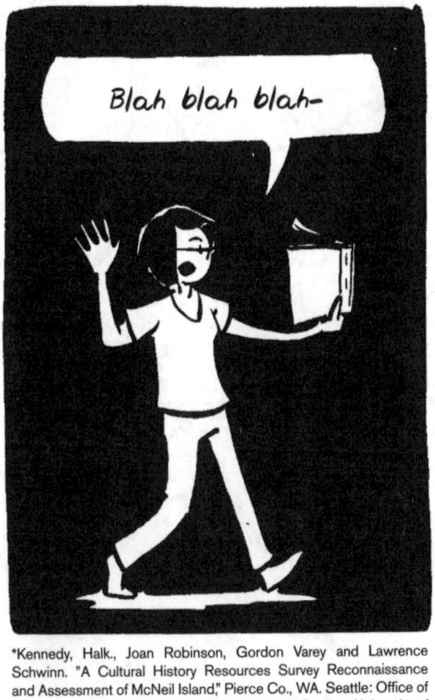
Blah blah blah-

*Kennedy, Halk., Joan Robinson, Gordon Varey and Lawrence Schwinn. "A Cultural History Resources Survey Reconnaissance and Assessment of McNeil Island," Pierce Co., WA. Seattle: Office of Public Archaeology, Institute for Environmental Studies, University of Washington, 1981. *Full bibliography in the back of the book.*

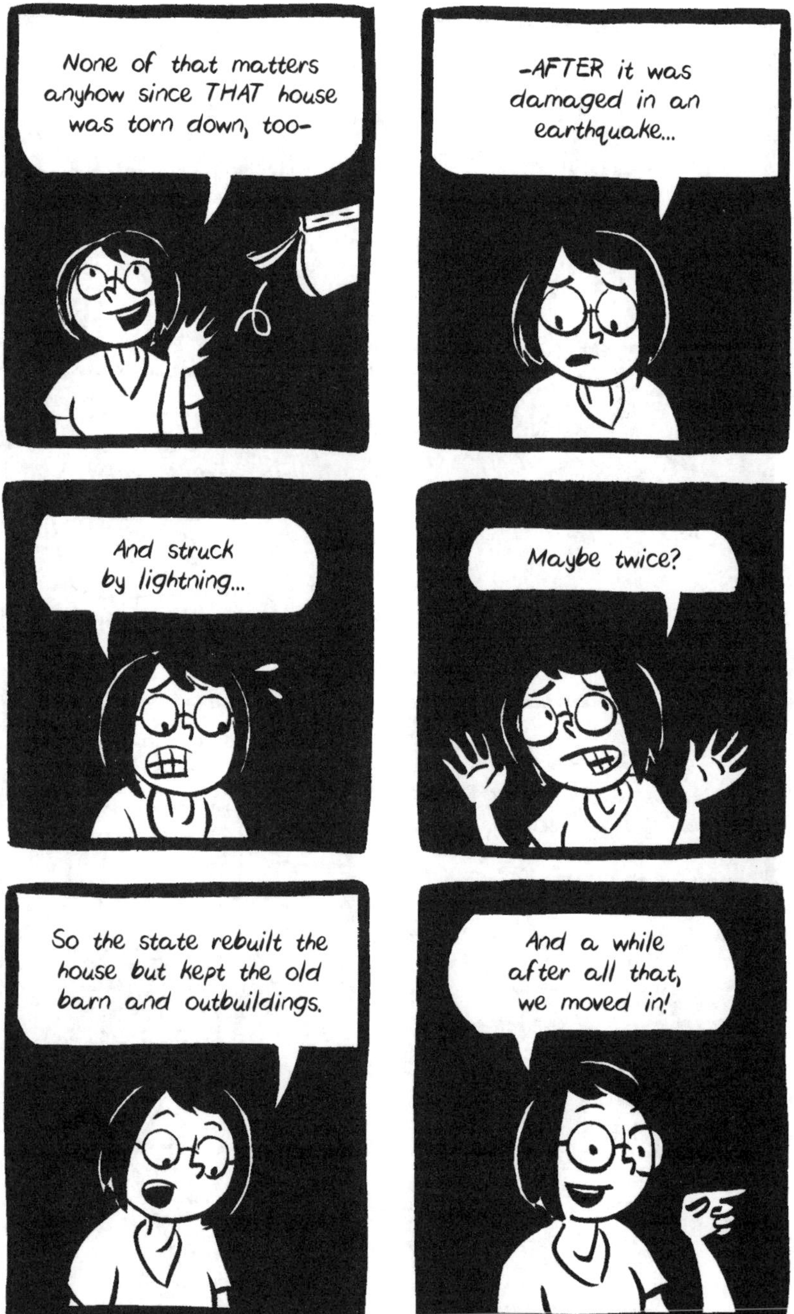
None of that matters anyhow since THAT house was torn down, too-
-AFTER it was damaged in an earthquake...
And struck by lightning...
Maybe twice?
So the state rebuilt the house but kept the old barn and outbuildings.
And a while after all that, we moved in!

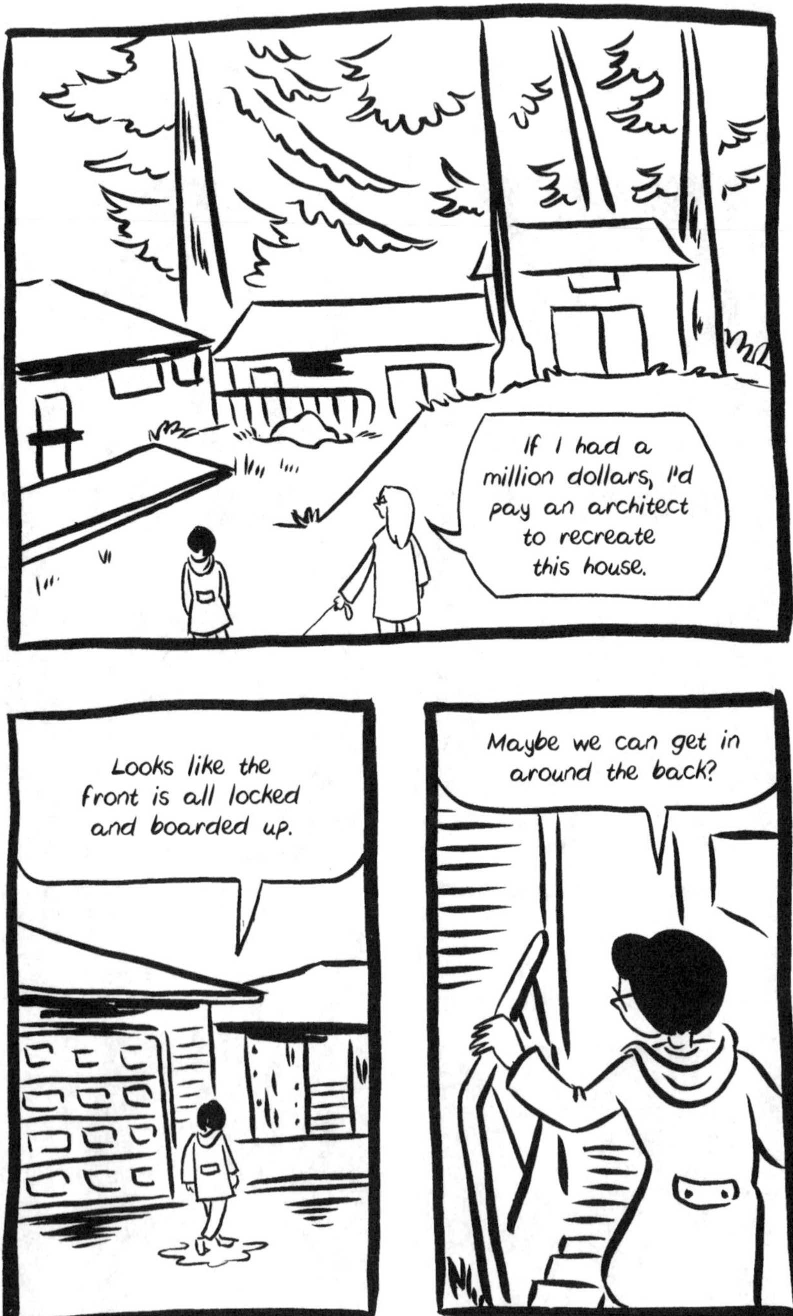
If I had a million dollars, I'd pay an architect to recreate this house.
Looks like the front is all locked and boarded up.
Maybe we can get in around the back?

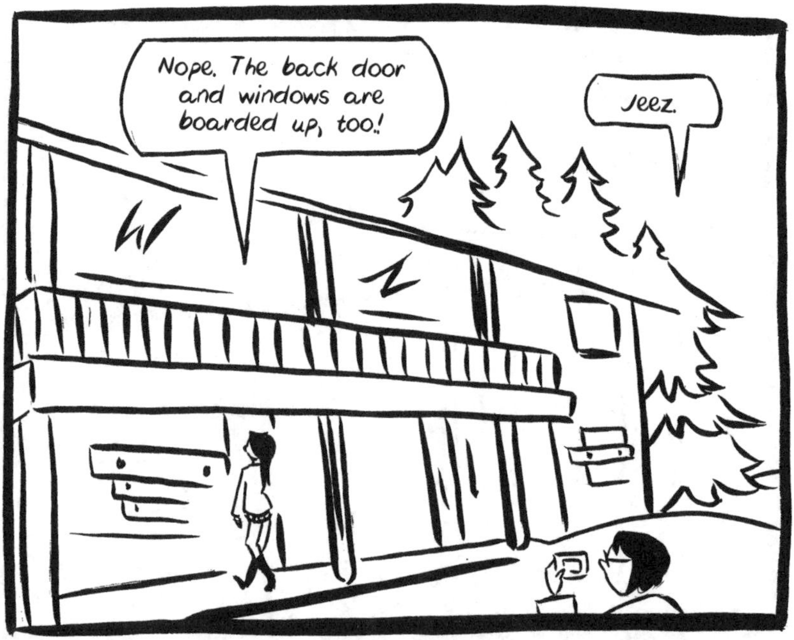
Nope. The back door and windows are boarded up, too!
Jeez.

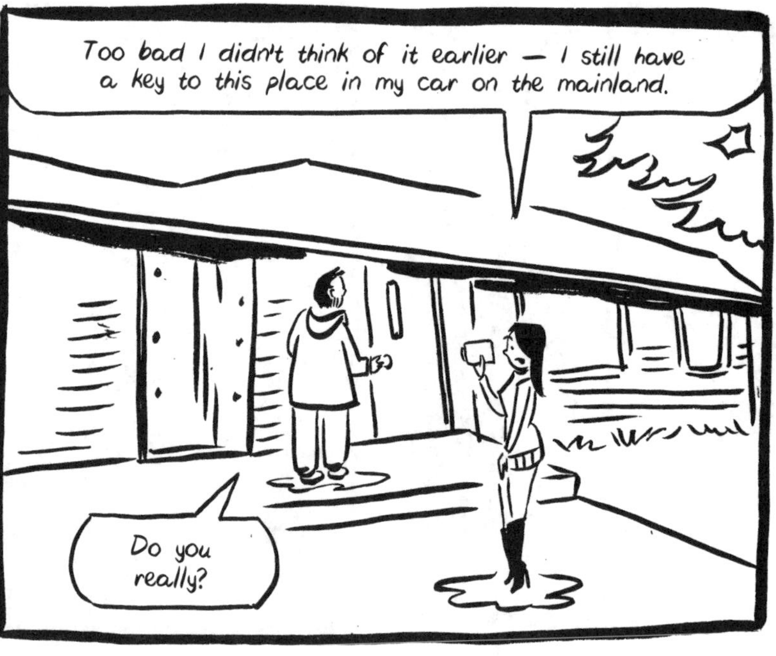
Too bad I didn't think of it earlier — I still have a key to this place in my car on the mainland.
Do you really?

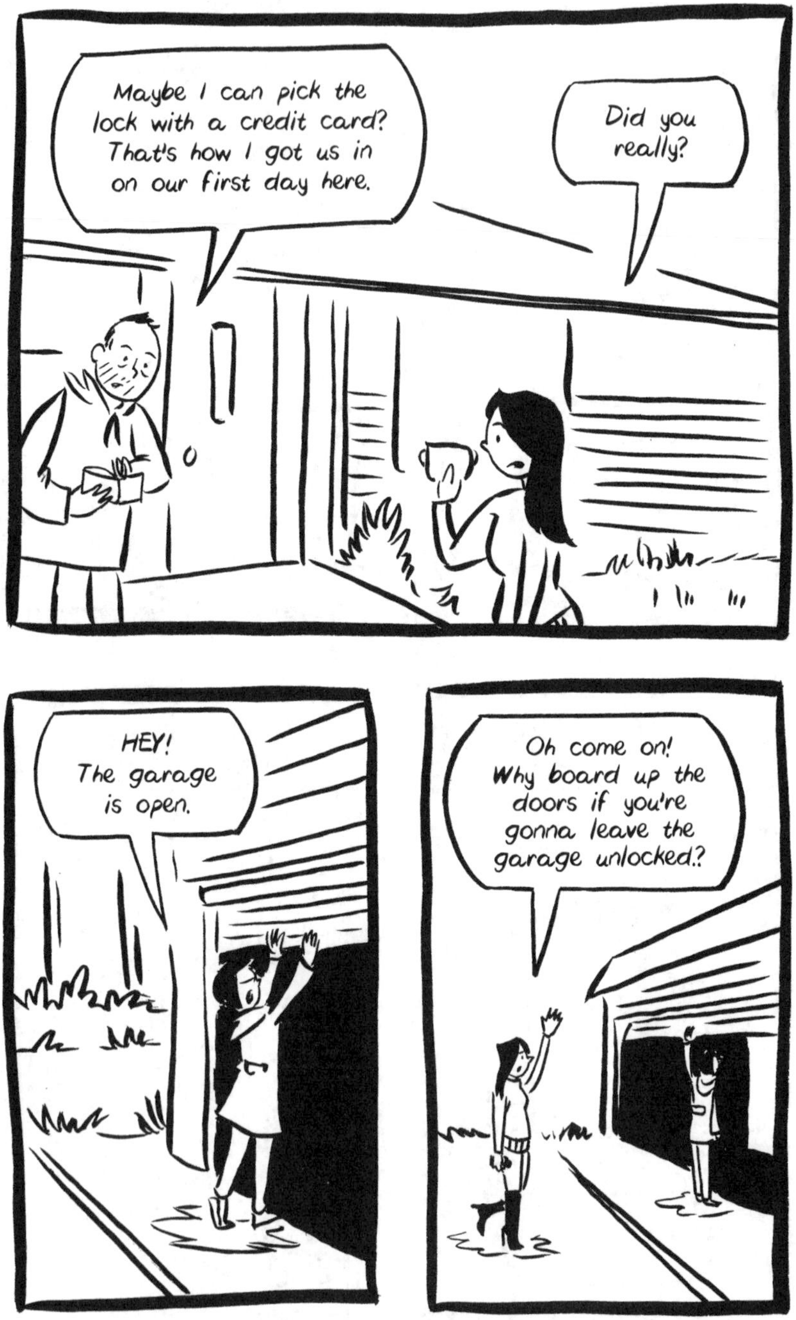
Maybe I can pick the lock with a credit card? That's how I got us in on our first day here.
Did you really?
HEY! The garage is open.
Oh come on! Why board up the doors if you're gonna leave the garage unlocked.?

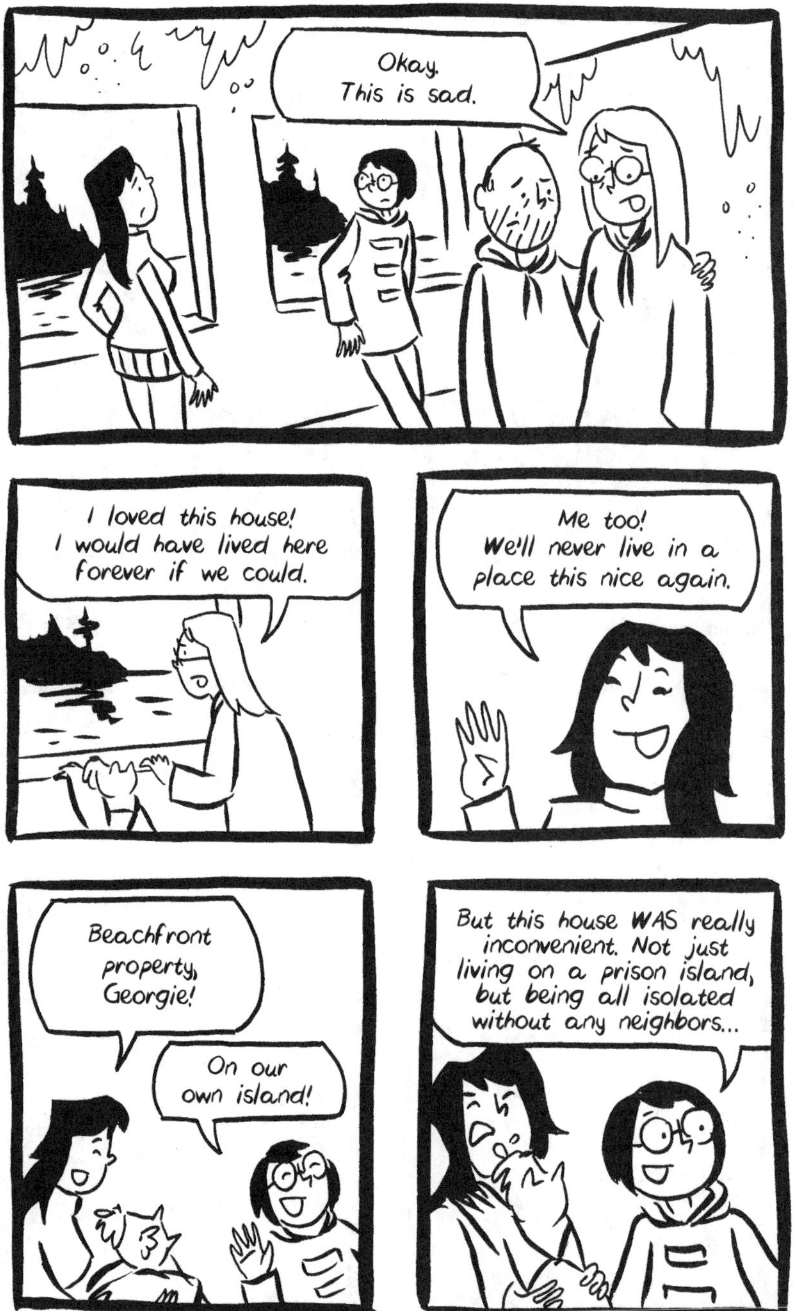
Okay. This is sad.
I loved this house! I would have lived here forever if we could.
Me too! We'll never live in a place this nice again.
Beachfront property, Georgie!
On our own island!
But this house WAS really inconvenient. Not just living on a prison island, but being all isolated without any neighbors...

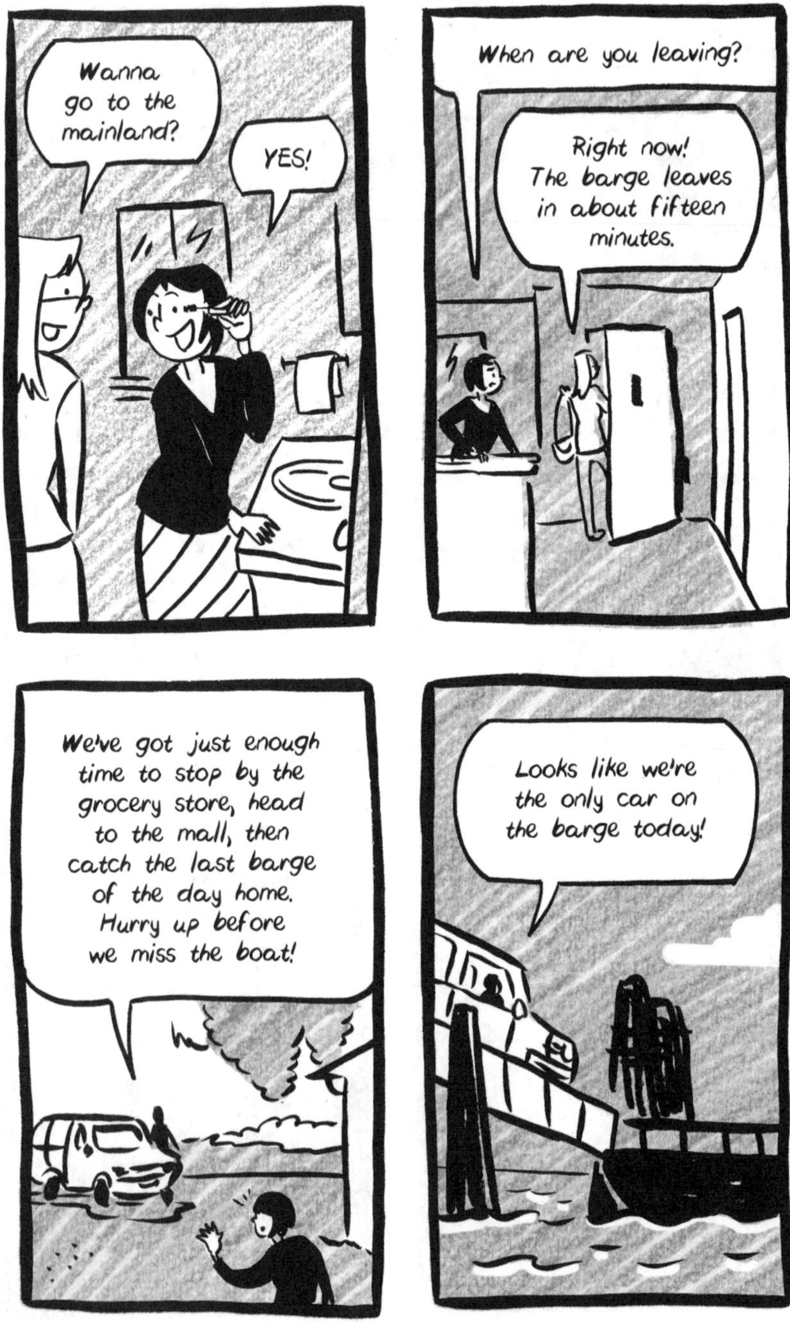
Wanna go to the mainland?
YES!
When are you leaving?
Right now! The barge leaves in about fifteen minutes.
We've got just enough time to stop by the grocery store, head to the mall, then catch the last barge of the day home. Hurry up before we miss the boat!
Looks like we're the only car on the barge today!

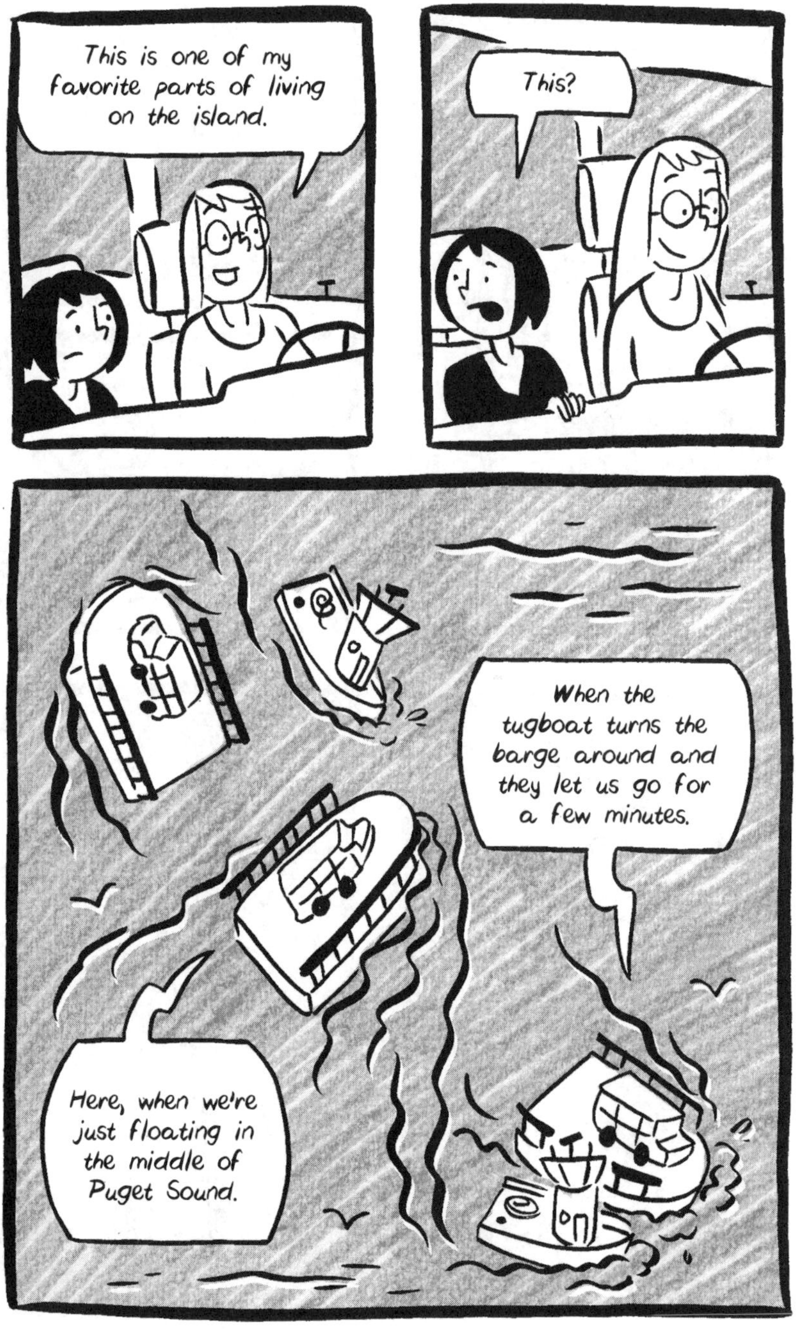
This is one of my favorite parts of living on the island.
This?
When the tugboat turns the barge around and they let us go for a few minutes.
Here, when we're just floating in the middle of Puget Sound.

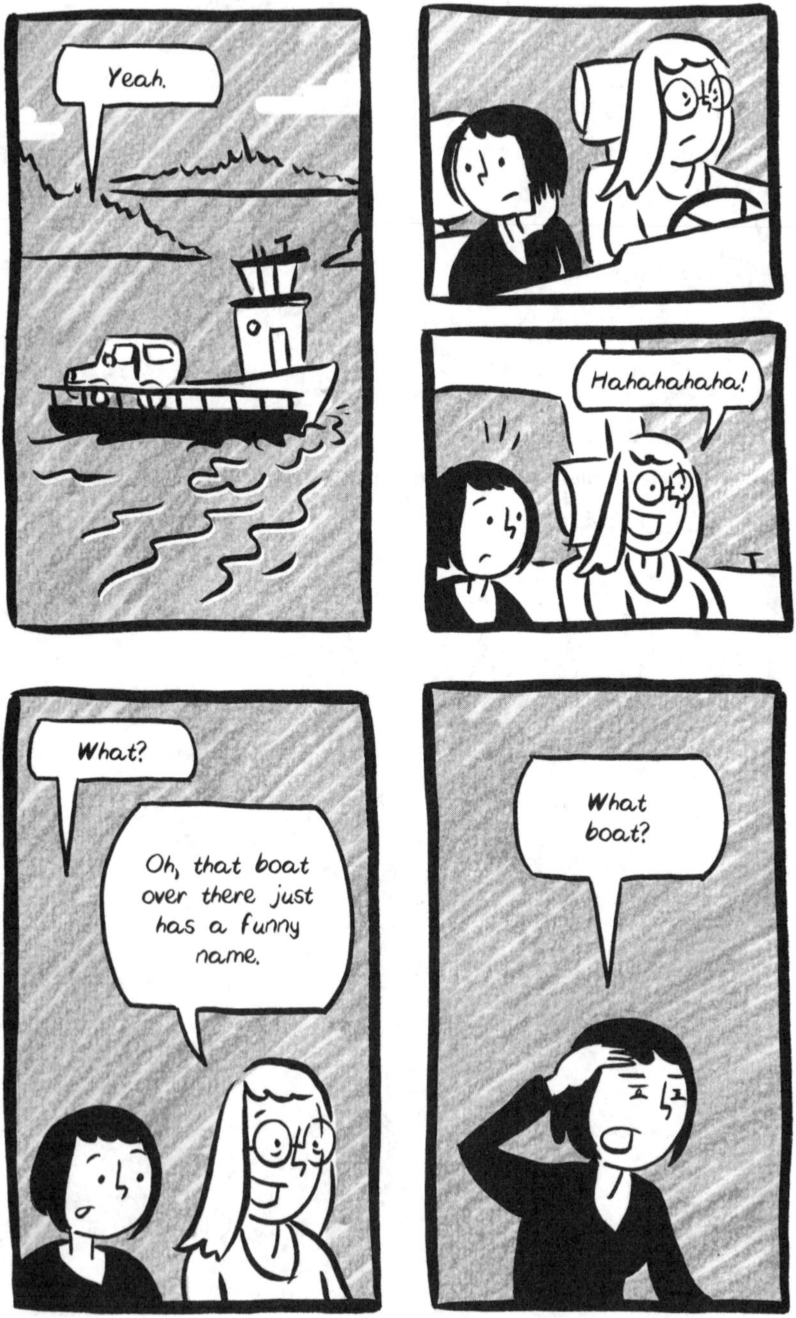
Yeah.
Hahahahaha!
What?
Oh, that boat over there just has a funny name.
What boat?

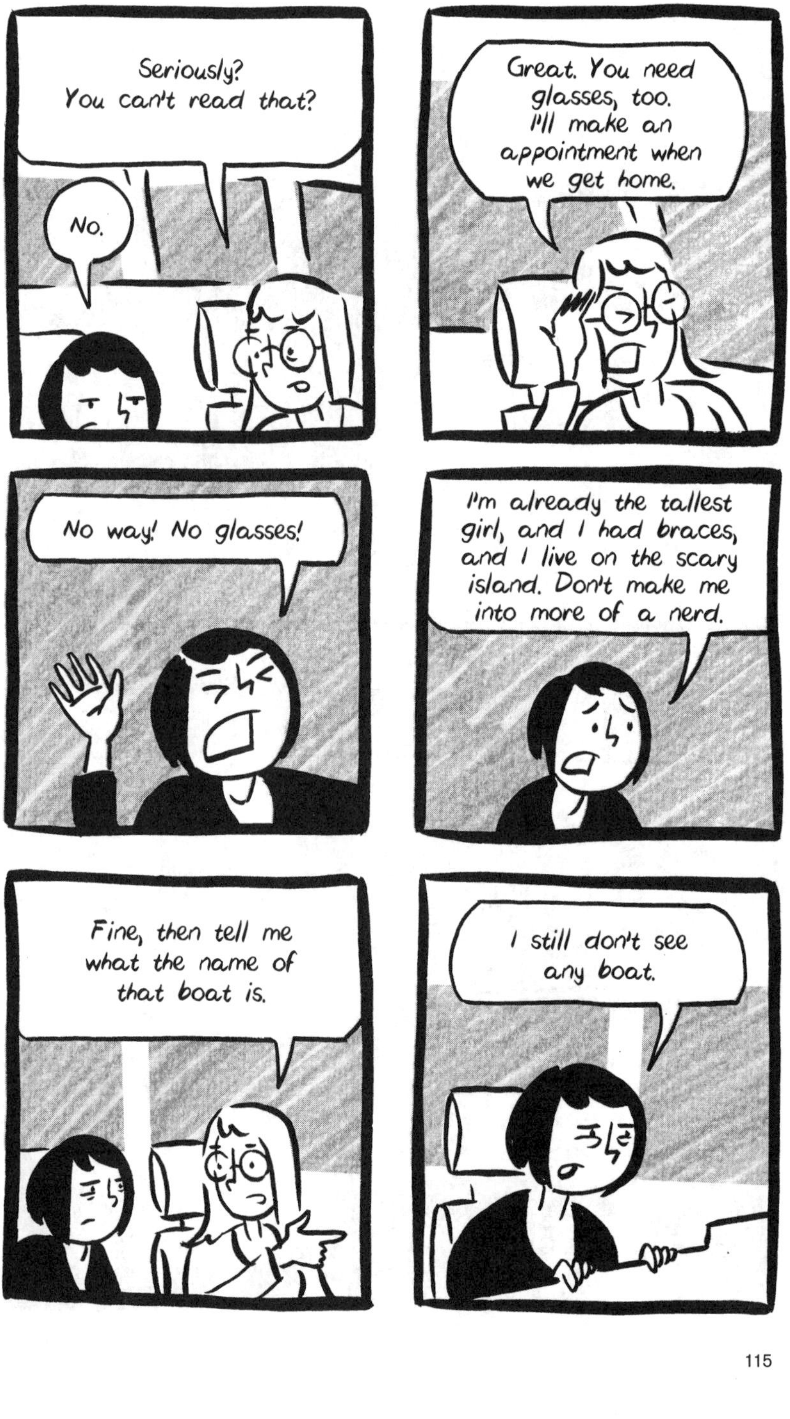
Seriously? You can't read that?
No.
Great. You need glasses, too. I'll make an appointment when we get home.
No way! No glasses!
I'm already the tallest girl, and I had braces, and I live on the scary island. Don't make me into more of a nerd.
Fine, then tell me what the name of that boat is.
I still don't see any boat.

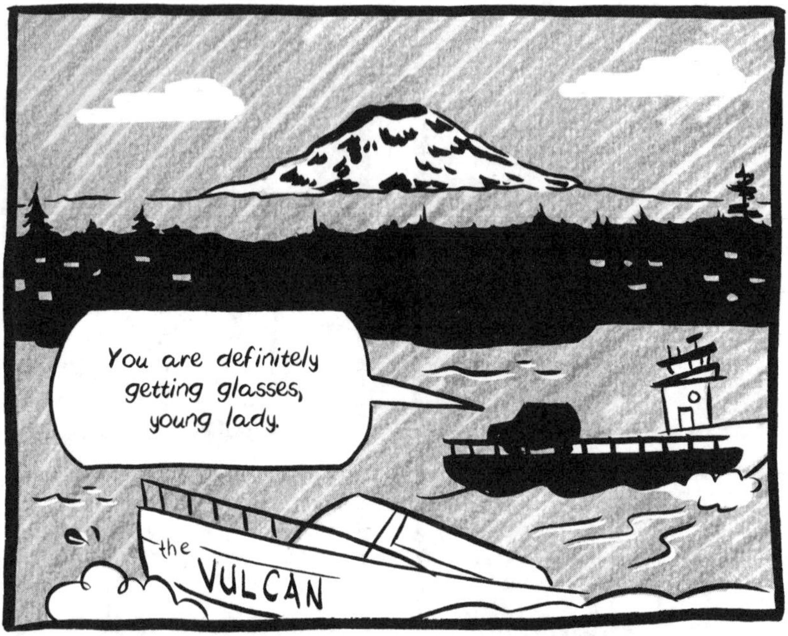
You are definitely getting glasses, young lady.
the VULCAN

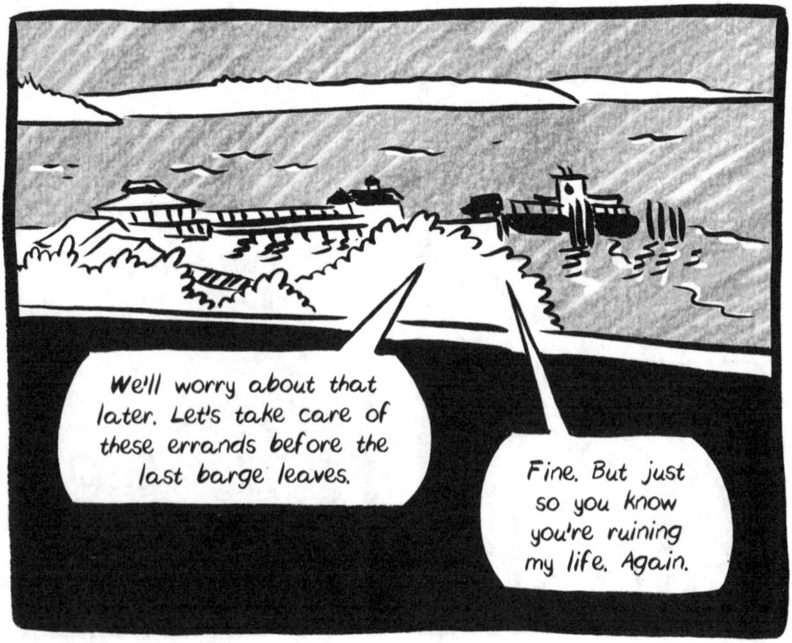
We'll worry about that later. Let's take care of these errands before the last barge leaves.
Fine. But just so you know you're ruining my life. Again.

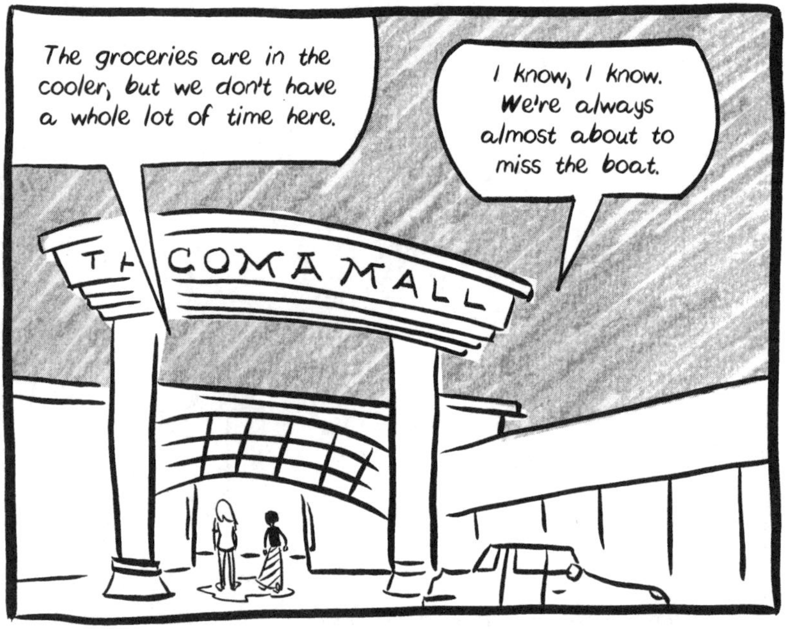
The groceries are in the cooler, but we don't have a whole lot of time here.
I know, I know. We're always almost about to miss the boat.
T COMA MALL

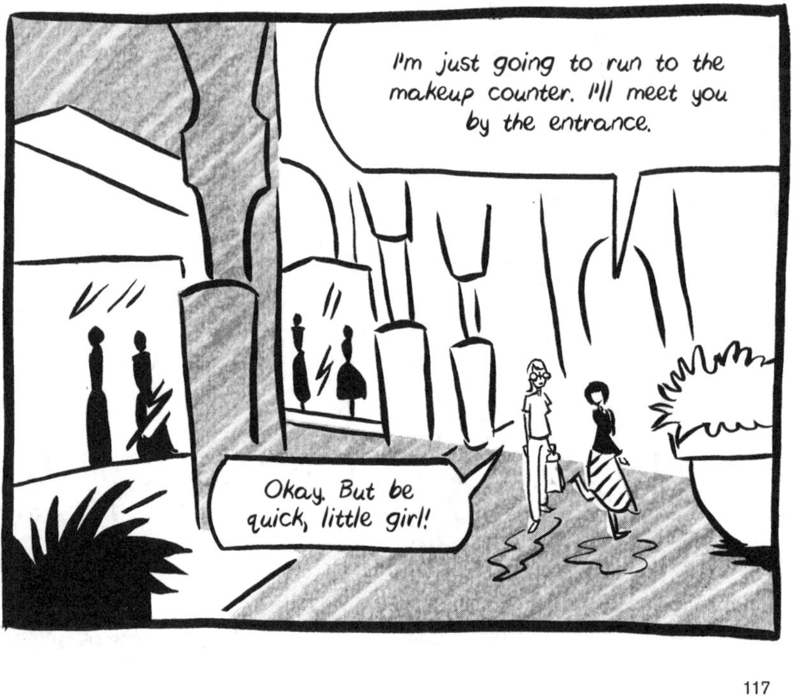
I'm just going to run to the makeup counter. I'll meet you by the entrance.
Okay. But be quick, little girl!

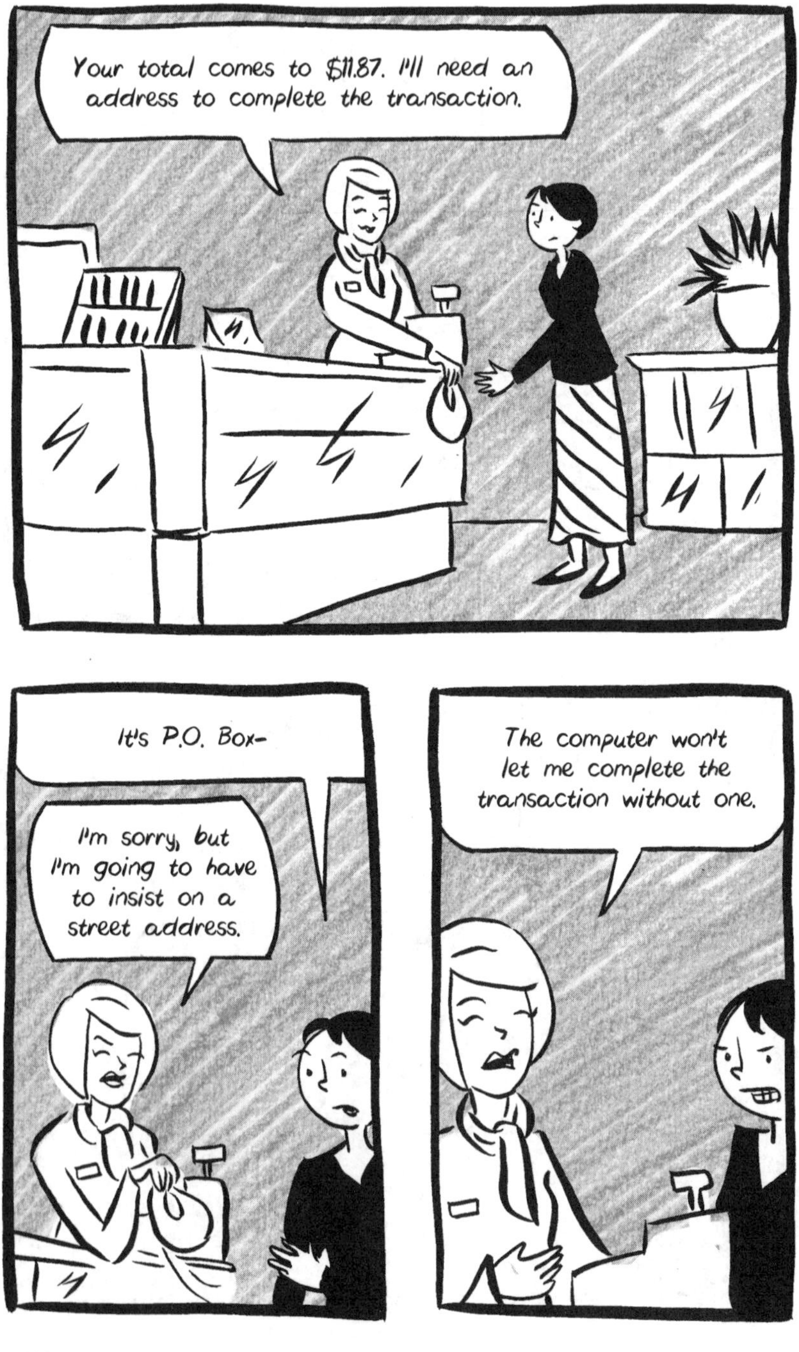
Your total comes to $11.87. I'll need an address to complete the transaction.
It's P.O. Box-
I'm sorry, but I'm going to have to insist on a street address.
The computer won't let me complete the transaction without one.

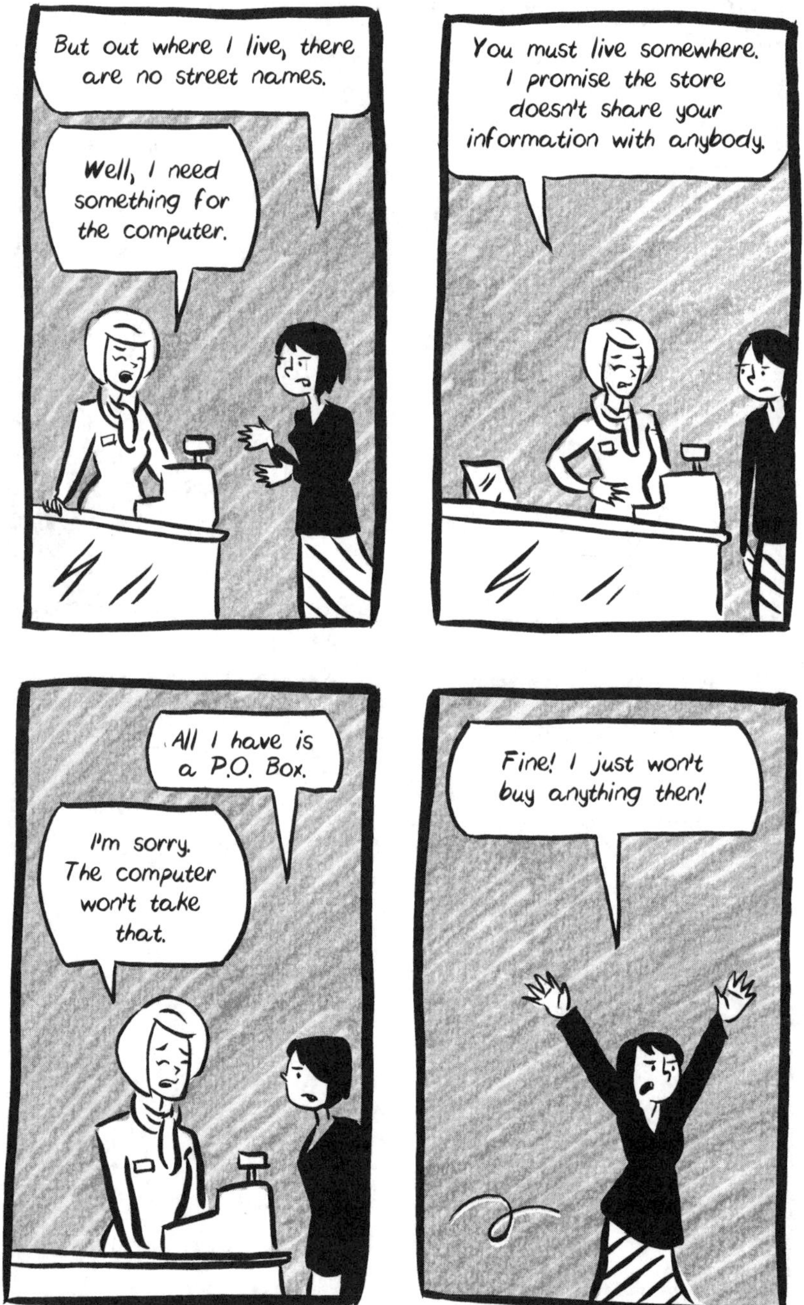
But out where I live, there are no street names.
Well, I need something for the computer.
You must live somewhere. I promise the store doesn't share your information with anybody.
All I have is a P.O. Box.
I'm sorry. The computer won't take that.
Fine! I just won't buy anything then!

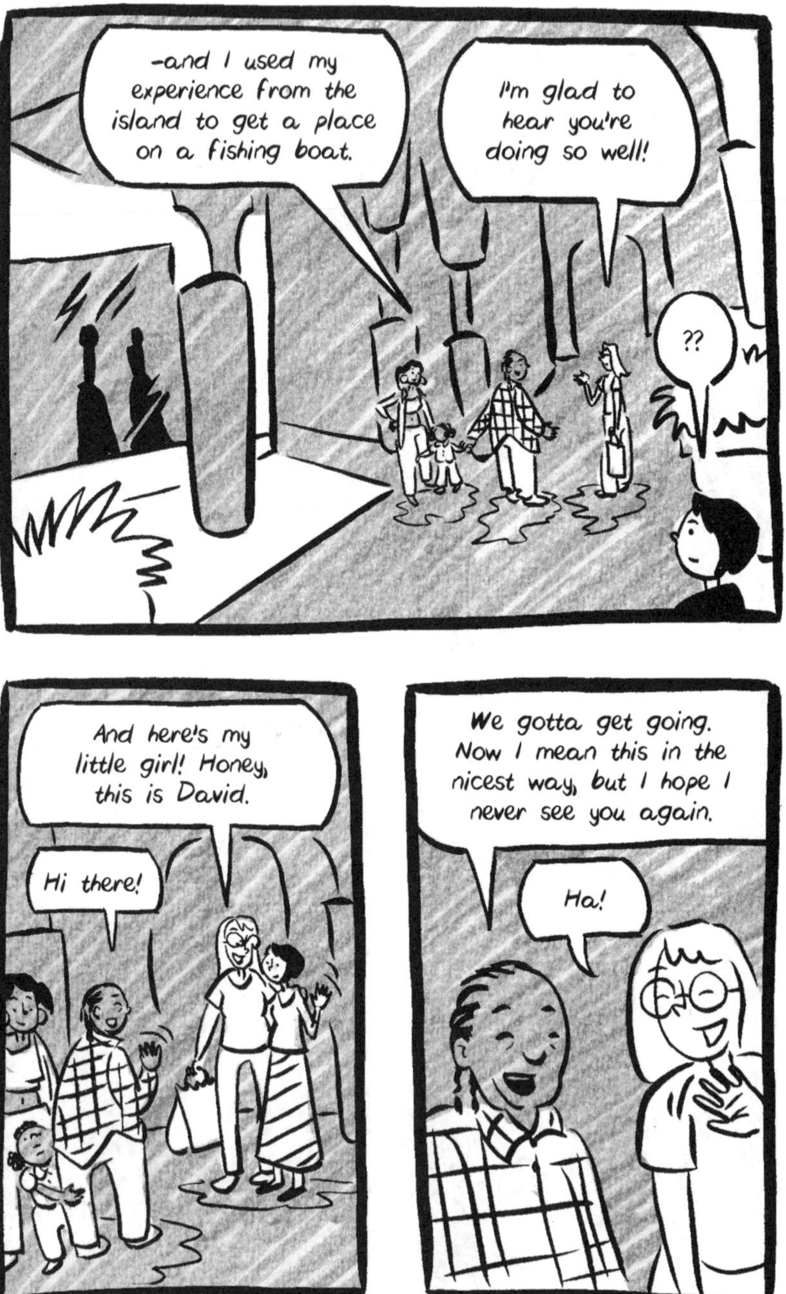
-and I used my experience from the island to get a place on a fishing boat.
I'm glad to hear you're doing so well!
??
And here's my little girl! Honey, this is David.
Hi there!
We gotta get going. Now I mean this in the nicest way, but I hope I never see you again.
Ha!

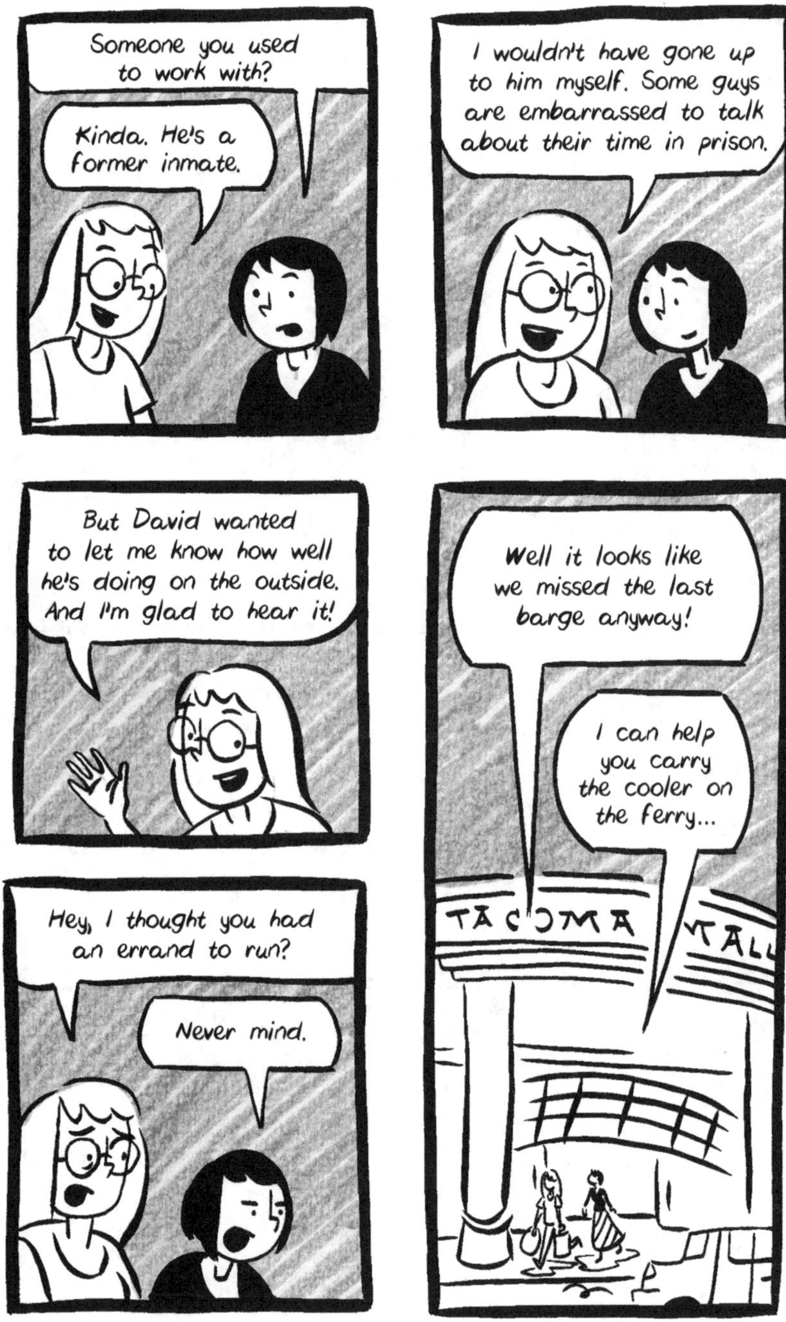
Someone you used to work with?
Kinda. He's a former inmate.
I wouldn't have gone up to him myself. Some guys are embarrassed to talk about their time in prison.
But David wanted to let me know how well he's doing on the outside. And I'm glad to hear it!
Hey, I thought you had an errand to run?
Never mind.
Well it looks like we missed the last barge anyway!
I can help you carry the cooler on the ferry...
TACOMA

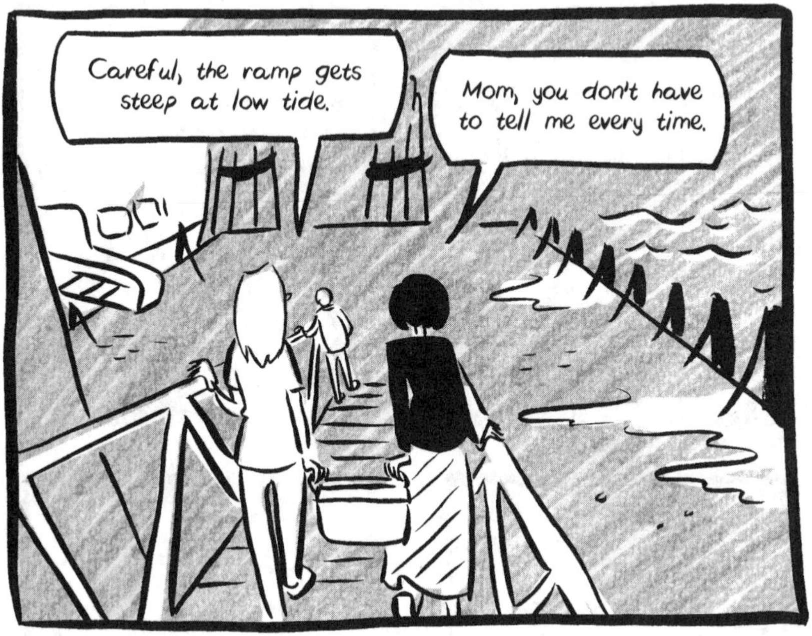
Careful, the ramp gets steep at low tide.
Mom, you don't have to tell me every time.

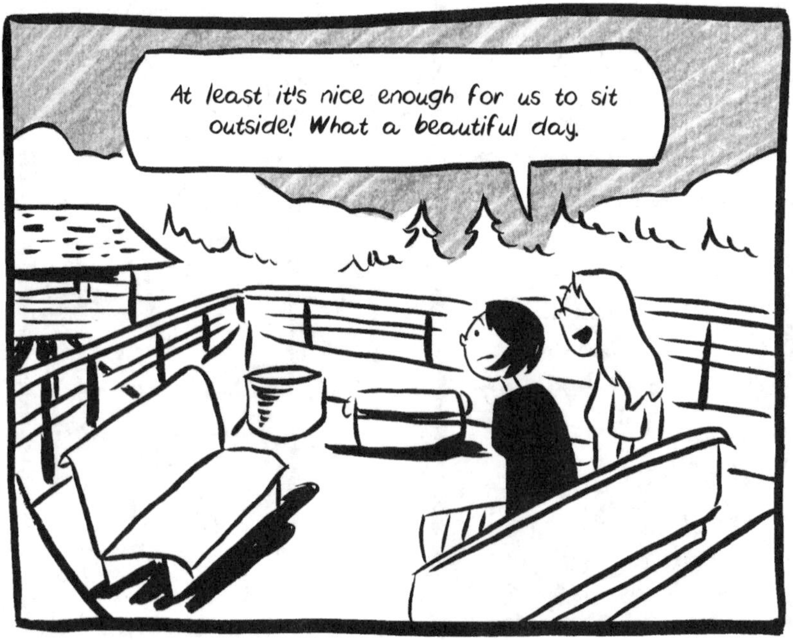
At least it's nice enough for us to sit outside! What a beautiful day.

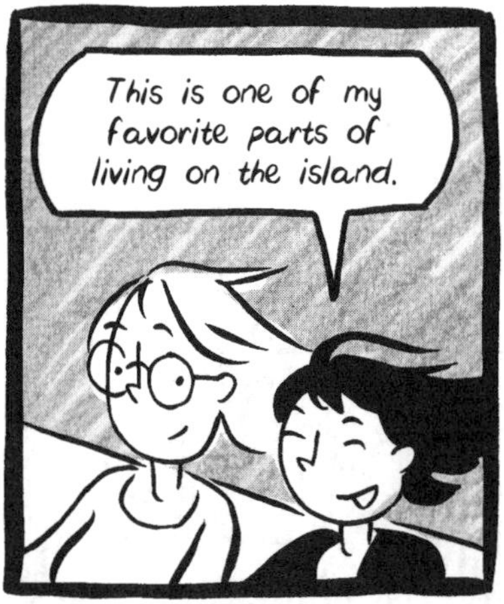
This is one of my favorite parts of living on the island.

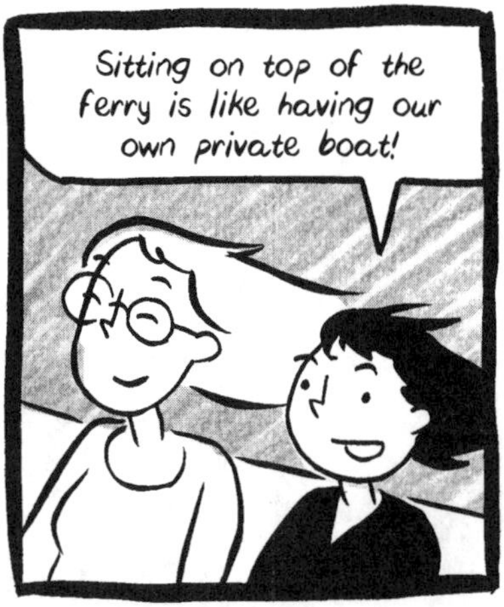
Sitting on top of the ferry is like having our own private boat!

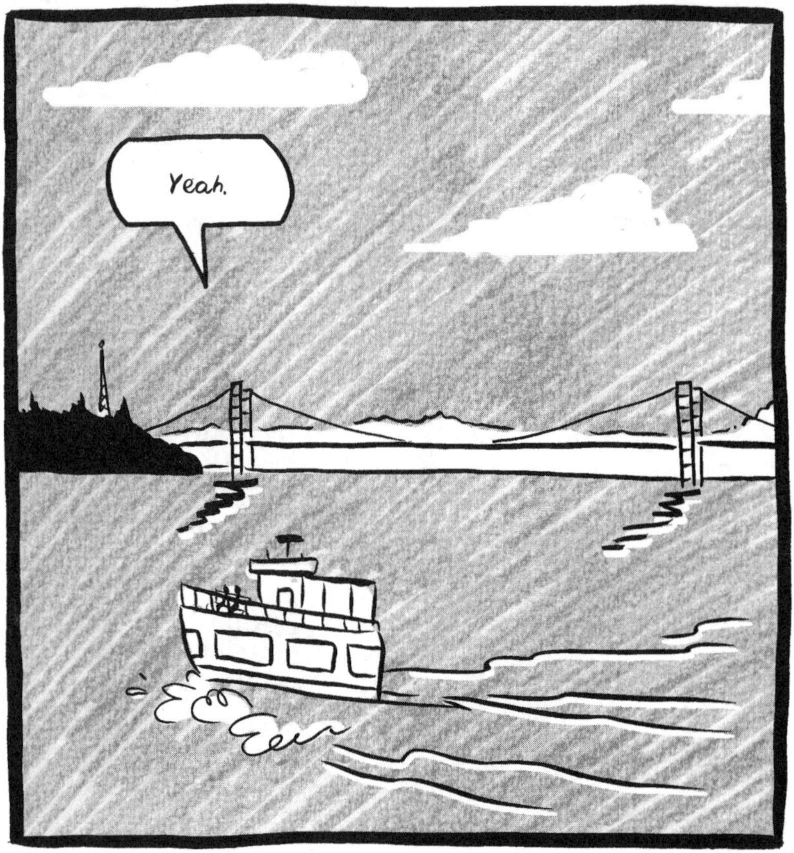
Yeah.

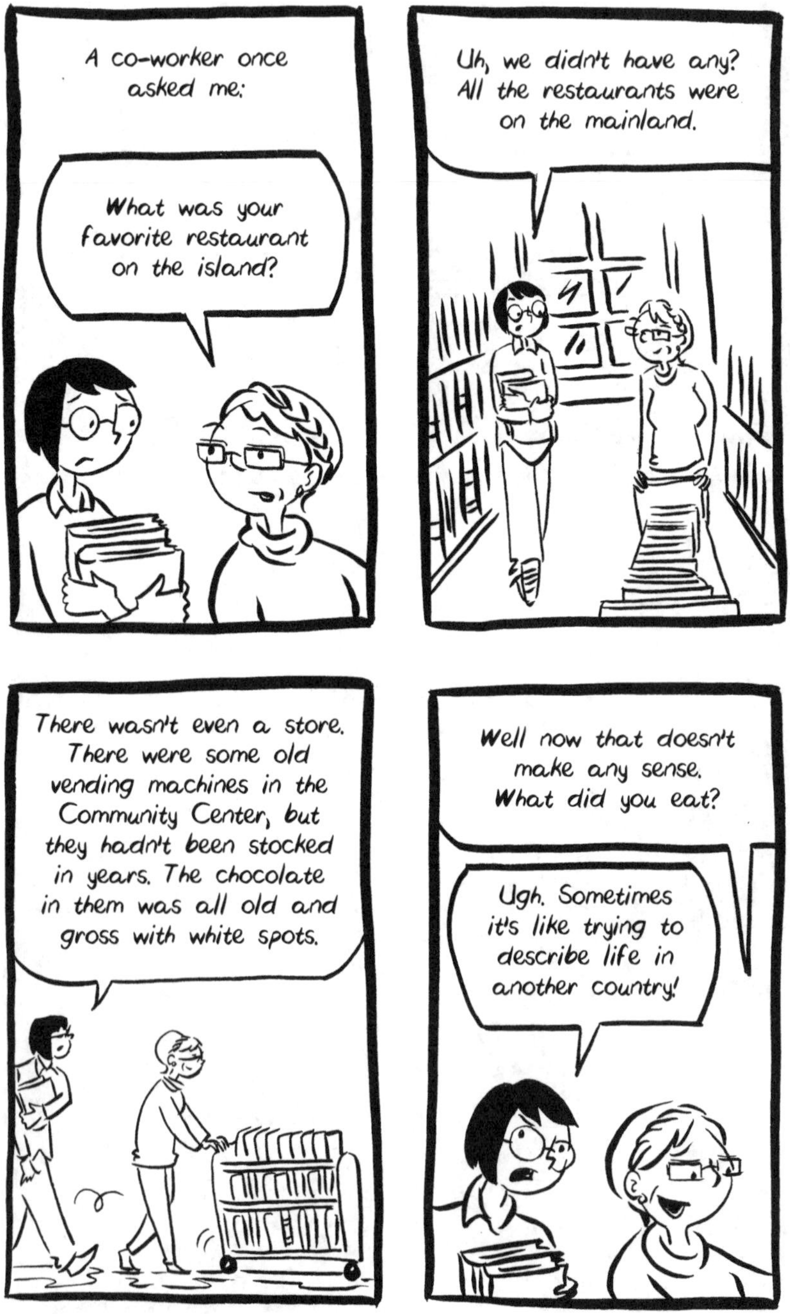
A co-worker once asked me:
What was your favorite restaurant on the island?
Uh, we didn't have any? All the restaurants were on the mainland.
There wasn't even a store. There were some old vending machines in the Community Center, but they hadn't been stocked in years. The chocolate in them was all old and gross with white spots.
Well now that doesn't make any sense. What did you eat?
Ugh. Sometimes it's like trying to describe life in another country!

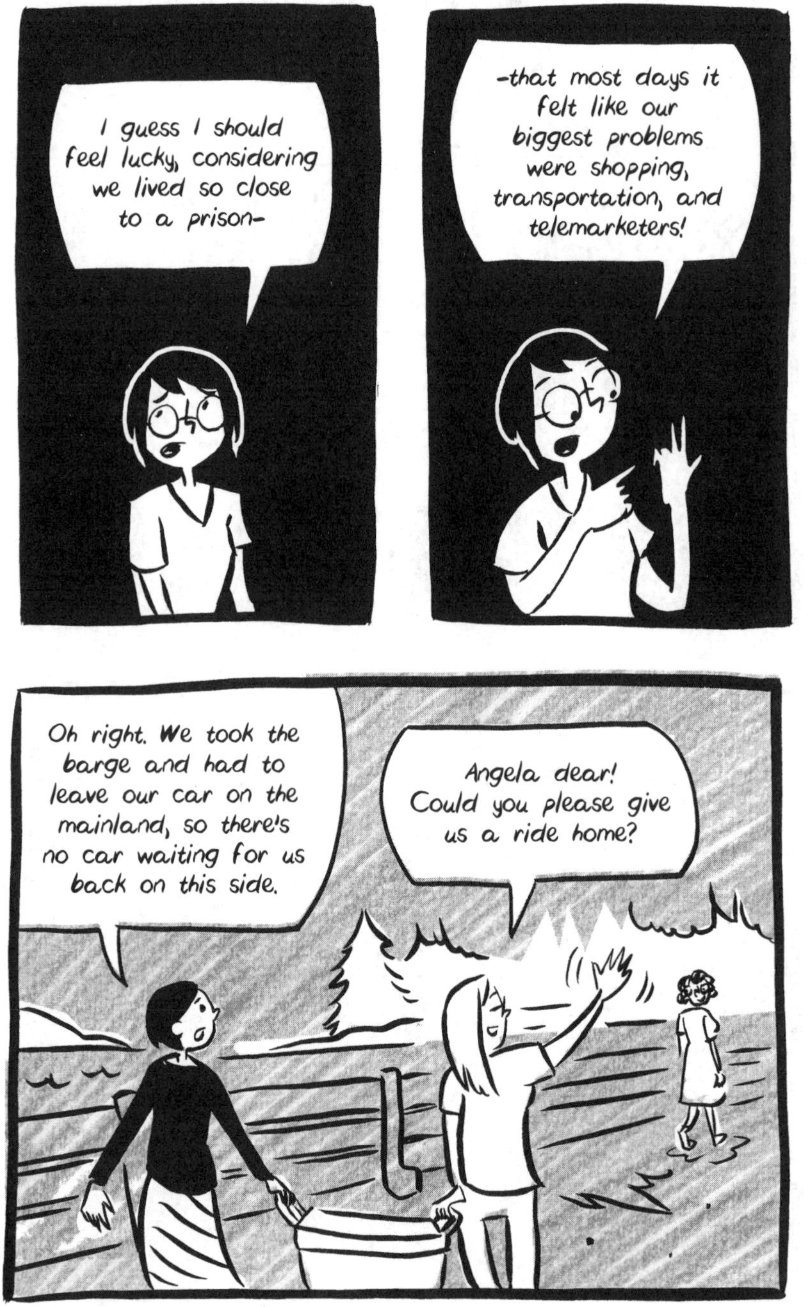
I guess I should feel lucky, considering we lived so close to a prison-
-that most days it felt like our biggest problems were shopping, transportation, and telemarketers!
Oh right. We took the barge and had to leave our car on the mainland, so there's no car waiting for us back on this side.
Angela dear! Could you please give us a ride home?

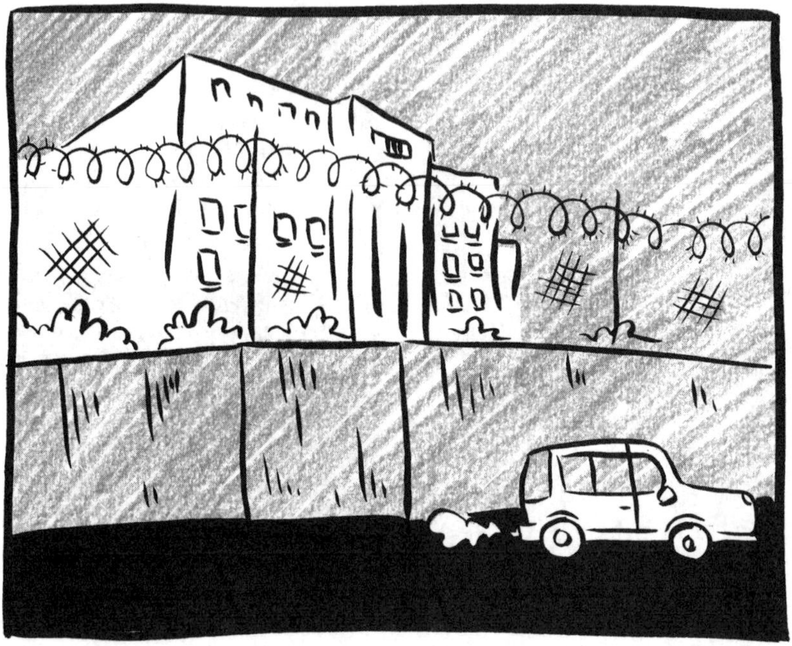

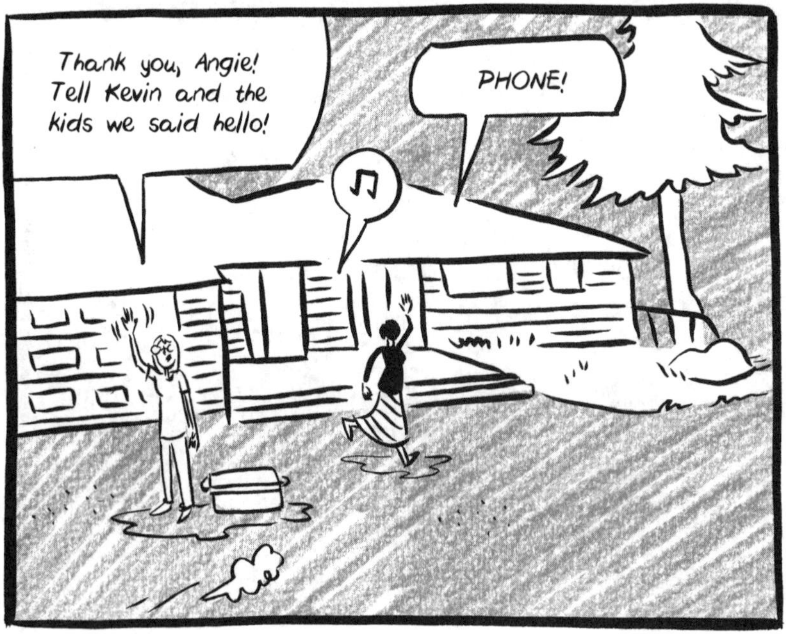
Thank you, Angie! Tell Kevin and the kids we said hello!
PHONE!

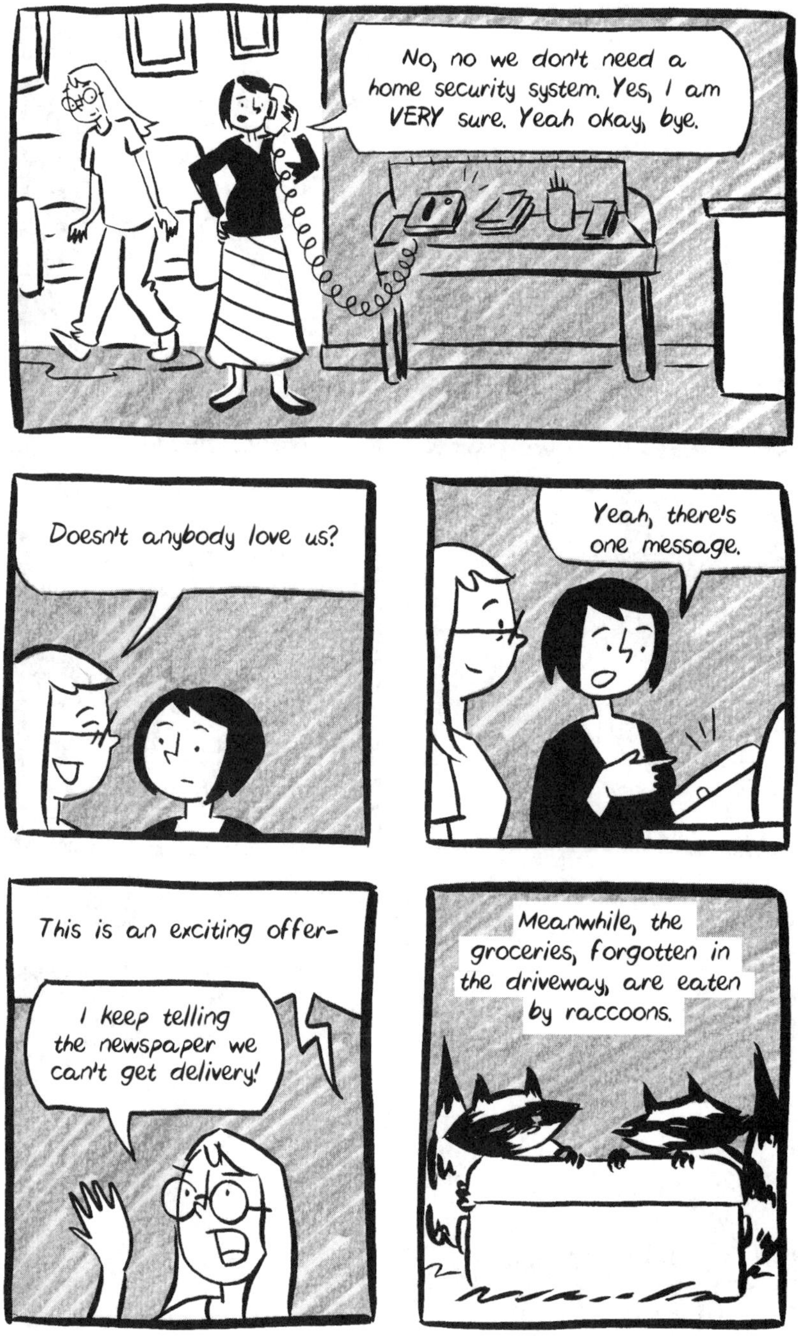
No, no we don't need a home security system. Yes, I am VERY sure. Yeah okay, bye.
Doesn't anybody love us?
Yeah, there's one message.
This is an exciting offer-
I keep telling the newspaper we can't get delivery!
Meanwhile, the groceries, forgotten in the driveway, are eaten by raccoons.

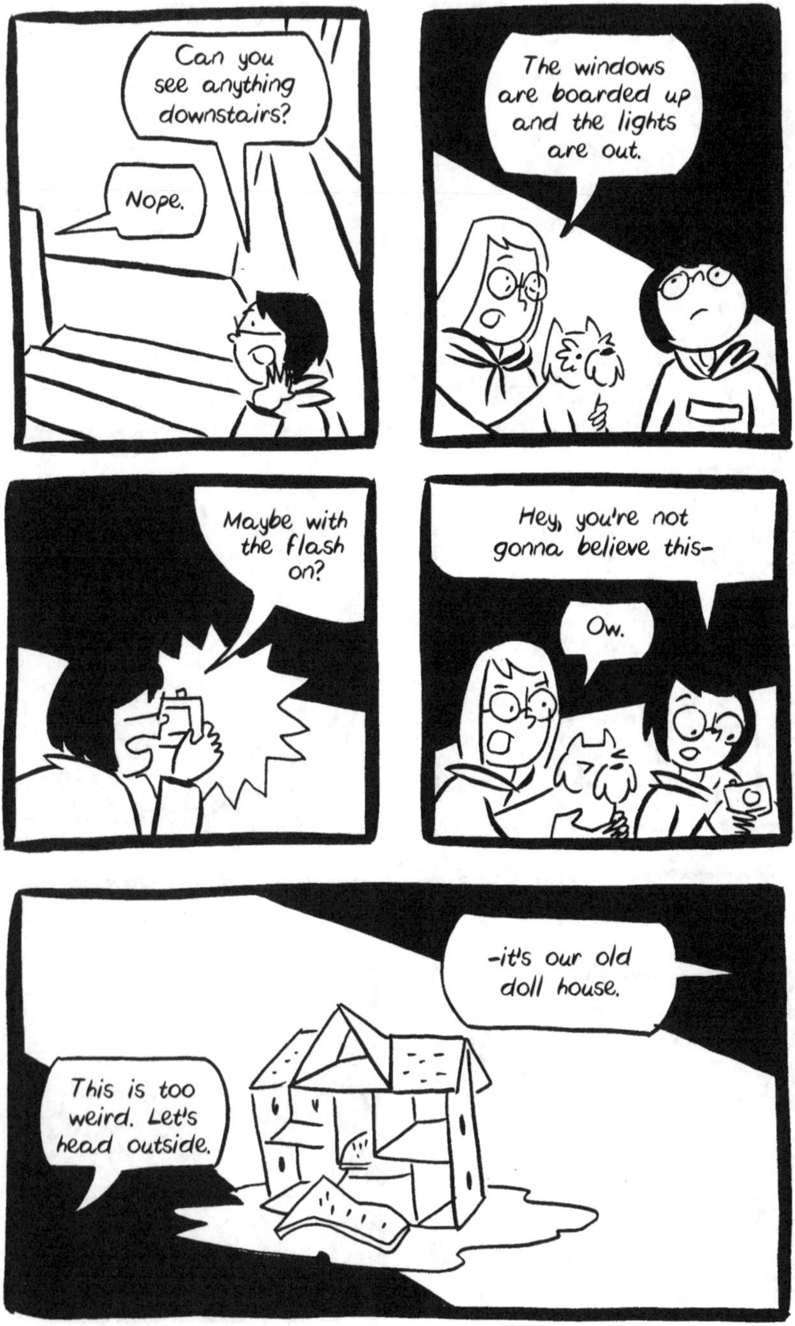
Can you see anything downstairs?
Nope.
The windows are boarded up and the lights are out.
Maybe with the flash on?
Hey, you're not gonna believe this-
Ow.
-it's our old doll house.
This is too weird. Let's head outside.

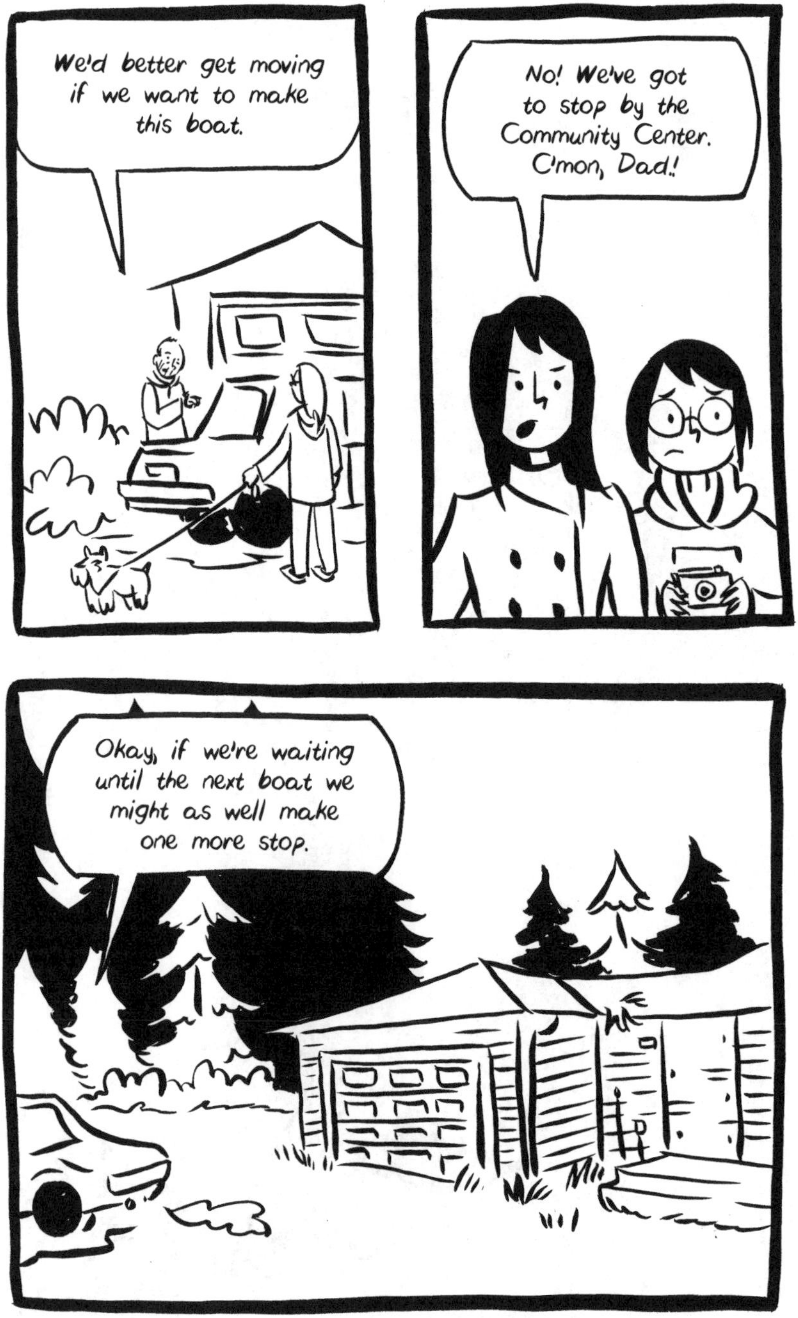
We'd better get moving if we want to make this boat.
No! We've got to stop by the Community Center. C'mon, Dad!
Okay, if we're waiting until the next boat we might as well make one more stop.

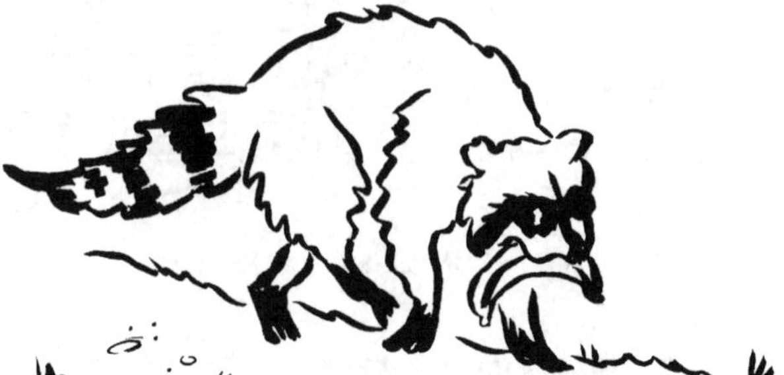

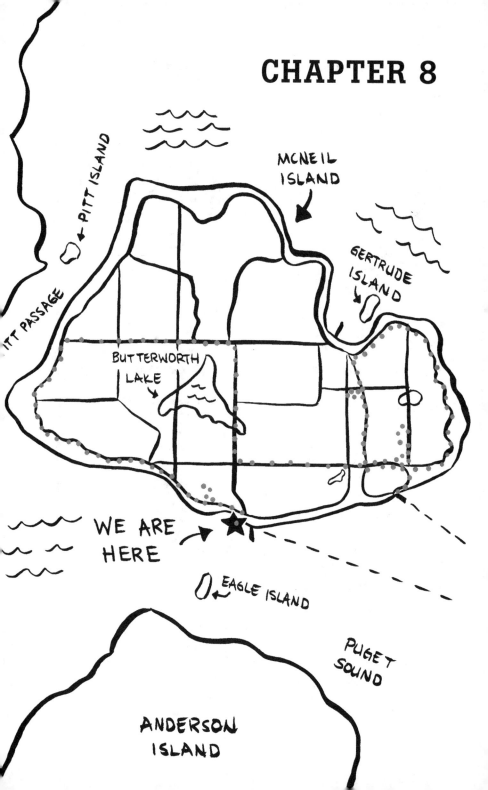

CHAPTER 8

MCNEIL
ISLAND

GERTRUDE
ISLAND

PITT ISLAND

ITT PASSAGE

BUTTERWORTH
LAKE

WE ARE
HERE

EAGLE ISLAND

PUGET
SOUND

ANDERSON
ISLAND

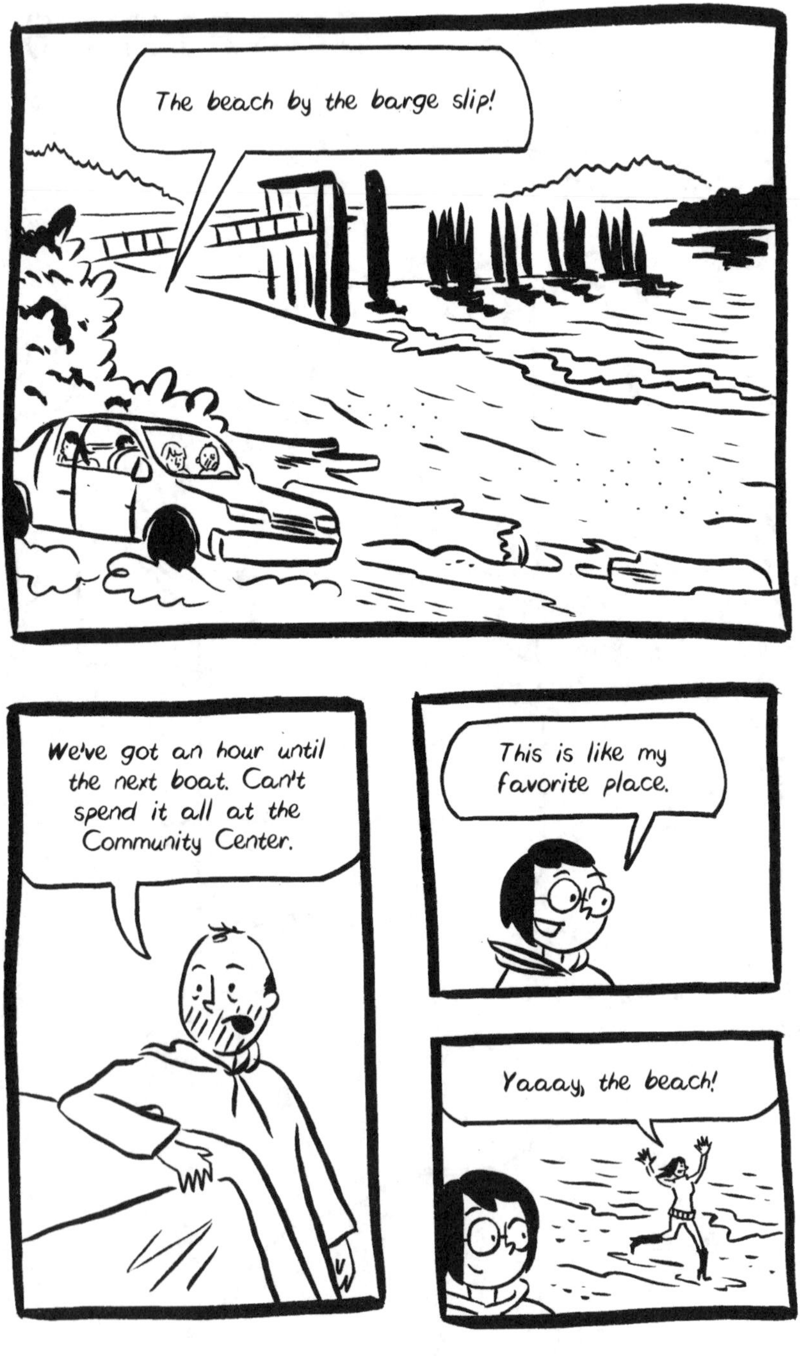
The beach by the barge slip!
We've got an hour until the next boat. Can't spend it all at the Community Center.
This is like my favorite place.
Yaaay, the beach!

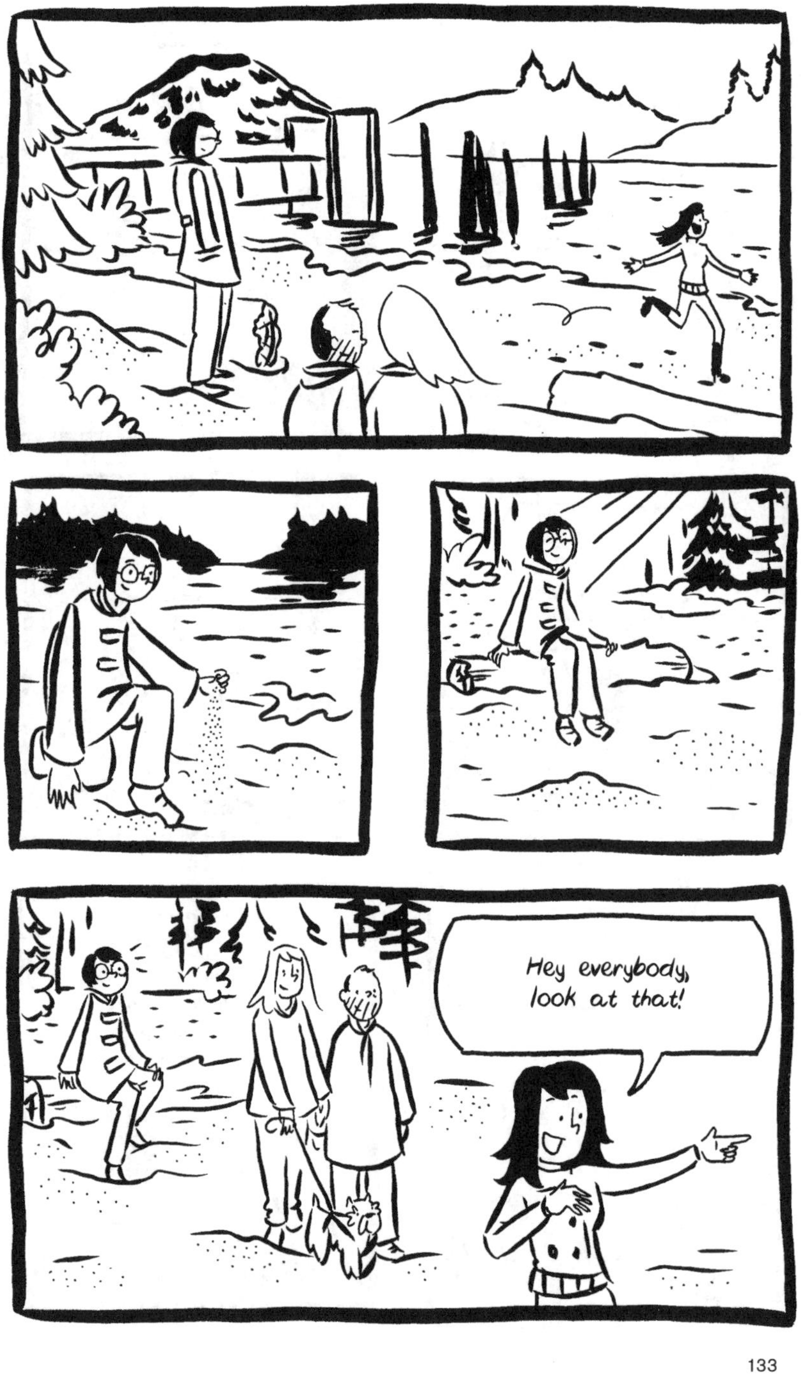
Hey everybody, look at that!

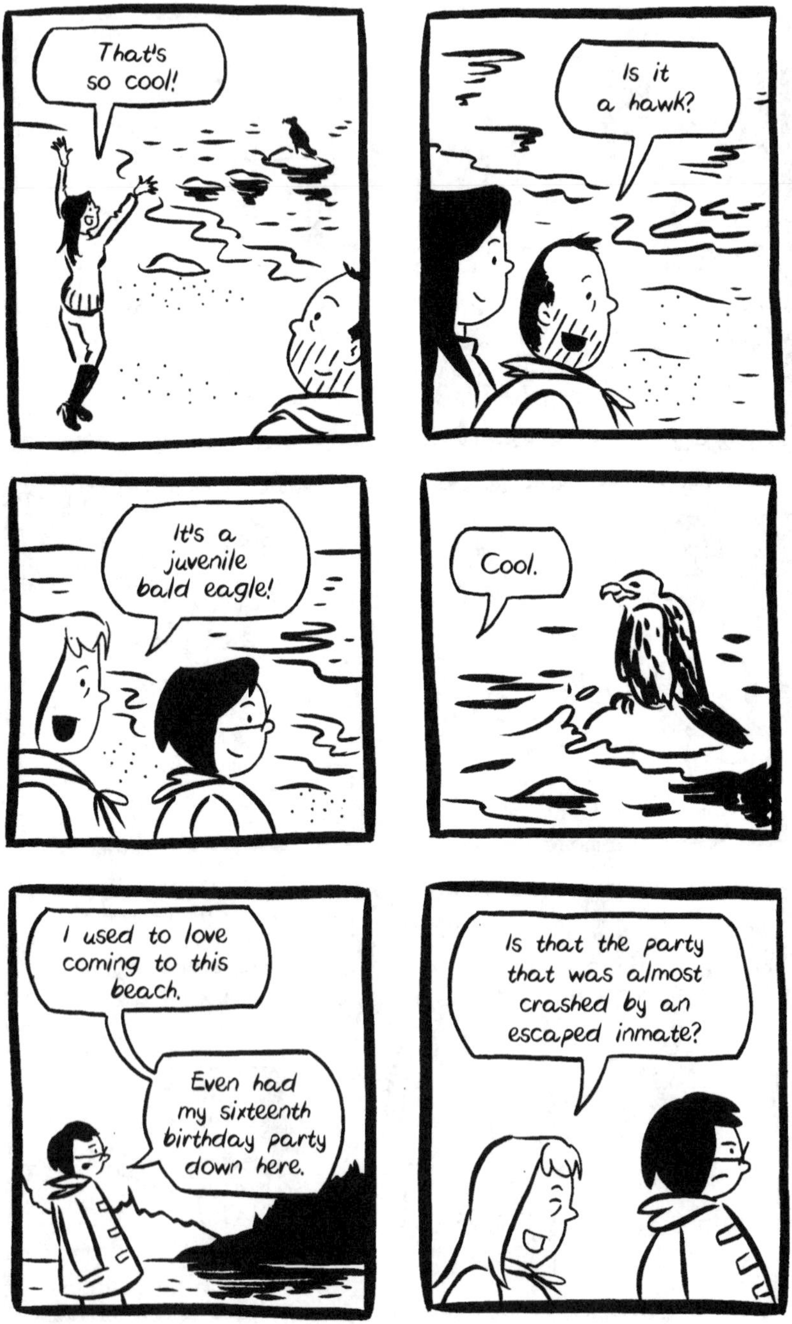
That's so cool!
Is it a hawk?
It's a juvenile bald eagle!
Cool.
I used to love coming to this beach.
Even had my sixteenth birthday party down here.
Is that the party that was almost crashed by an escaped inmate?

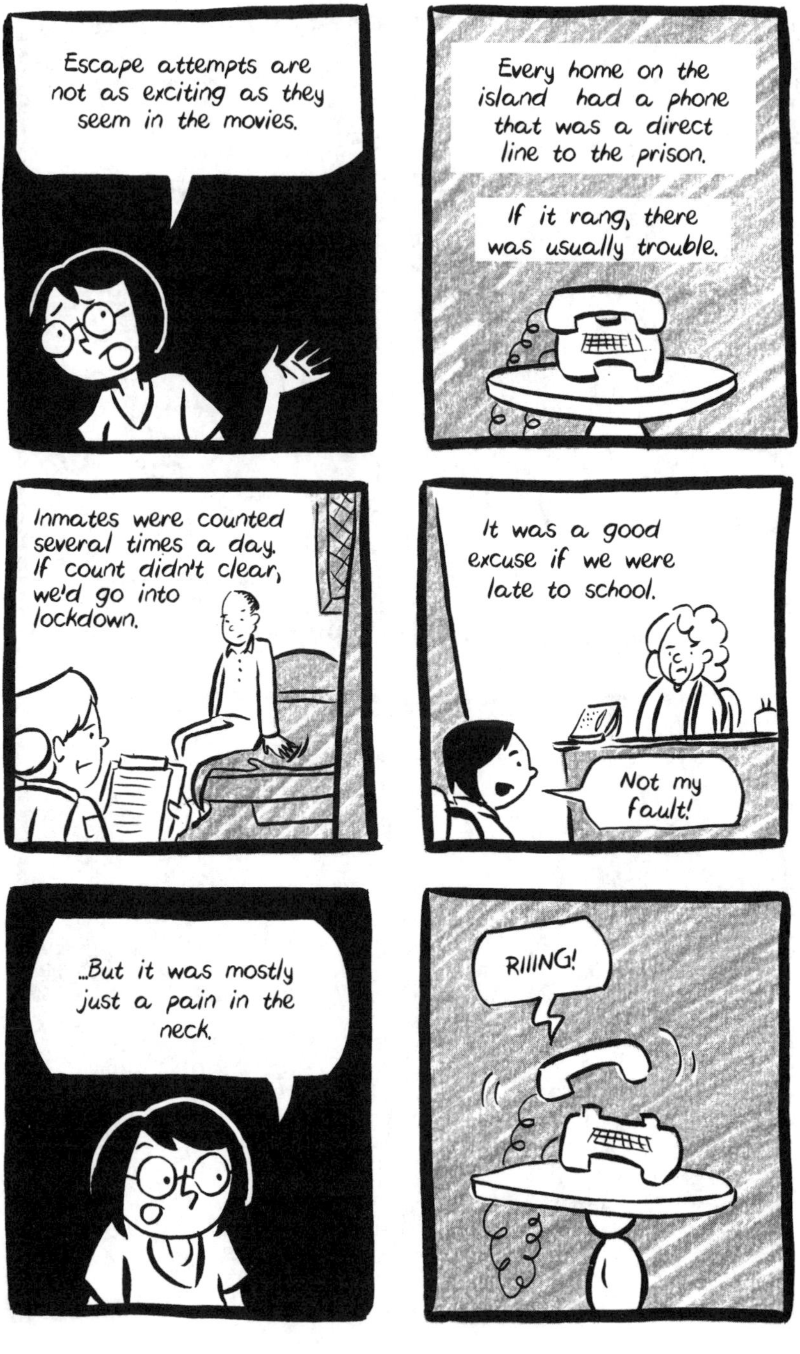
Escape attempts are not as exciting as they seem in the movies.
Every home on the island had a phone that was a direct line to the prison.
If it rang, there was usually trouble.
Inmates were counted several times a day. If count didn't clear, we'd go into lockdown.
It was a good excuse if we were late to school.
Not my fault!
...But it was mostly just a pain in the neck.
RIIING!

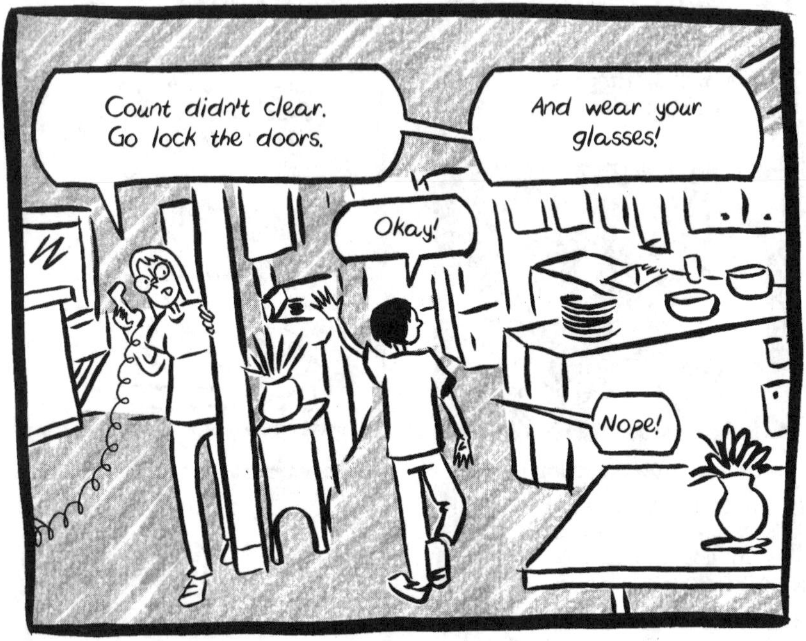
Count didn't clear.
Go lock the doors.
And wear your glasses!
Okay!
Nope!

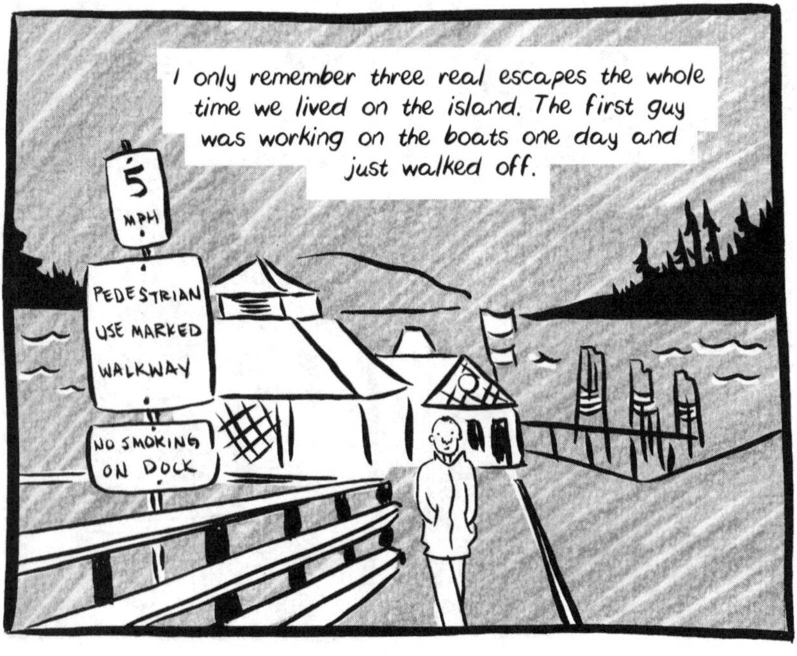
I only remember three real escapes the whole time we lived on the island. The first guy was working on the boats one day and just walked off.
5 MPH
PEDESTRIAN USE MARKED WALKWAY
NO SMOKING ON DOCK

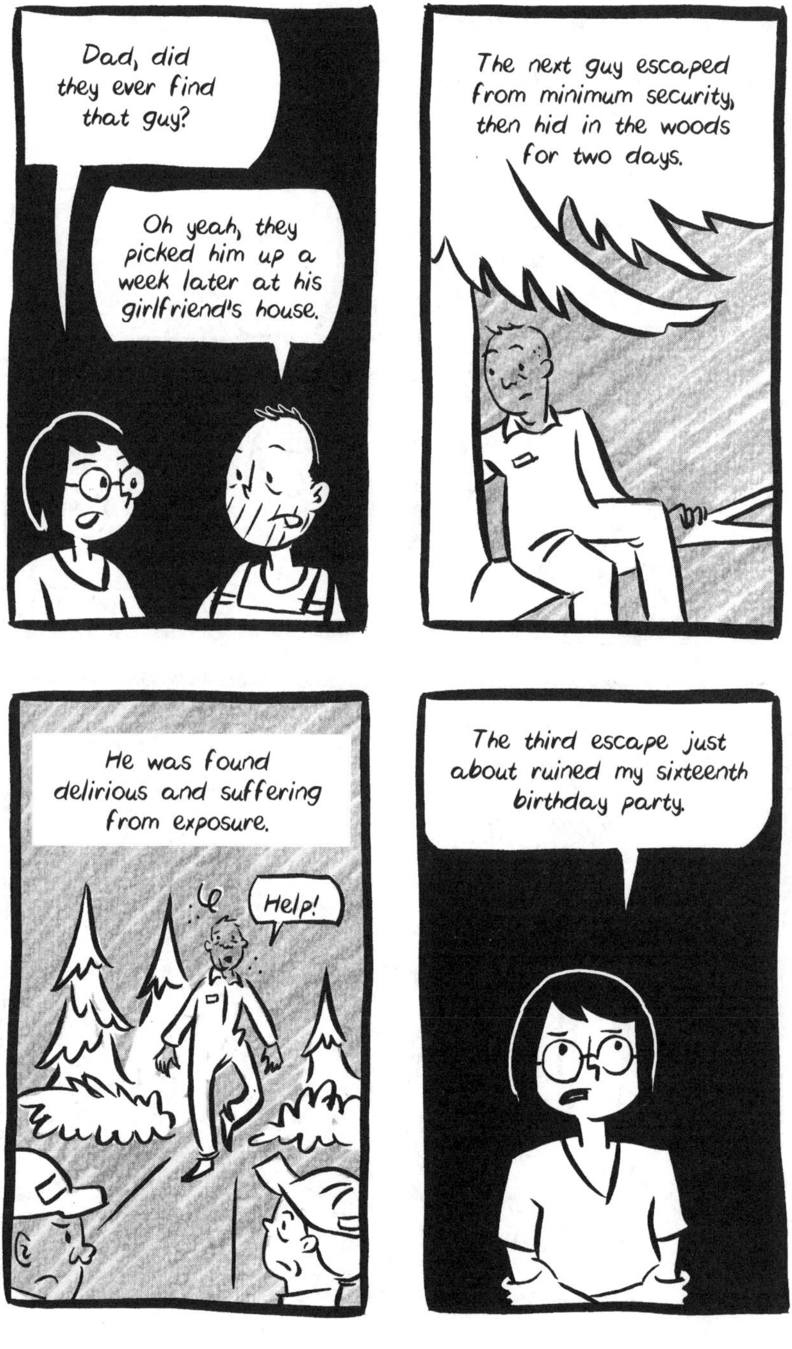
Dad, did they ever find that guy?
Oh yeah, they picked him up a week later at his girlfriend's house.
The next guy escaped from minimum security, then hid in the woods for two days.
He was found delirious and suffering from exposure.
Help!
The third escape just about ruined my sixteenth birthday party.

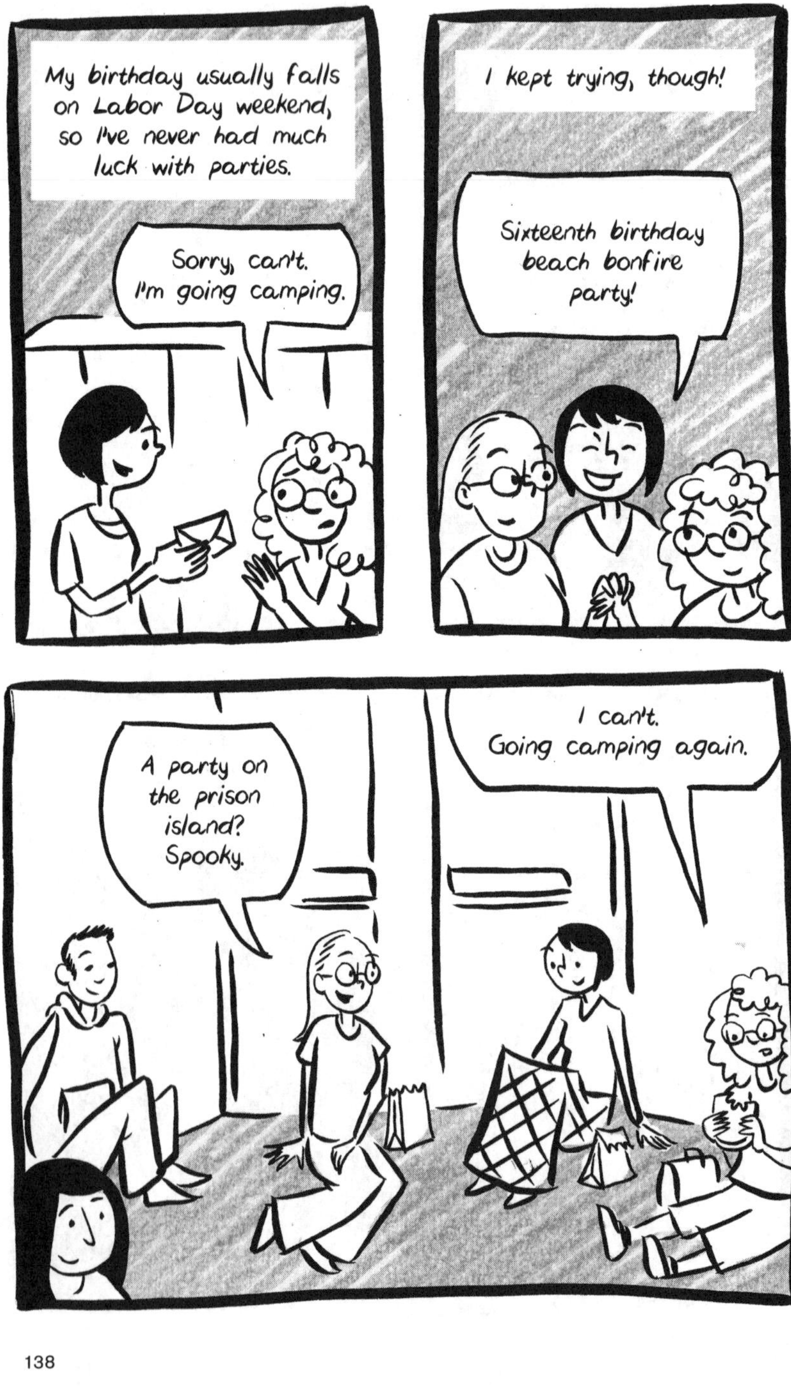
My birthday usually falls on Labor Day weekend, so I've never had much luck with parties.
Sorry, can't. I'm going camping.
I kept trying, though!
Sixteenth birthday beach bonfire party!
A party on the prison island? Spooky.
I can't. Going camping again.

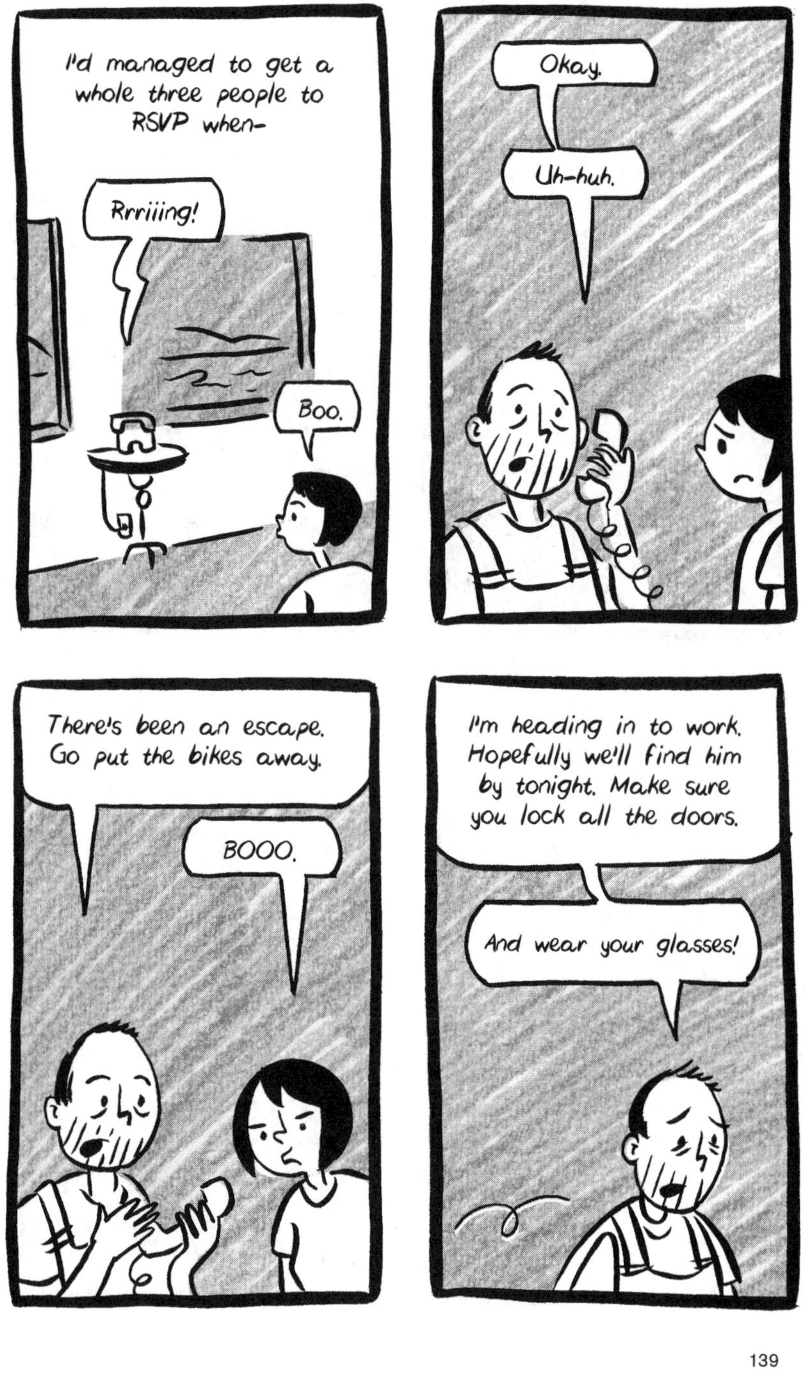
I'd managed to get a whole three people to RSVP when-
Rrriiing!
Boo.
Okay.
Uh-huh.
There's been an escape. Go put the bikes away.
BOOO.
I'm heading in to work. Hopefully we'll find him by tonight. Make sure you lock all the doors.
And wear your glasses!

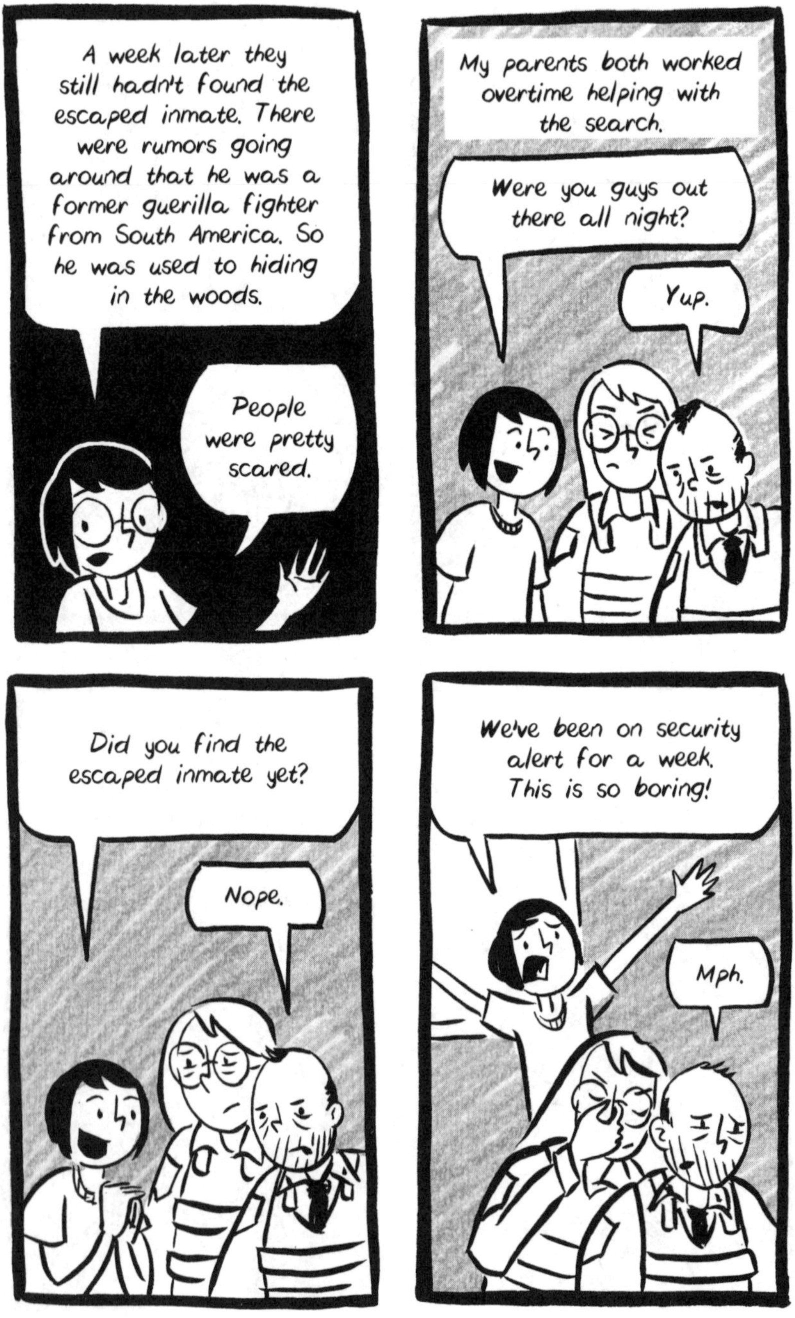
A week later they still hadn't found the escaped inmate. There were rumors going around that he was a former guerilla fighter from South America. So he was used to hiding in the woods.
People were pretty scared.
My parents both worked overtime helping with the search.
Were you guys out there all night?
Yup.
Did you find the escaped inmate yet?
Nope.
We've been on security alert for a week. This is so boring!
Mph.

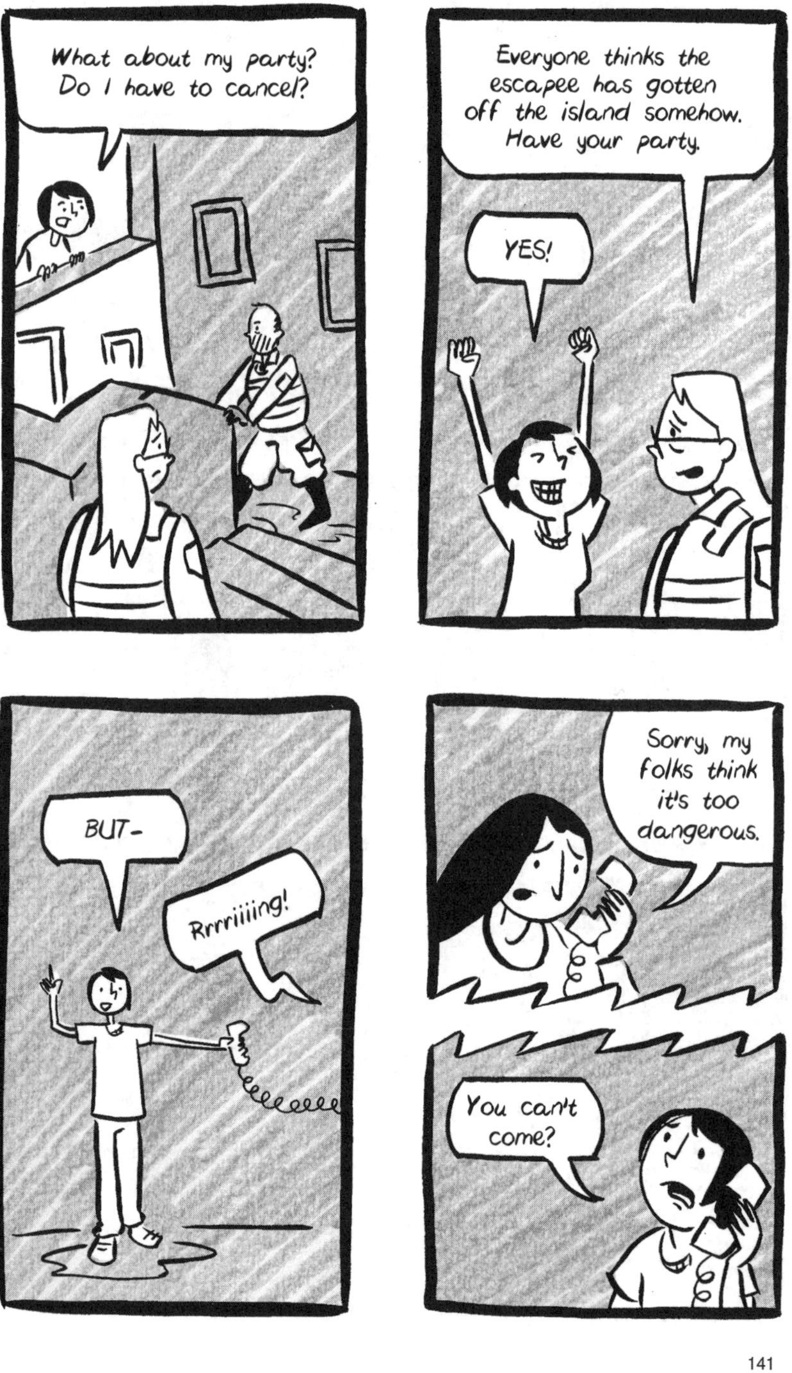
What about my party? Do I have to cancel?
Everyone thinks the escapee has gotten off the island somehow. Have your party.
YES!
BUT-
Rrrriiiing!
Sorry, my folks think it's too dangerous.
You can't come?

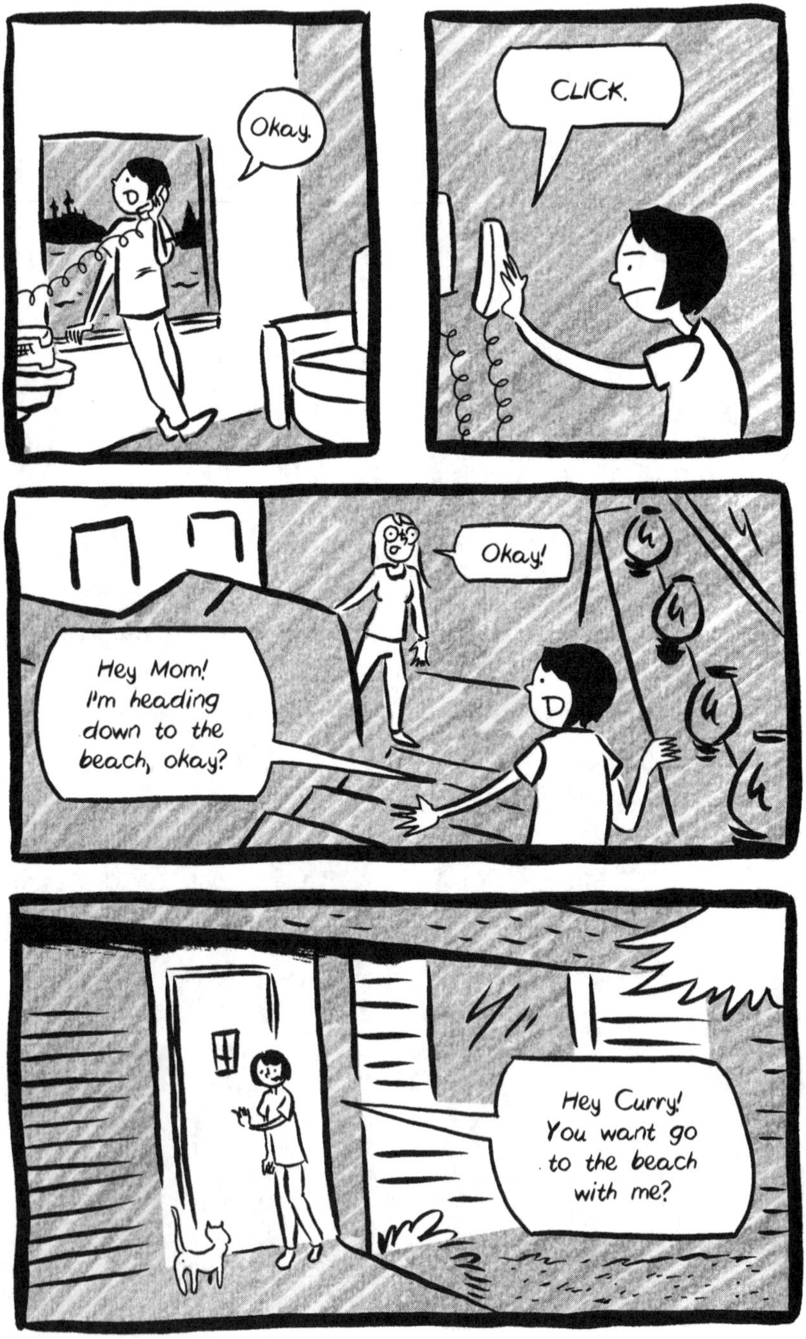
Okay.
CLICK.
Okay!
Hey Mom! I'm heading down to the beach, okay?
Hey Curry! You want go to the beach with me?

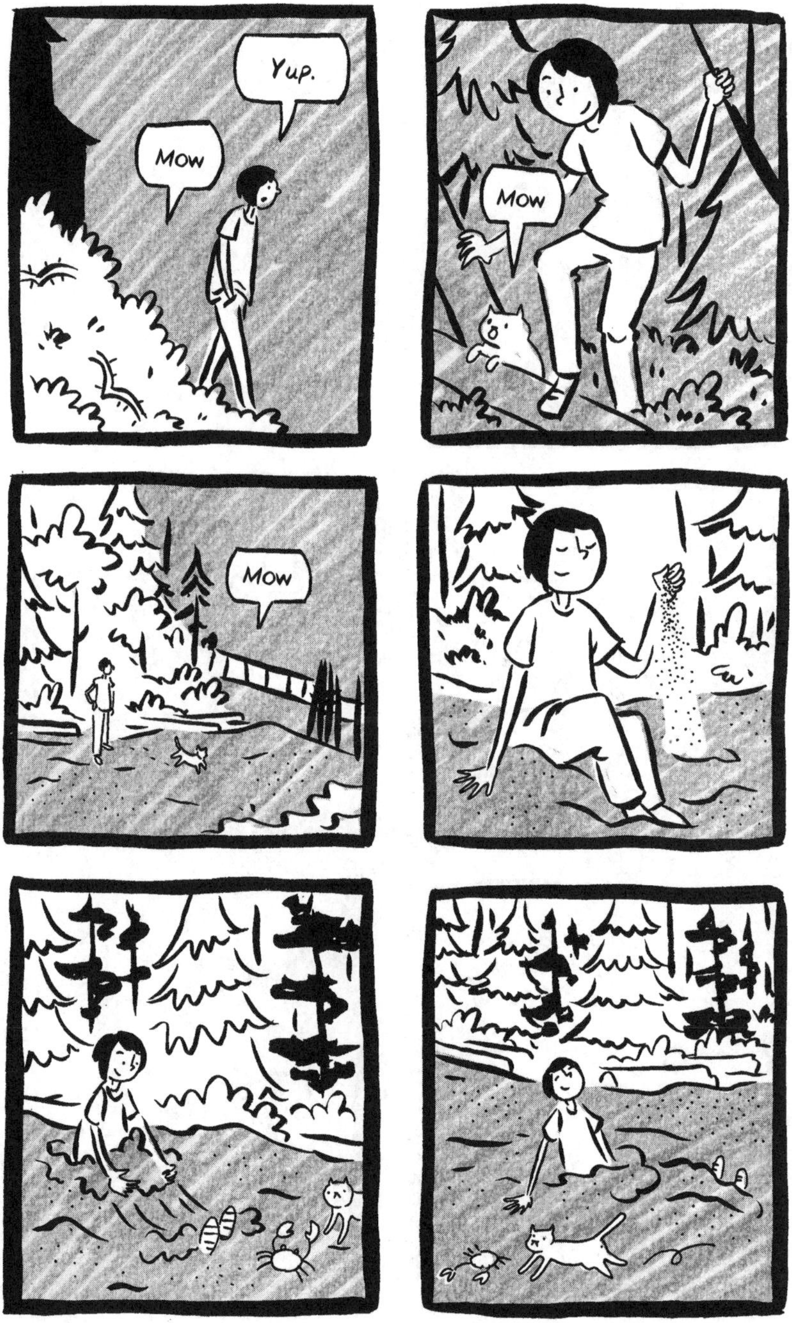
Mow
Yup.
Mow
Mow

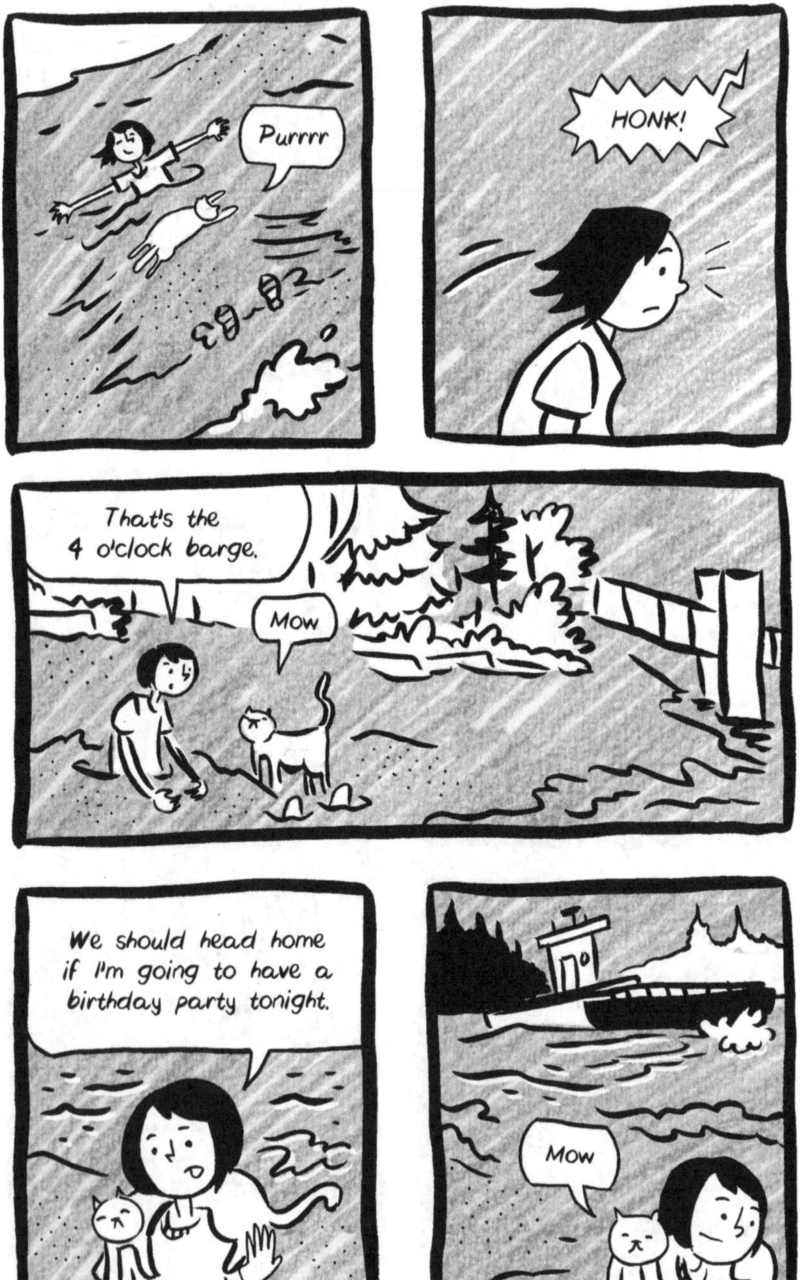
Purrrr
HONK!
That's the 4 o'clock barge.
Mow
We should head home if I'm going to have a birthday party tonight.
Mow

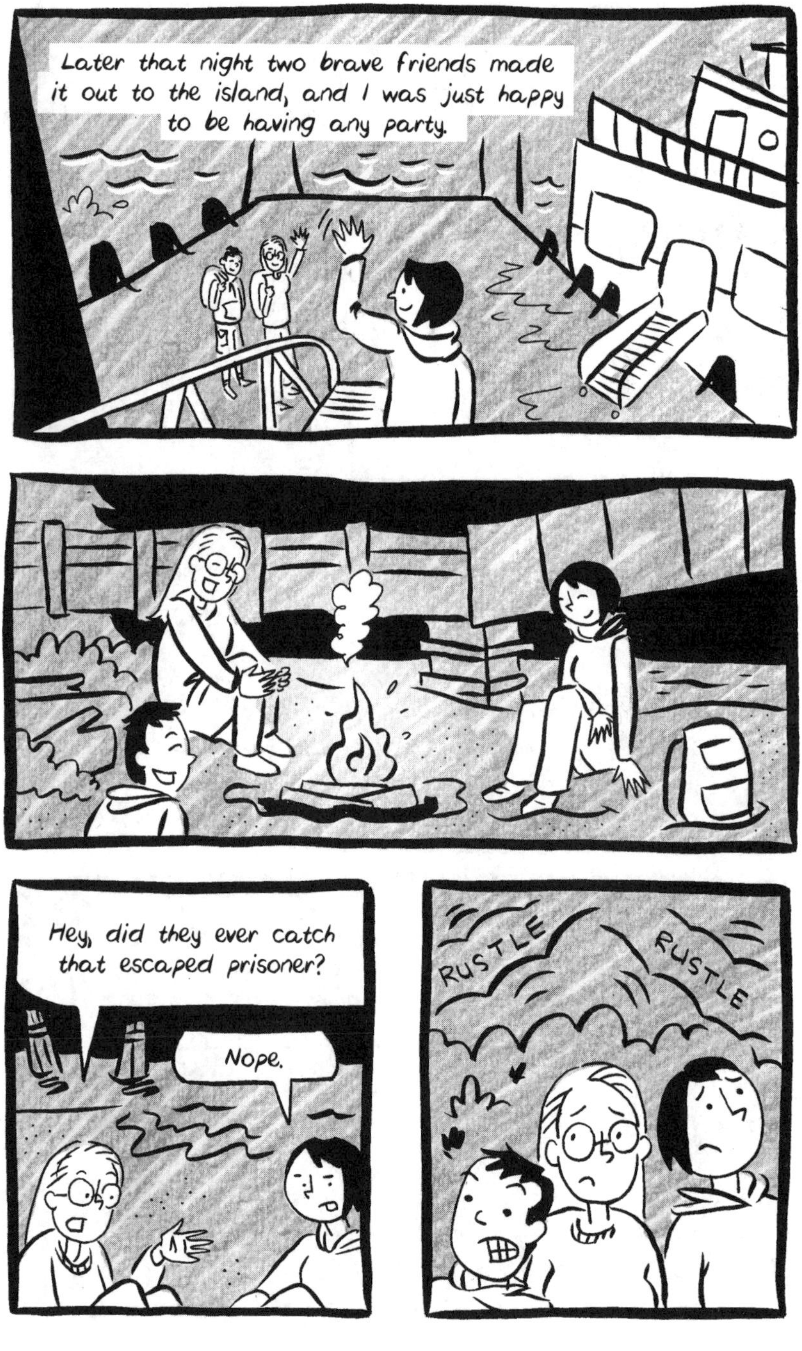
Later that night two brave friends made it out to the island, and I was just happy to be having any party.
Hey, did they ever catch that escaped prisoner?
Nope.
RUSTLE
RUSTLE

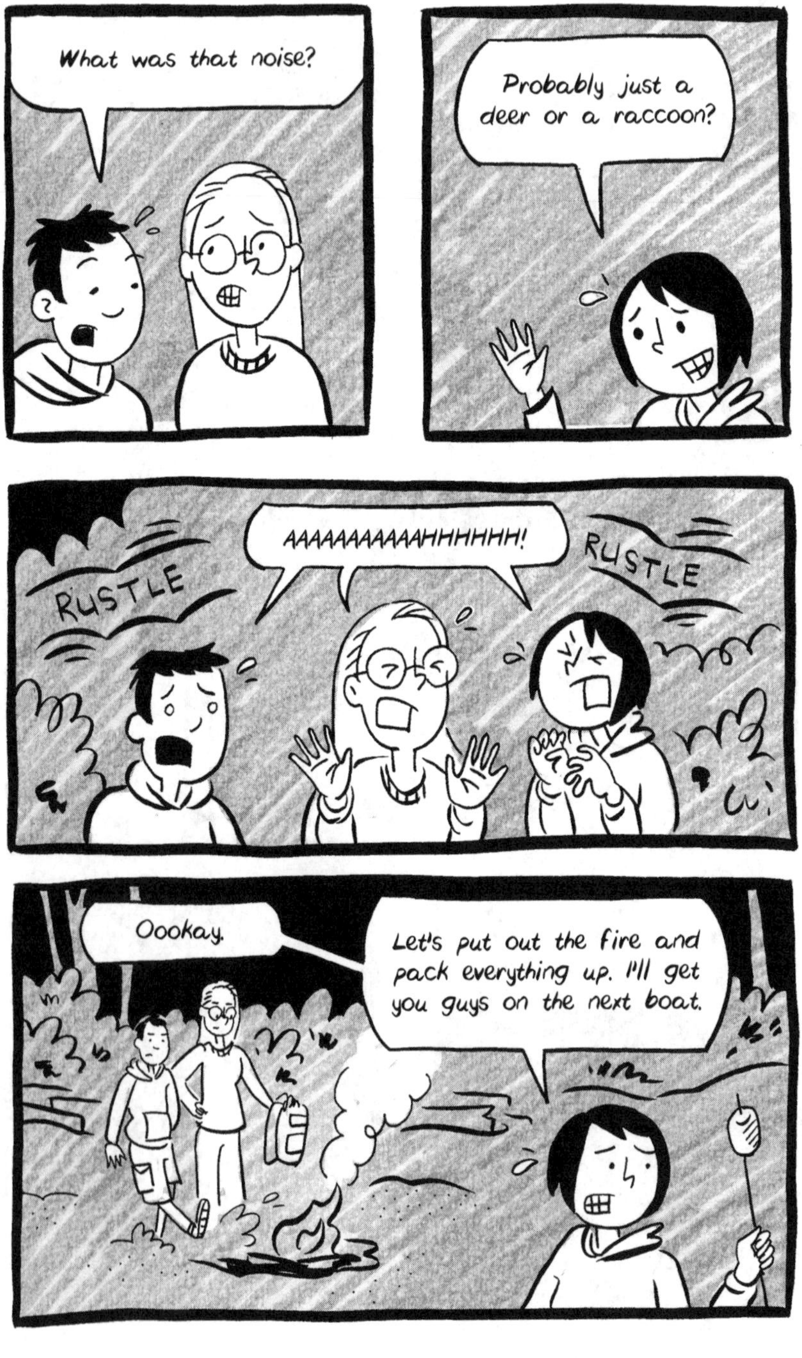
What was that noise?
Probably just a deer or a raccoon?
RUSTLE
AAAAAAAAAAAAHHHHHH!
RUSTLE
Oookay.
Let's put out the fire and pack everything up. I'll get you guys on the next boat.

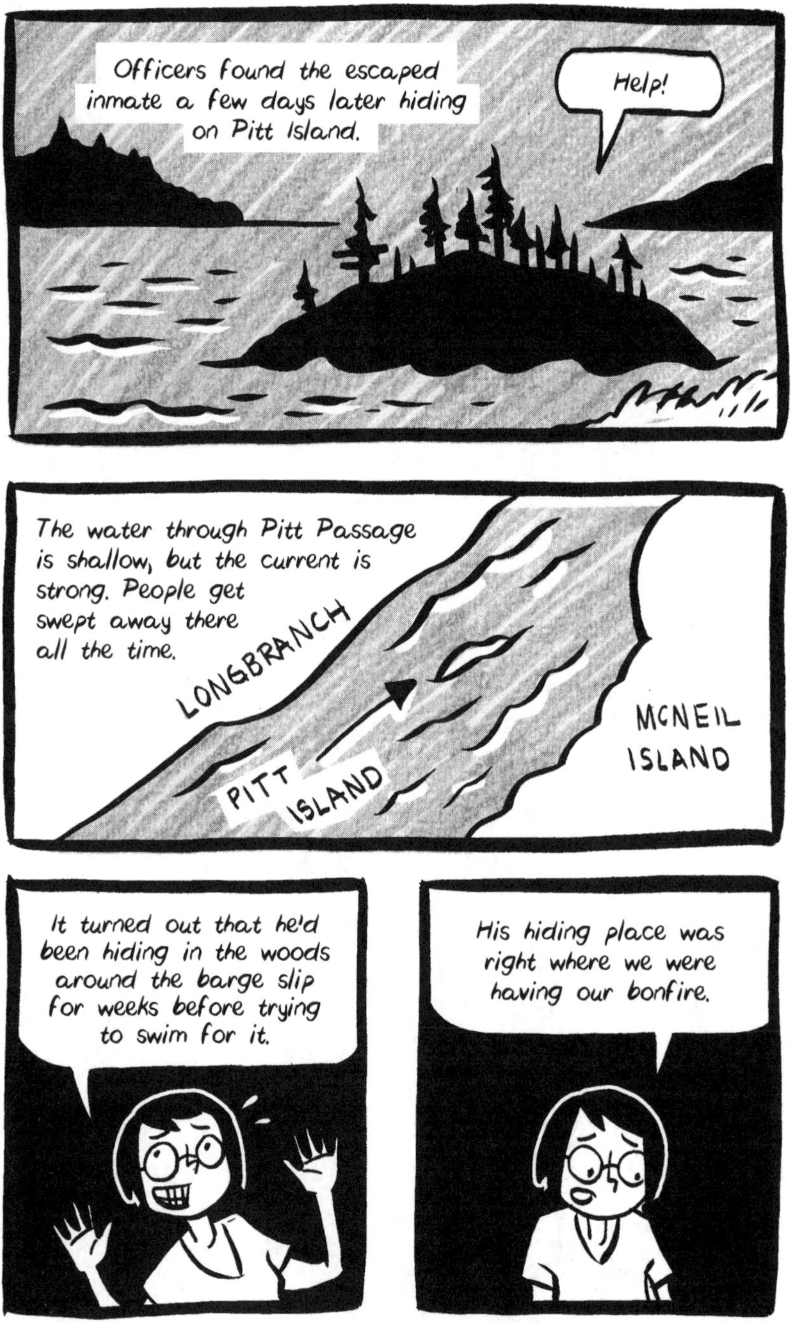
Officers found the escaped inmate a few days later hiding on Pitt Island.
Help!
The water through Pitt Passage is shallow, but the current is strong. People get swept away there all the time.
LONGBRANCH
PITT ISLAND
MCNEIL ISLAND
It turned out that he'd been hiding in the woods around the barge slip for weeks before trying to swim for it.
His hiding place was right where we were having our bonfire.

CHAPTER 9

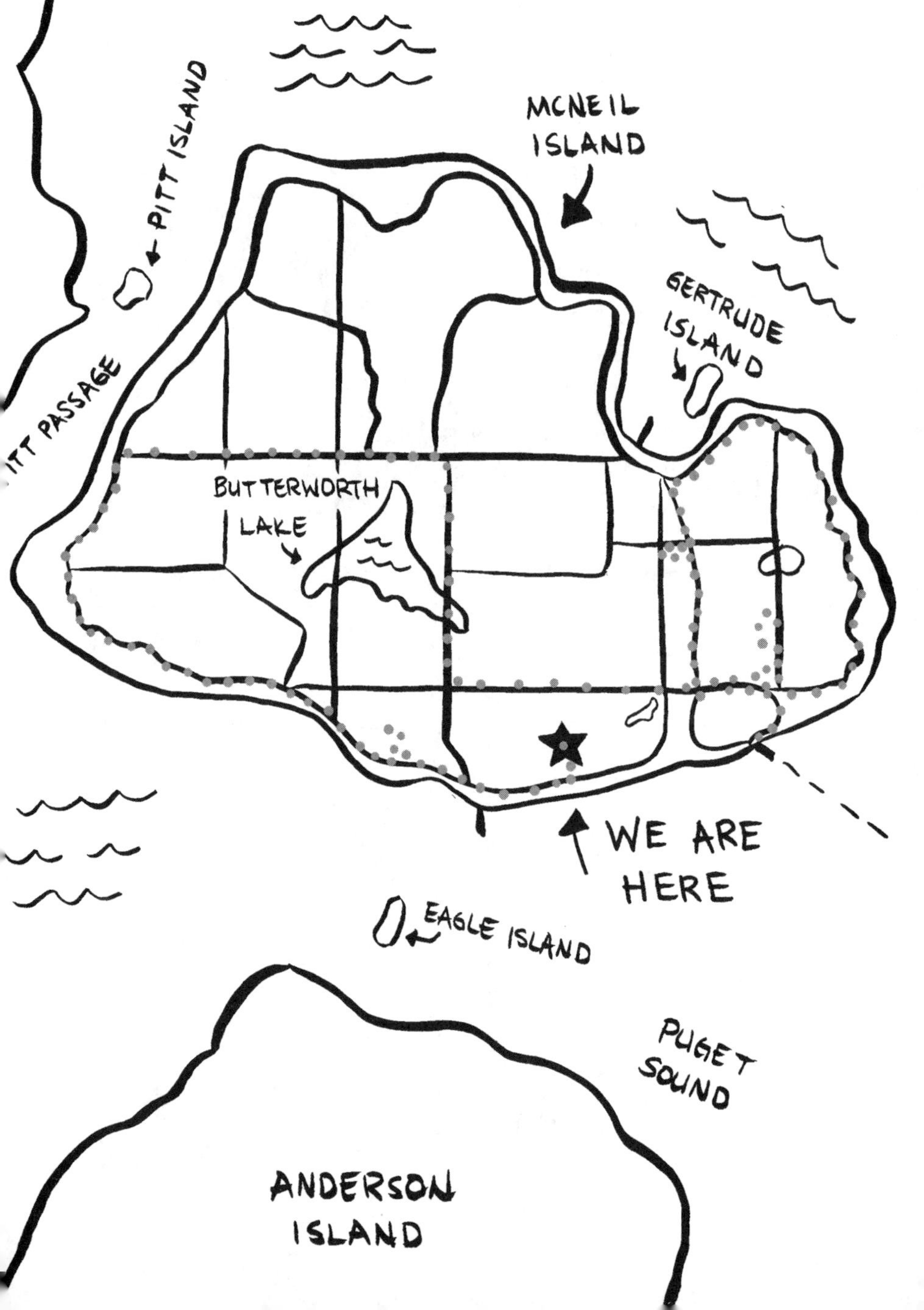

PITT ISLAND
MCNEIL ISLAND
GERTRUDE ISLAND
ITT PASSAGE
BUTTERWORTH LAKE
WE ARE HERE
EAGLE ISLAND
PUGET SOUND
ANDERSON ISLAND

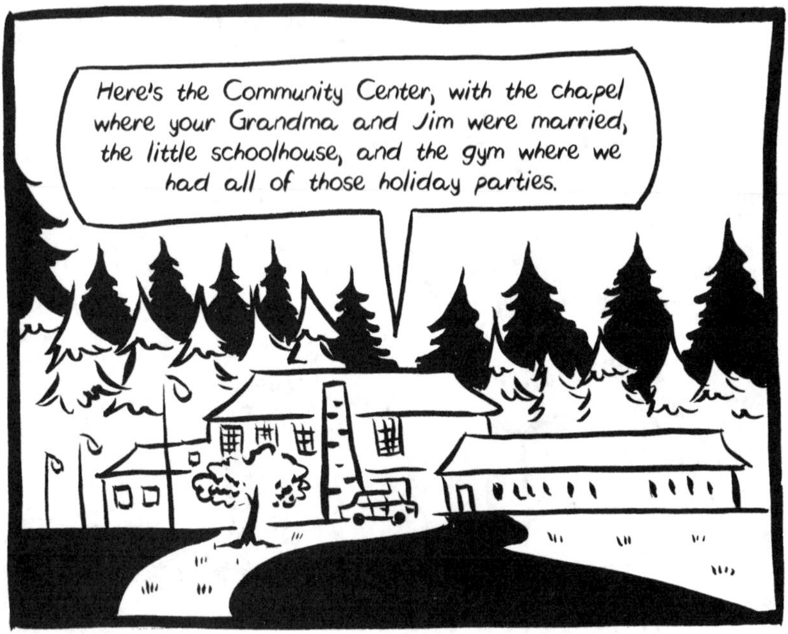
Here's the Community Center, with the chapel where your Grandma and Jim were married, the little schoolhouse, and the gym where we had all of those holiday parties.

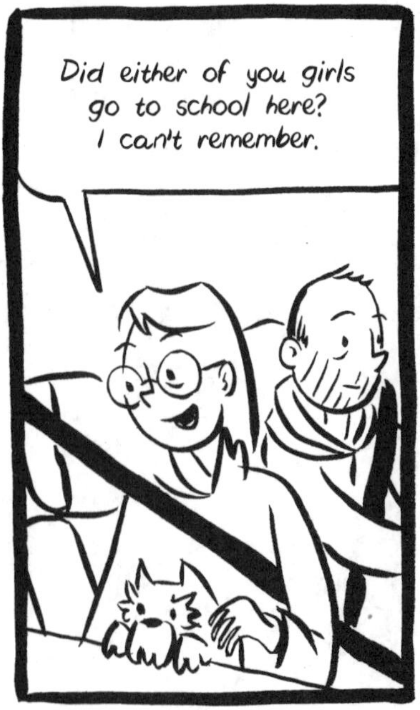
Did either of you girls go to school here? I can't remember.

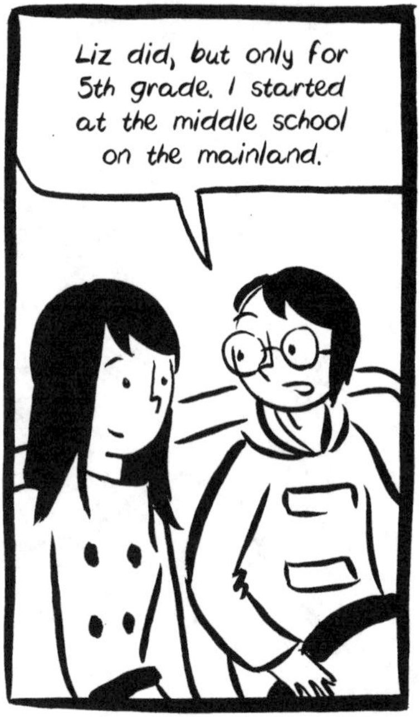
Liz did, but only for 5th grade. I started at the middle school on the mainland.

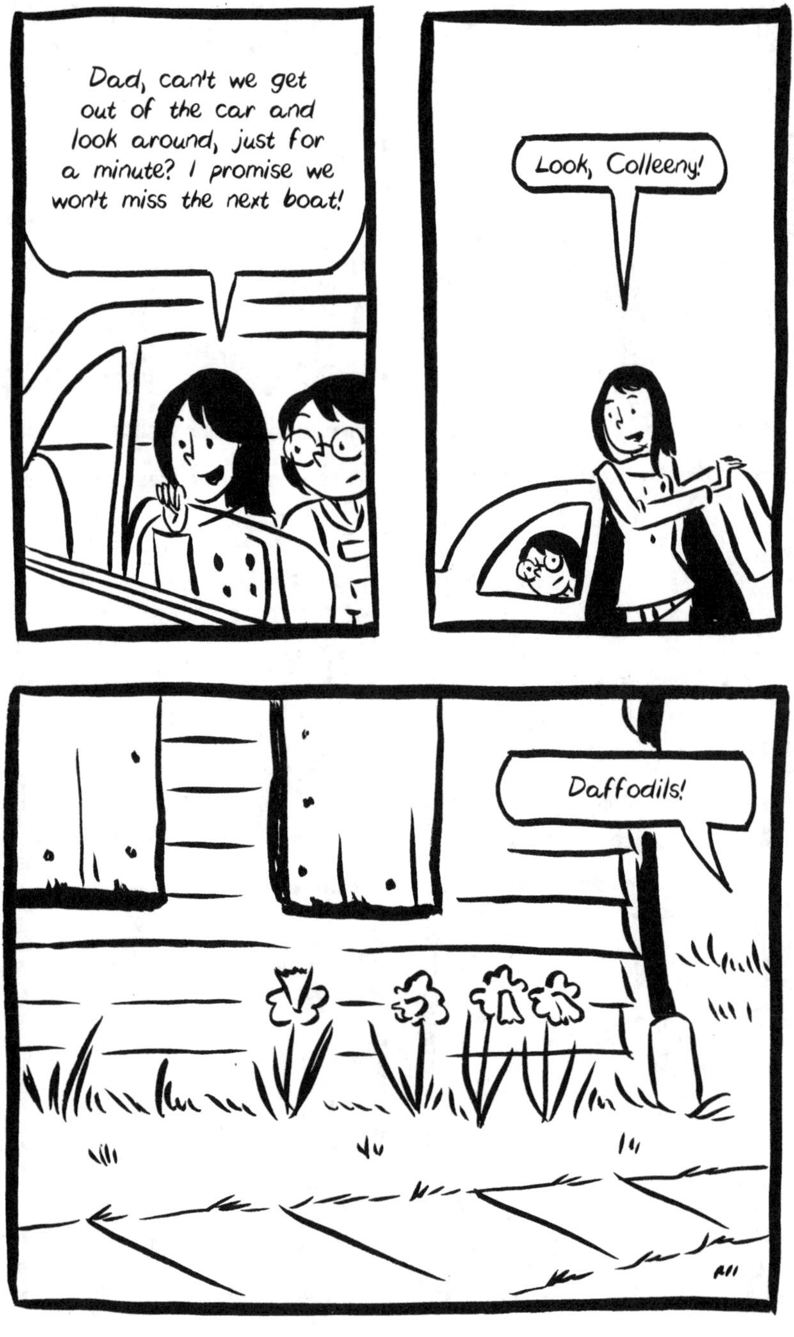
Dad, can't we get out of the car and look around, just for a minute? I promise we won't miss the next boat!
Look, Colleeny!
Daffodils!

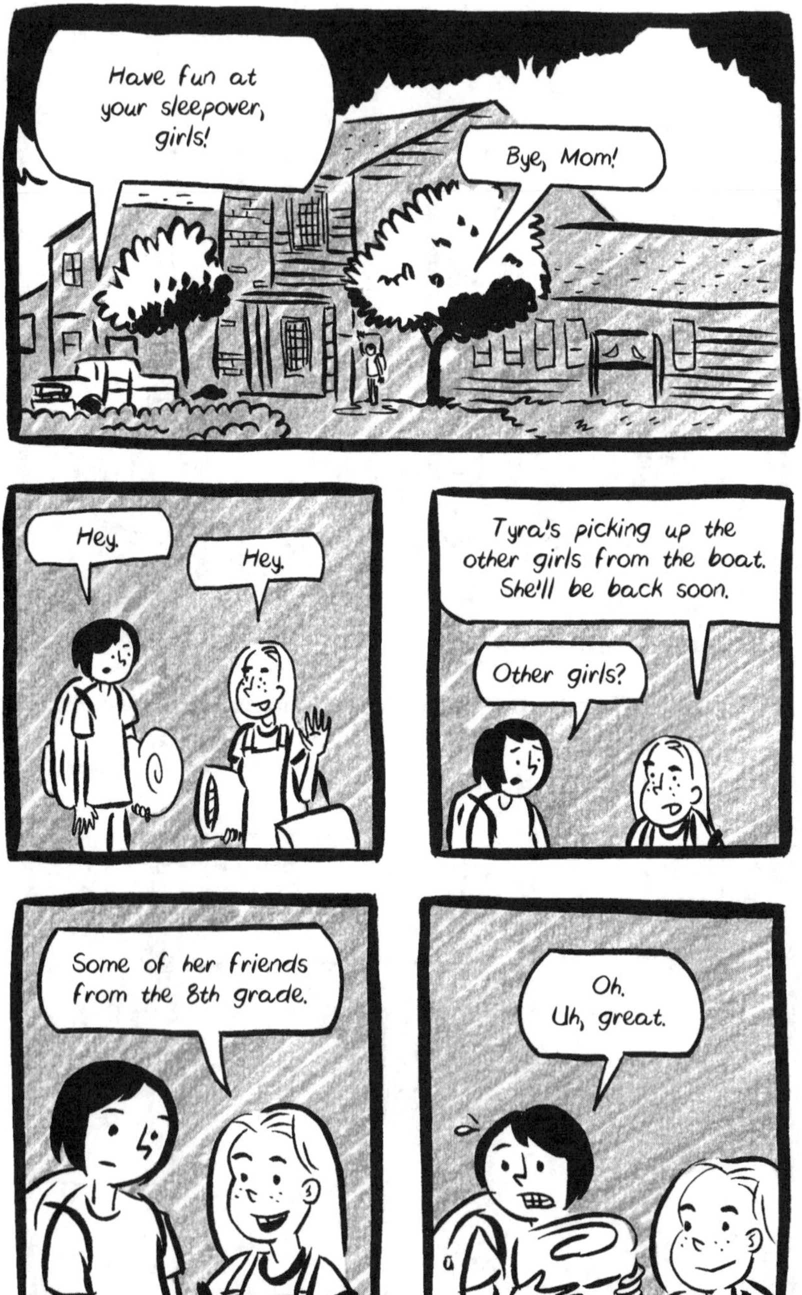
Have fun at your sleepover, girls!
Bye, Mom!
Hey.
Hey.
Tyra's picking up the other girls from the boat. She'll be back soon.
Other girls?
Some of her friends from the 8th grade.
Oh.
Uh, great.

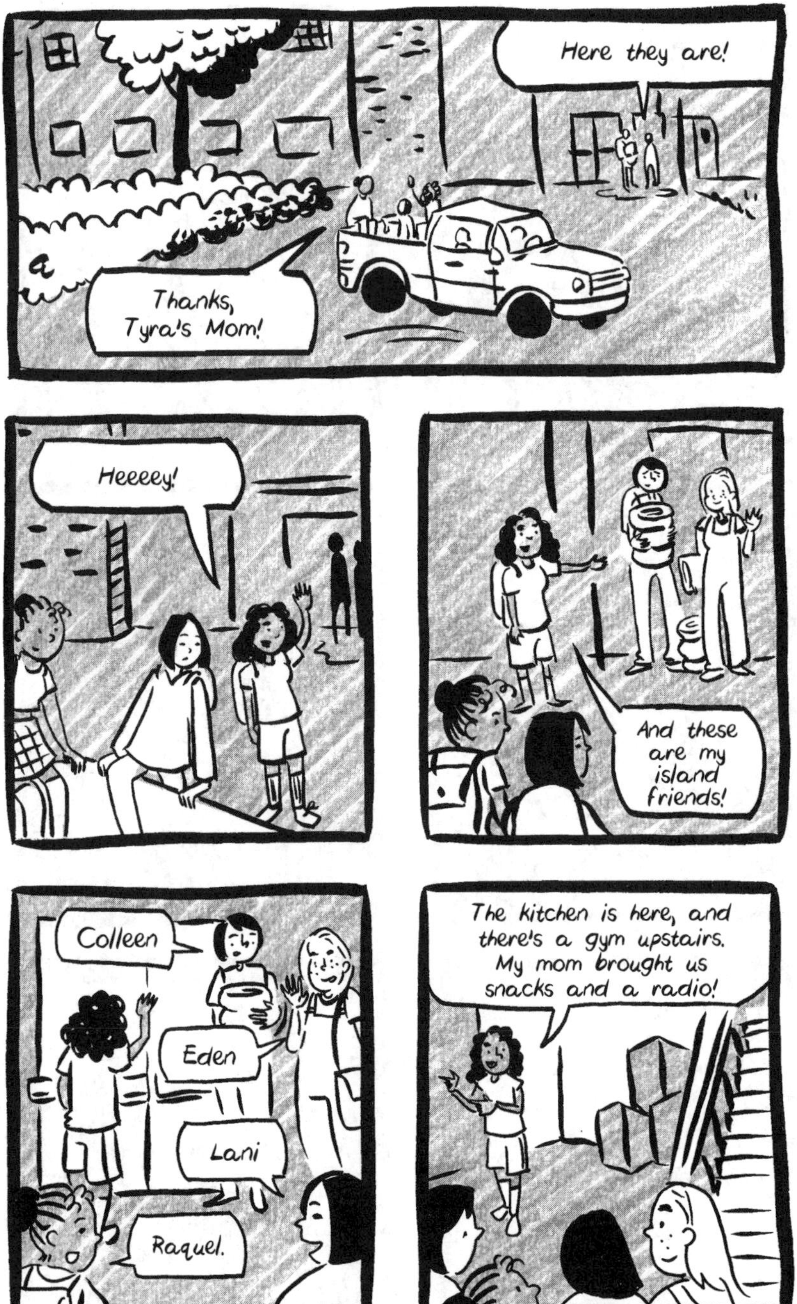
Here they are!
Thanks, Tyra's Mom!
Heeeey!
And these are my island friends!
Colleen
Eden
Lani
Raquel.
The kitchen is here, and there's a gym upstairs. My mom brought us snacks and a radio!

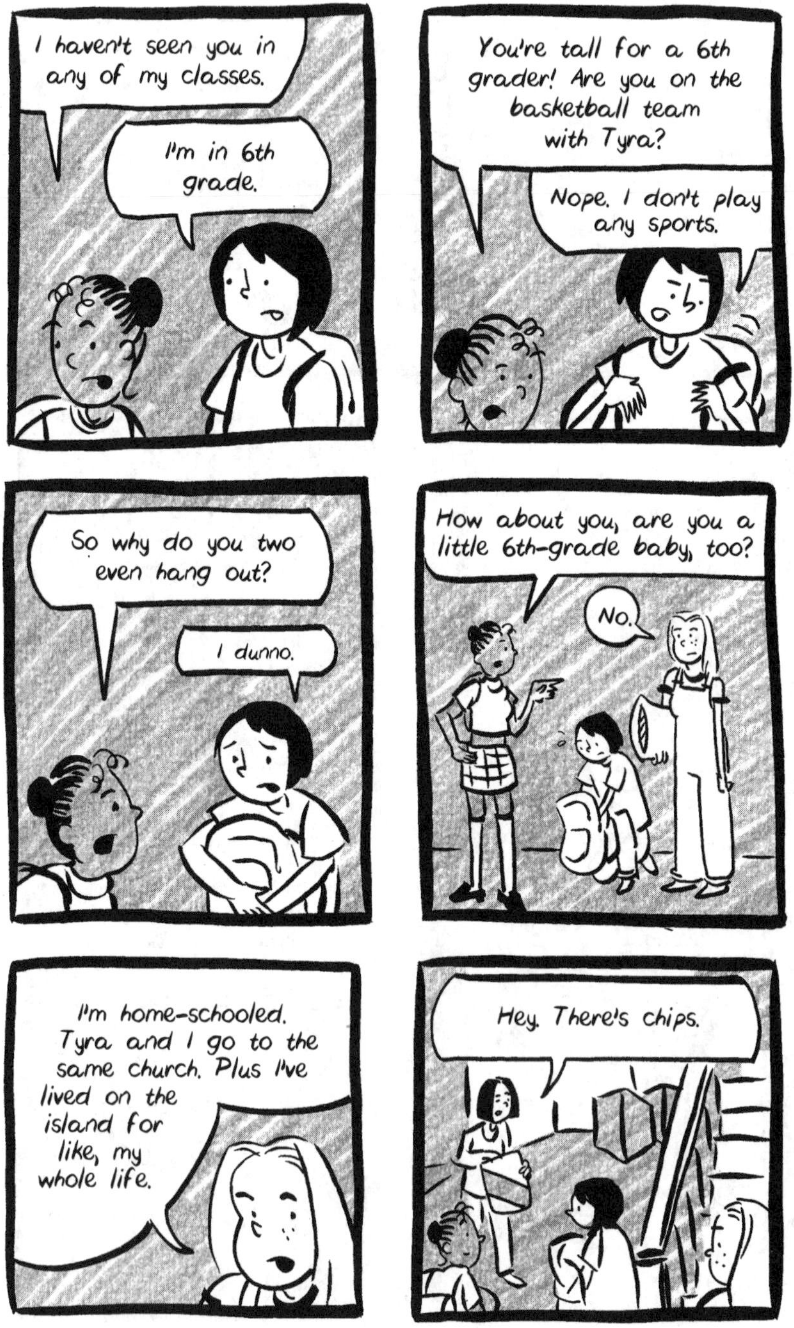
I haven't seen you in any of my classes.
I'm in 6th grade.
You're tall for a 6th grader! Are you on the basketball team with Tyra?
Nope. I don't play any sports.
So why do you two even hang out?
I dunno.
How about you, are you a little 6th-grade baby, too?
No.
I'm home-schooled. Tyra and I go to the same church. Plus I've lived on the island for like, my whole life.
Hey. There's chips.

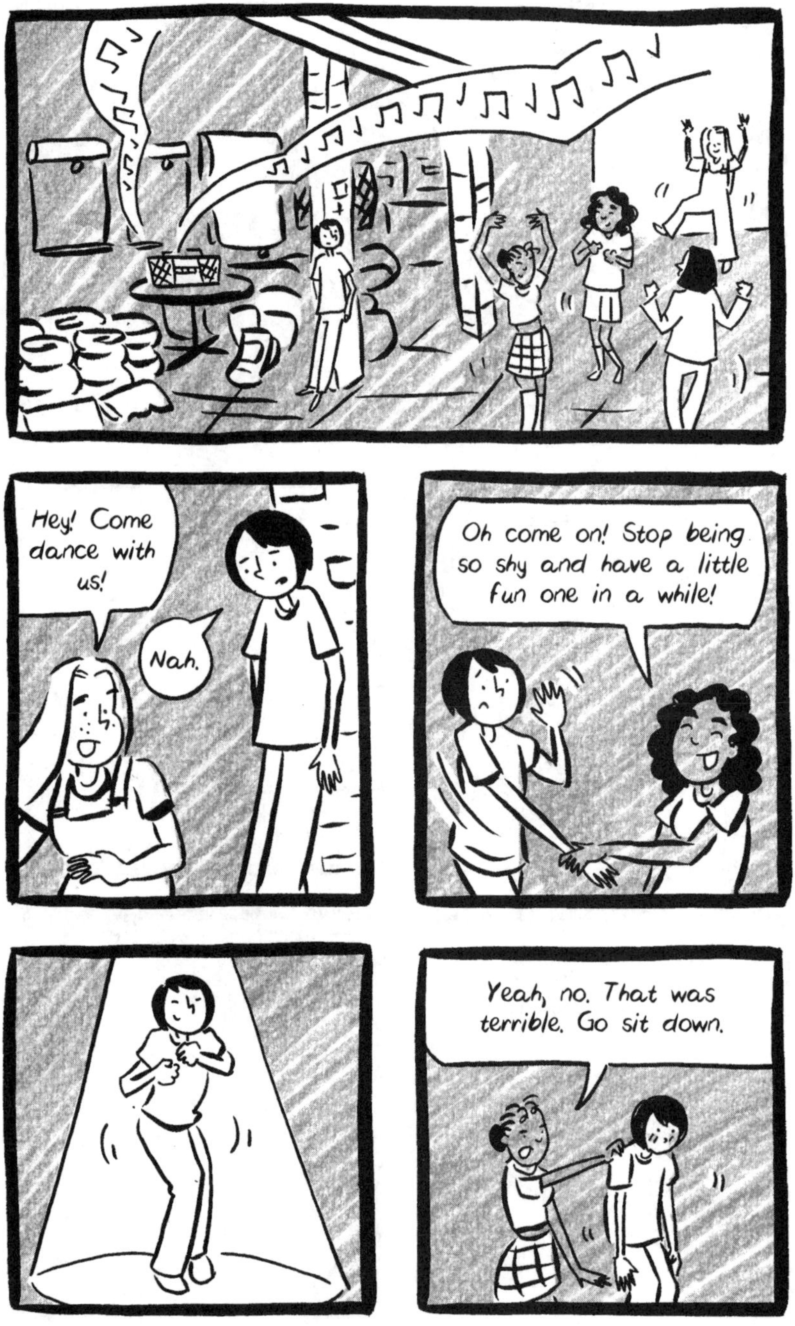
Hey! Come dance with us!
Nah.
Oh come on! Stop being so shy and have a little fun one in a while!
Yeah, no. That was terrible. Go sit down.

The radio is boring, got any CDs?

Nope.

We could call the radio station and make a request?

Great idea!

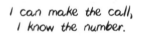

I can make the call, I know the number.

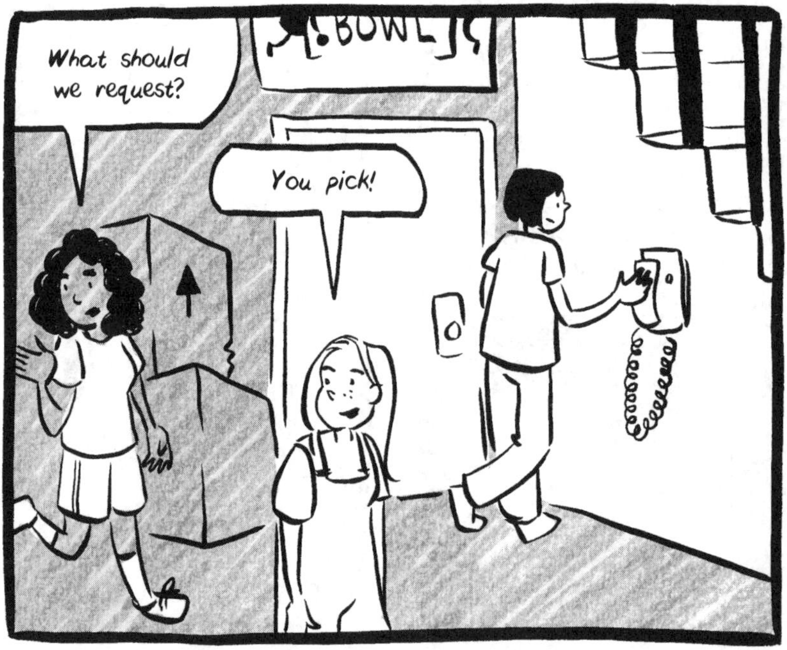
What should we request?
You pick!
BOWL

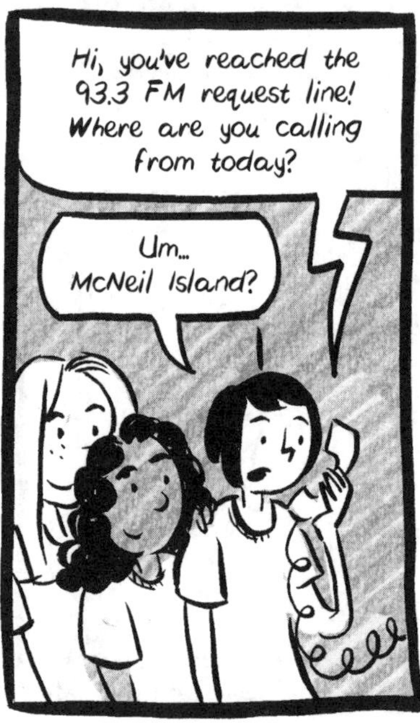
Hi, you've reached the 93.3 FM request line! Where are you calling from today?
Um... McNeil Island?

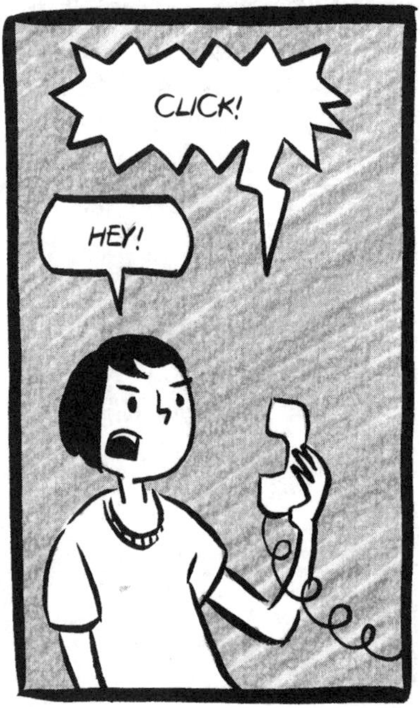
CLICK!
HEY!

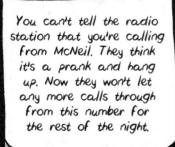

You can't tell the radio station that you're calling from McNeil. They think it's a prank and hang up. Now they won't let any more calls through from this number for the rest of the night.

Good job there, 6th grade baby.

How was I supposed to know?

Great. Now what are we supposed to do, stuck out here in the middle of nowhere?

BOWL

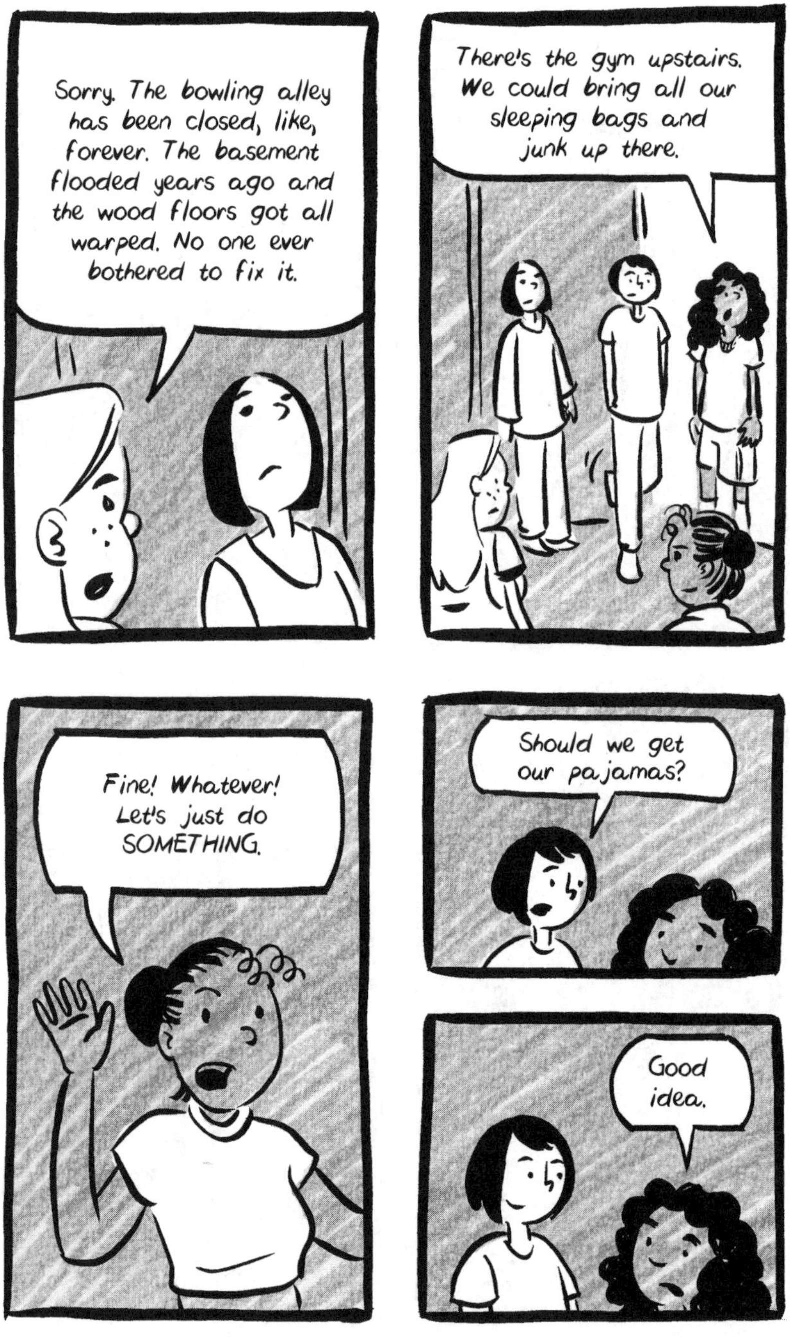
Sorry. The bowling alley has been closed, like, forever. The basement flooded years ago and the wood floors got all warped. No one ever bothered to fix it.
There's the gym upstairs. We could bring all our sleeping bags and junk up there.
Fine! Whatever! Let's just do SOMETHING.
Should we get our pajamas?
Good idea.

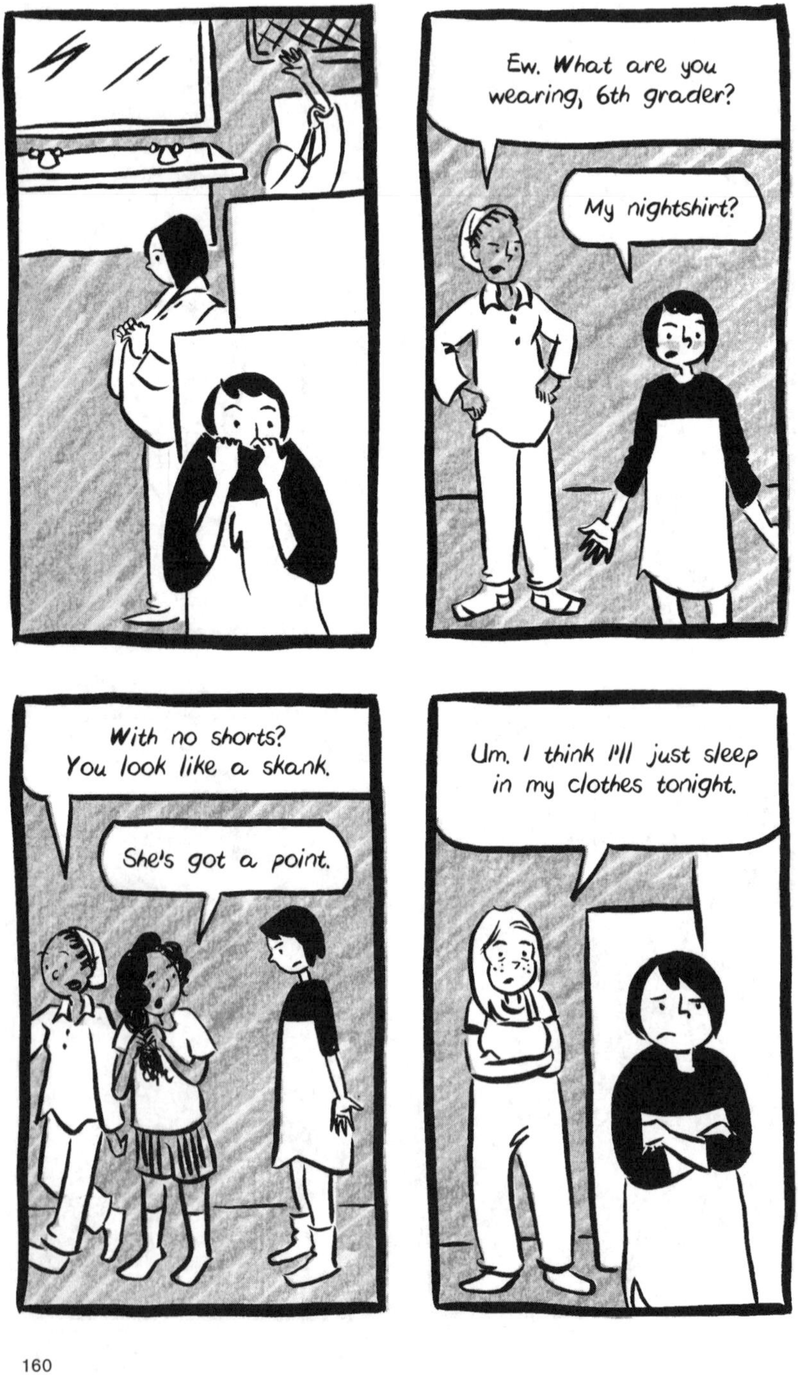
Ew. What are you wearing, 6th grader?
My nightshirt?
With no shorts? You look like a skank.
She's got a point.
Um. I think I'll just sleep in my clothes tonight.

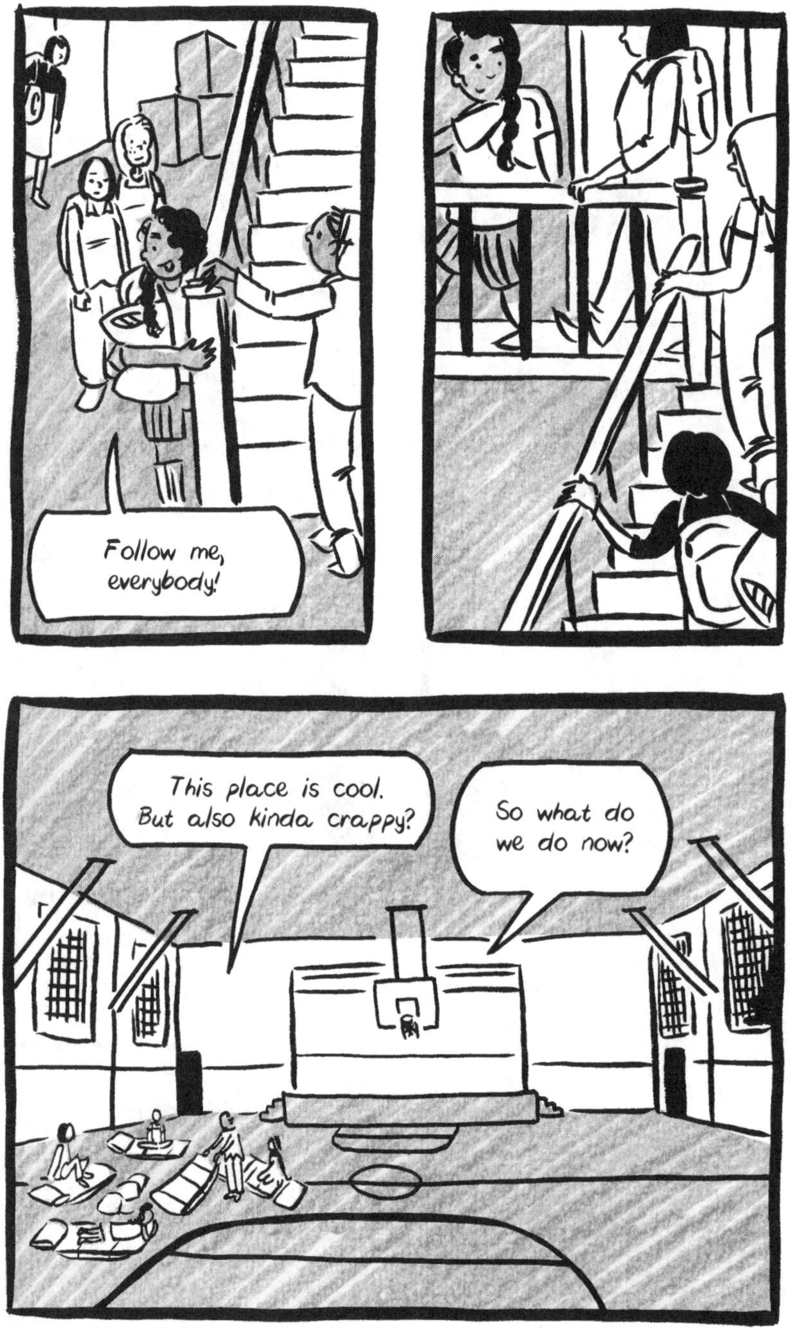
Follow me, everybody!
This place is cool. But also kinda crappy?
So what do we do now?

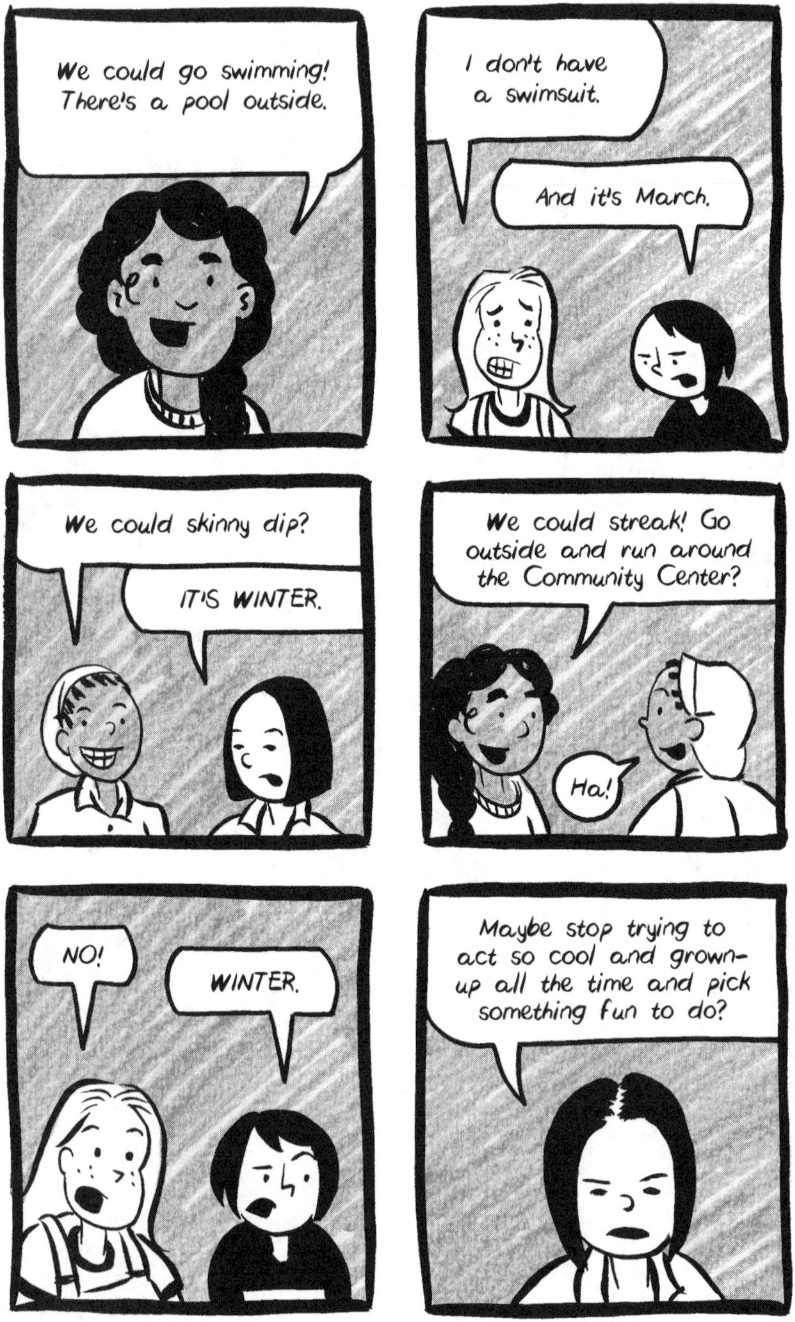

We could go swimming! There's a pool outside.
I don't have a swimsuit.
And it's March.
We could skinny dip?
IT'S WINTER.
We could streak! Go outside and run around the Community Center?
Ha!
NO!
WINTER.
Maybe stop trying to act so cool and grown-up all the time and pick something fun to do?

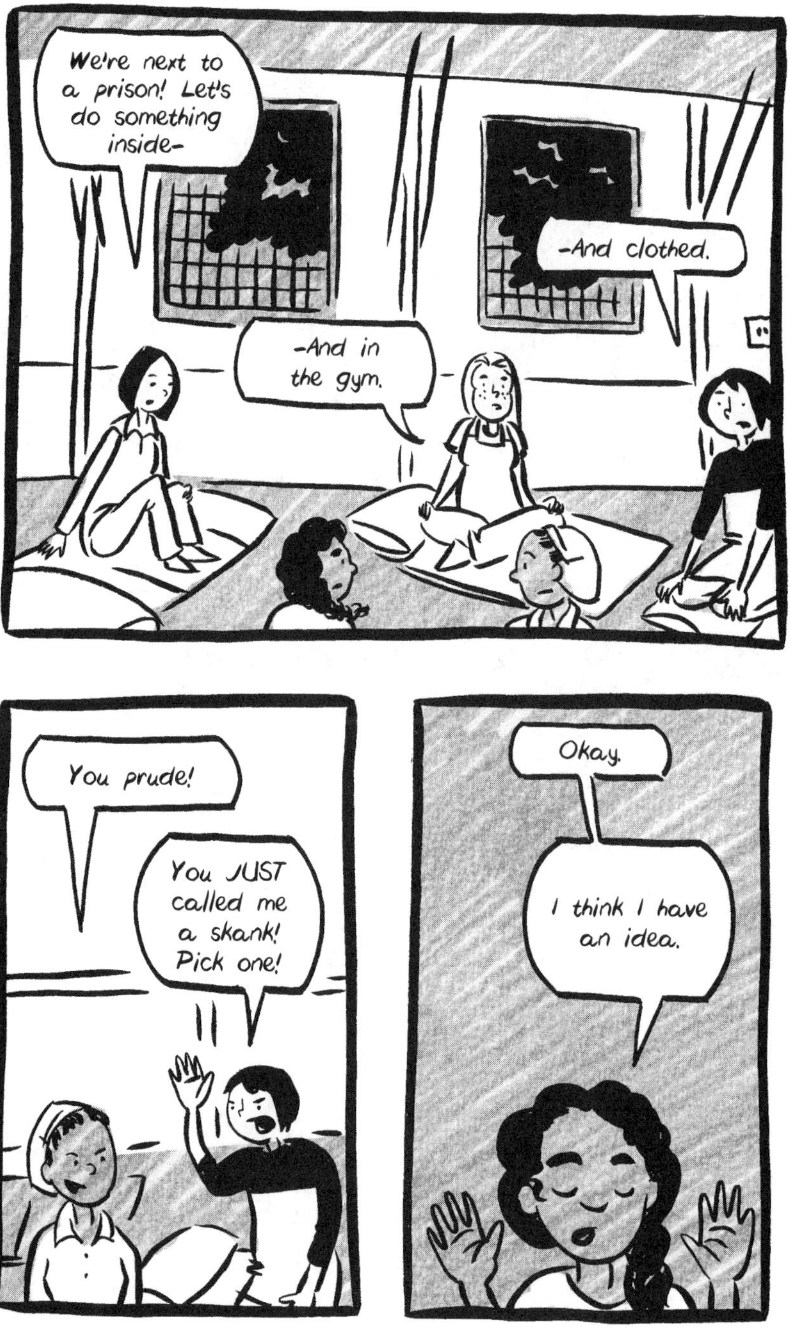
We're next to a prison! Let's do something inside-
-And in the gym.
-And clothed.
You prude!
You JUST called me a skank! Pick one!
Okay.
I think I have an idea.

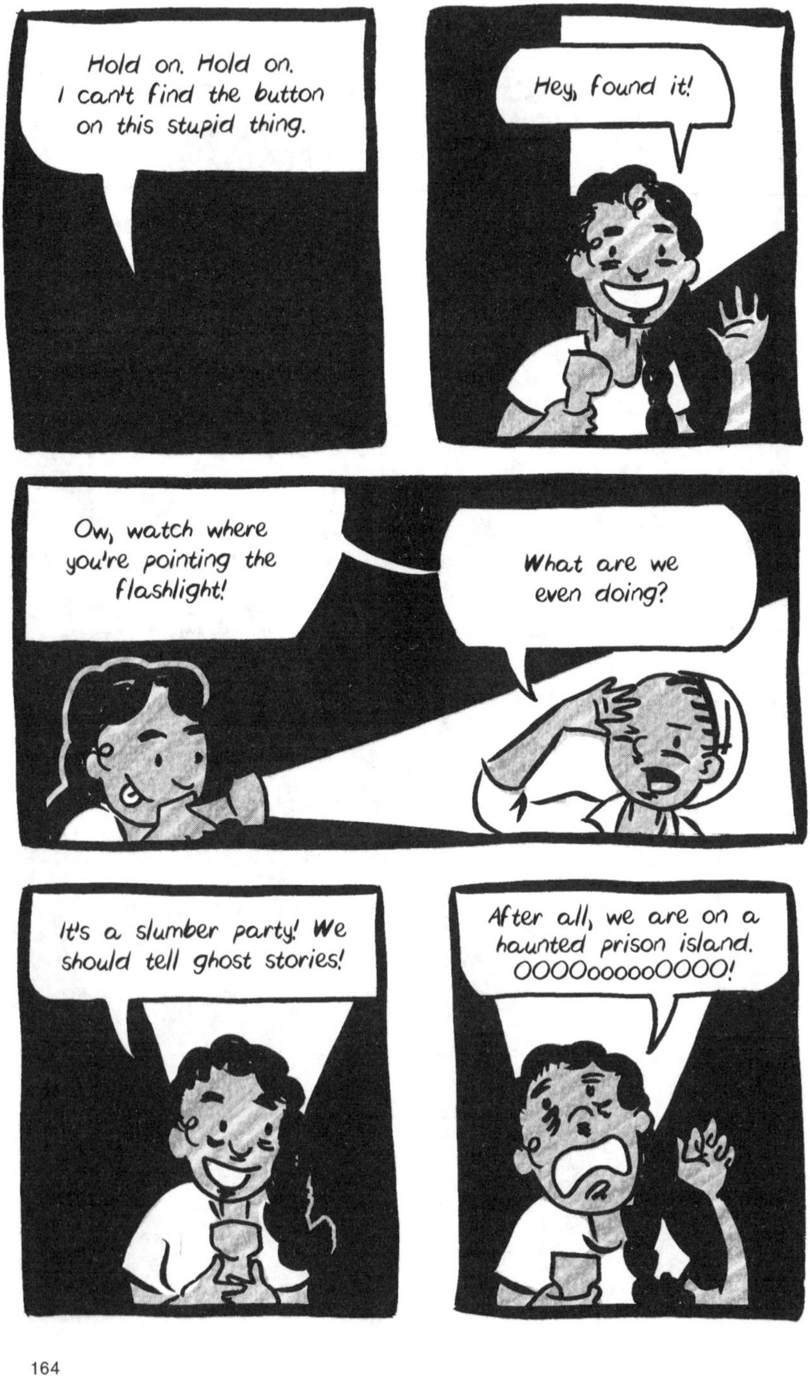
Hold on. Hold on. I can't find the button on this stupid thing.
Hey, found it!
Ow, watch where you're pointing the flashlight!
What are we even doing?
It's a slumber party! We should tell ghost stories!
After all, we are on a haunted prison island. OOOOoooooOOOO!

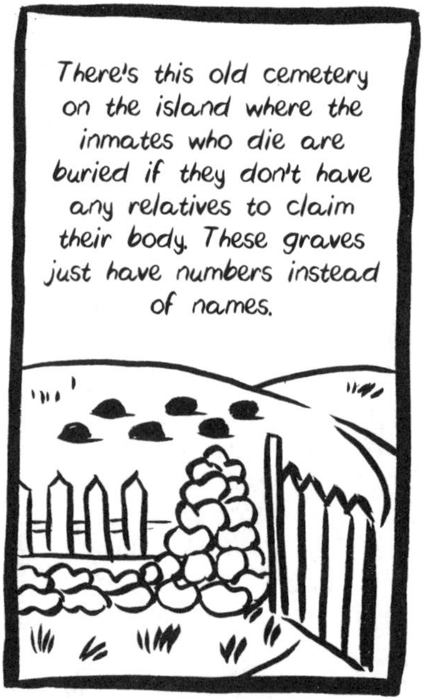
There's this old cemetery on the island where the inmates who die are buried if they don't have any relatives to claim their body. These graves just have numbers instead of names.

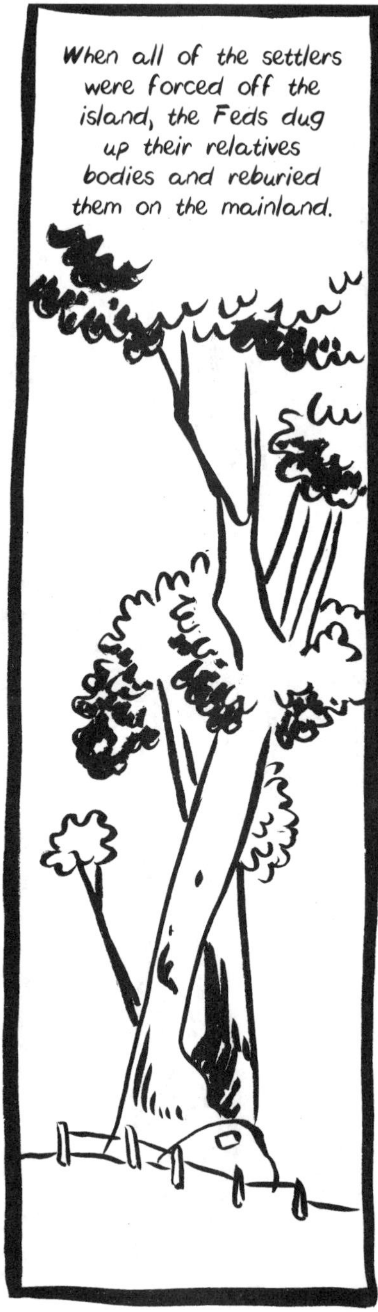
When all of the settlers were forced off the island, the Feds dug up their relatives bodies and reburied them on the mainland.

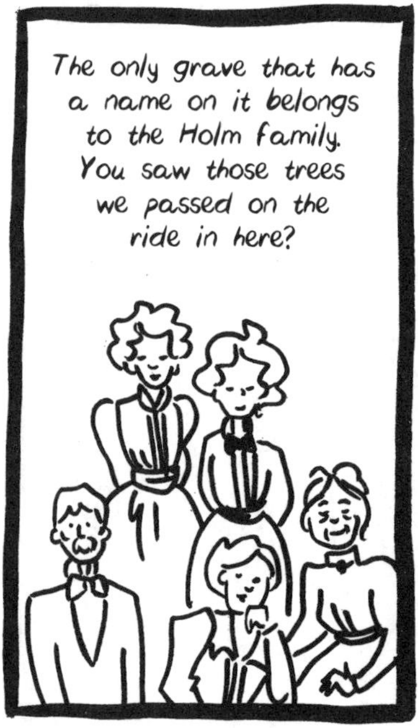
The only grave that has a name on it belongs to the Holm family. You saw those trees we passed on the ride in here?

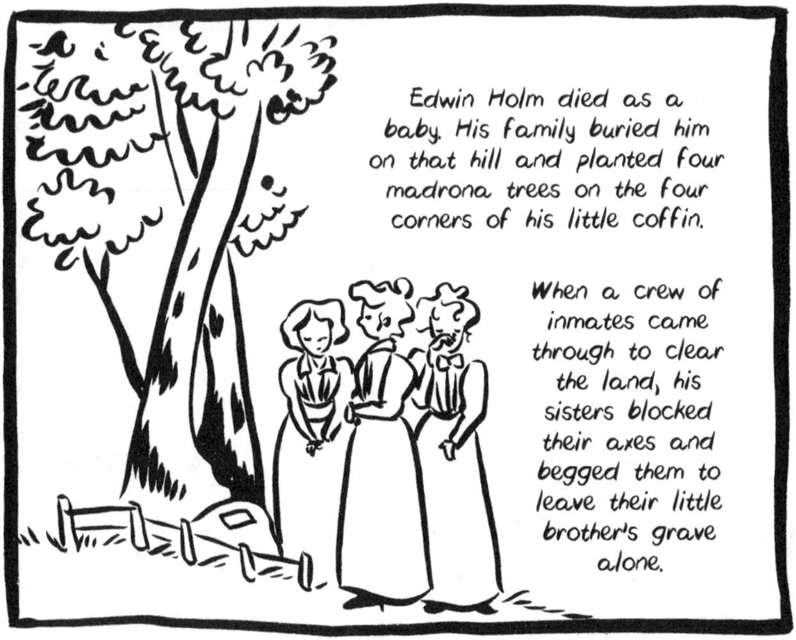
Edwin Holm died as a baby. His family buried him on that hill and planted four madrona trees on the four corners of his little coffin.
When a crew of inmates came through to clear the land, his sisters blocked their axes and begged them to leave their little brother's grave alone.

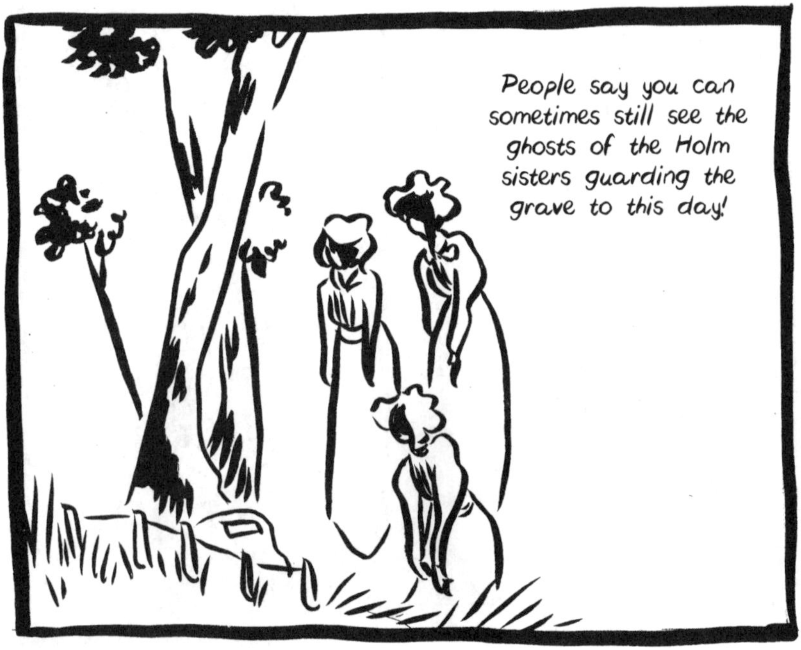
People say you can sometimes still see the ghosts of the Holm sisters guarding the grave to this day!

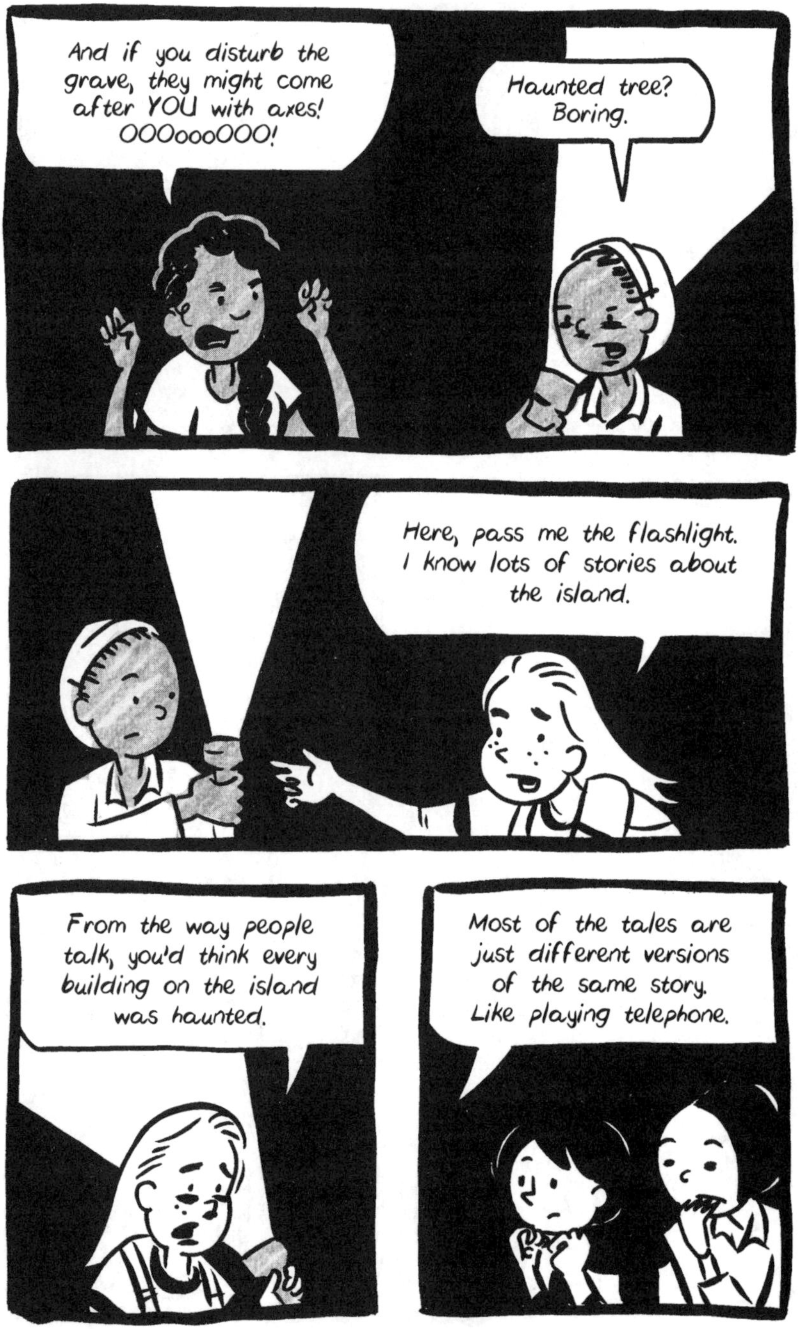
And if you disturb the grave, they might come after YOU with axes! OOOoooOOO!
Haunted tree? Boring.
Here, pass me the flashlight. I know lots of stories about the island.
From the way people talk, you'd think every building on the island was haunted.
Most of the tales are just different versions of the same story. Like playing telephone.

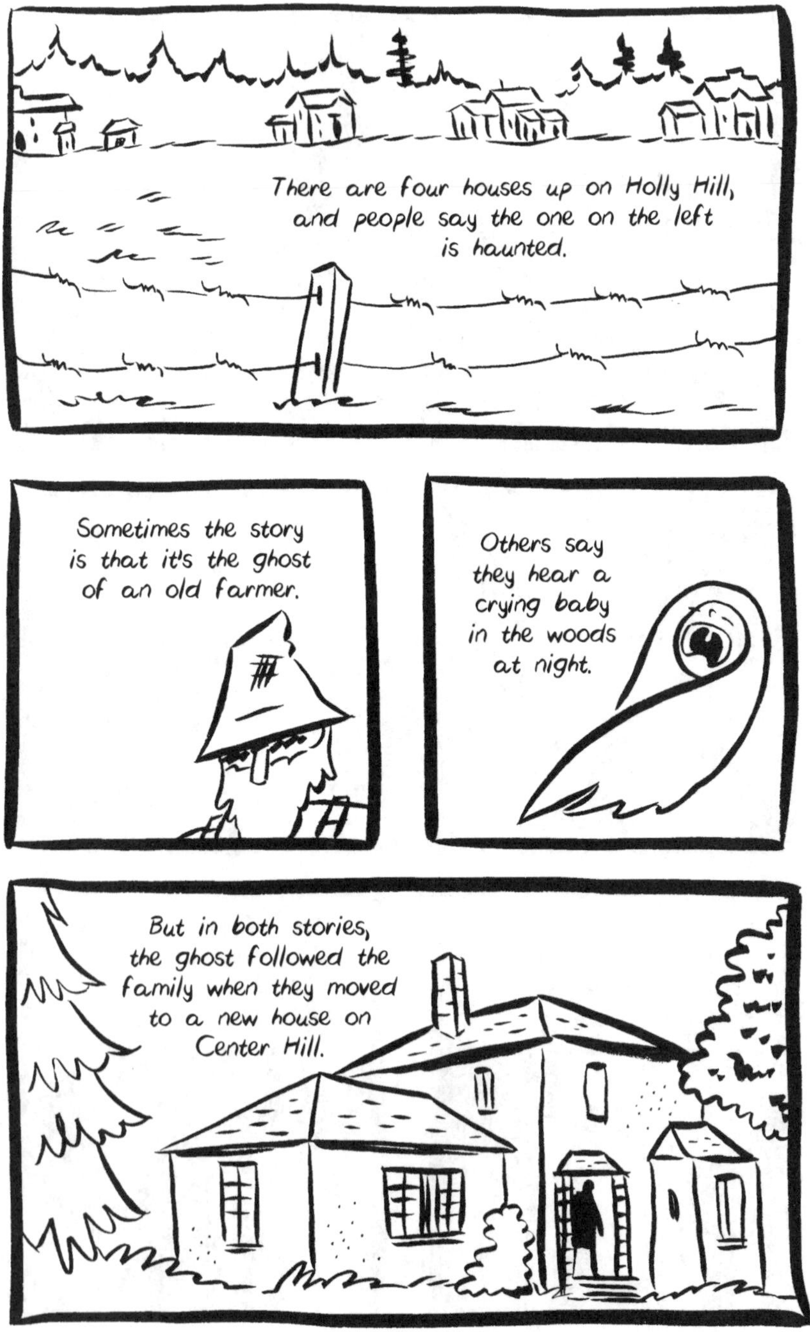
There are four houses up on Holly Hill, and people say the one on the left is haunted.
Sometimes the story is that it's the ghost of an old farmer.
Others say they hear a crying baby in the woods at night.
But in both stories, the ghost followed the family when they moved to a new house on Center Hill.

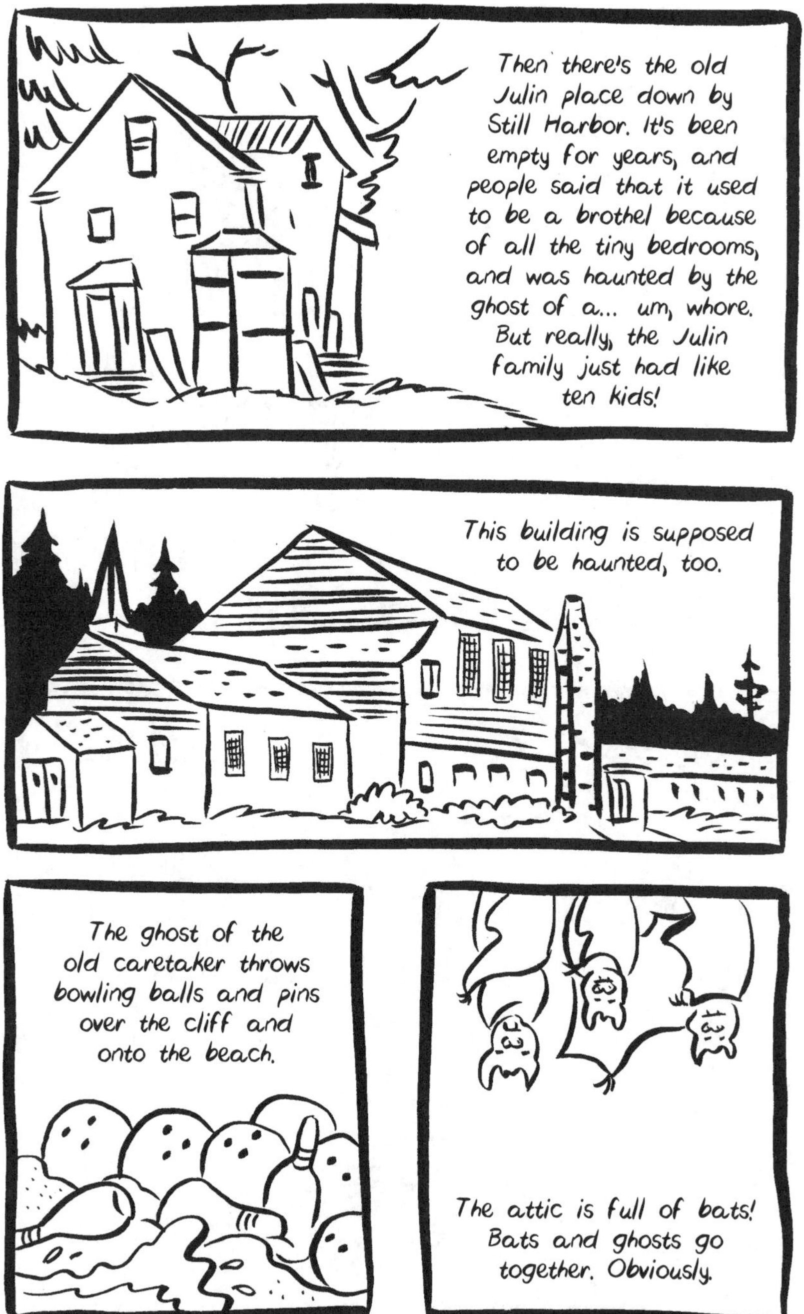
Then there's the old Julin place down by Still Harbor. It's been empty for years, and people said that it used to be a brothel because of all the tiny bedrooms, and was haunted by the ghost of a... um, whore. But really, the Julin family just had like ten kids!
This building is supposed to be haunted, too.
The ghost of the old caretaker throws bowling balls and pins over the cliff and onto the beach.
The attic is full of bats! Bats and ghosts go together. Obviously.

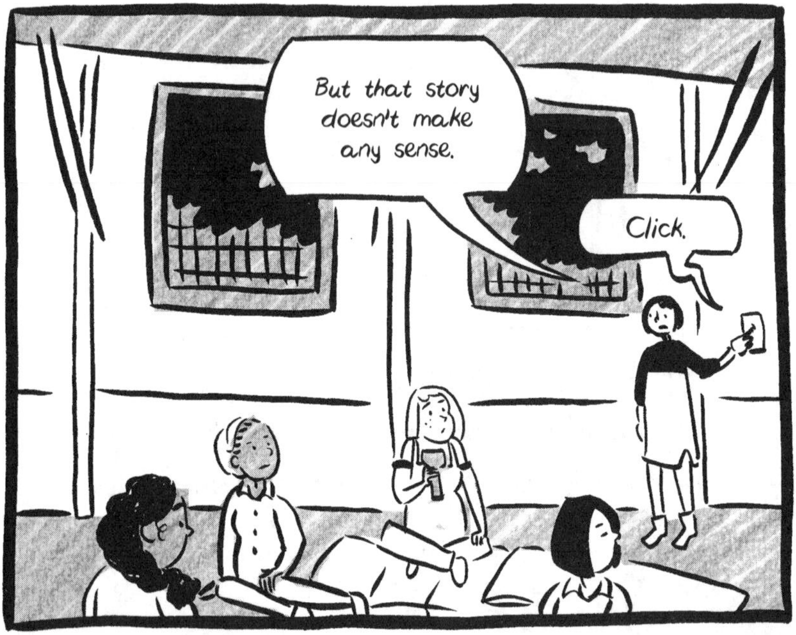
But that story doesn't make any sense.
Click.

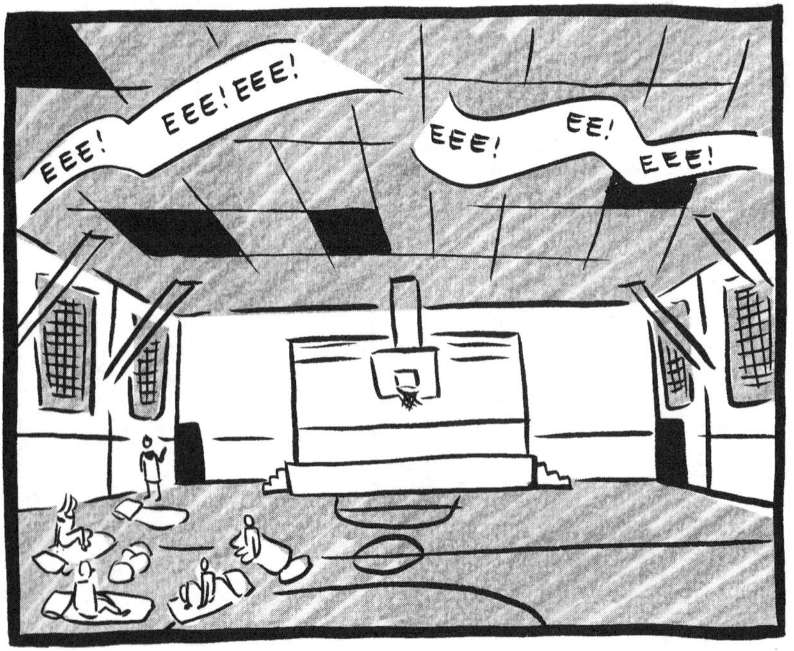
EEE! EEE! EEE!
EEE! EE! EEE!

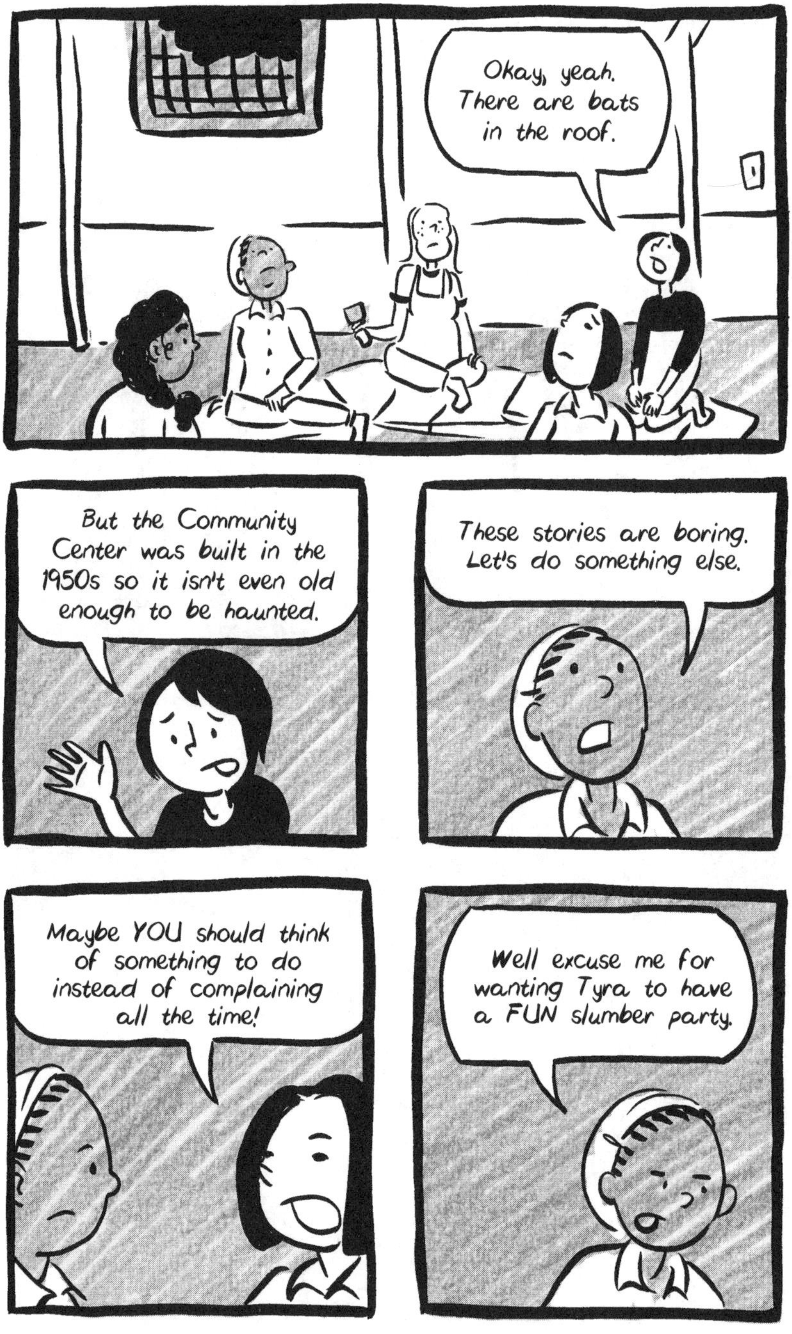

Okay, yeah. There are bats in the roof.
But the Community Center was built in the 1950s so it isn't even old enough to be haunted.
These stories are boring. Let's do something else.
Maybe YOU should think of something to do instead of complaining all the time!
Well excuse me for wanting Tyra to have a FUN slumber party.

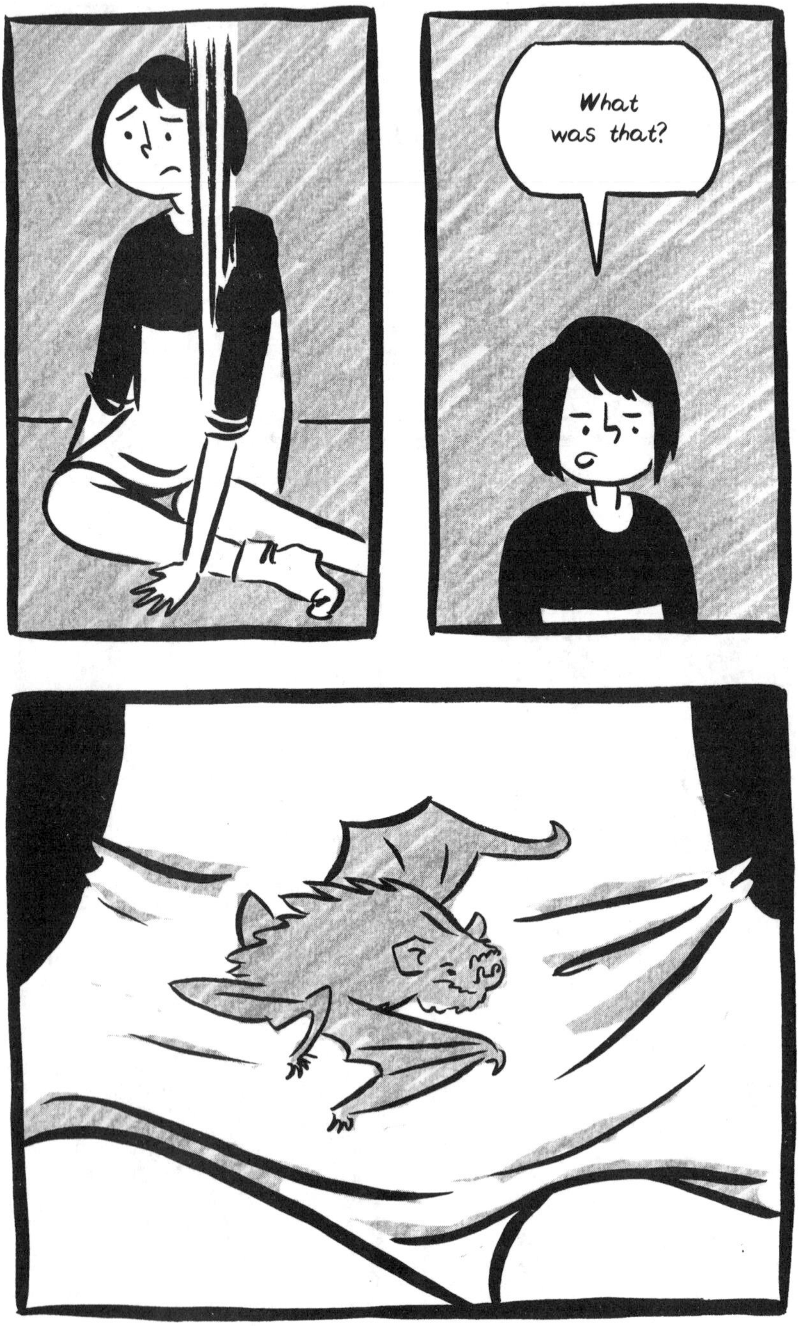
What was that?

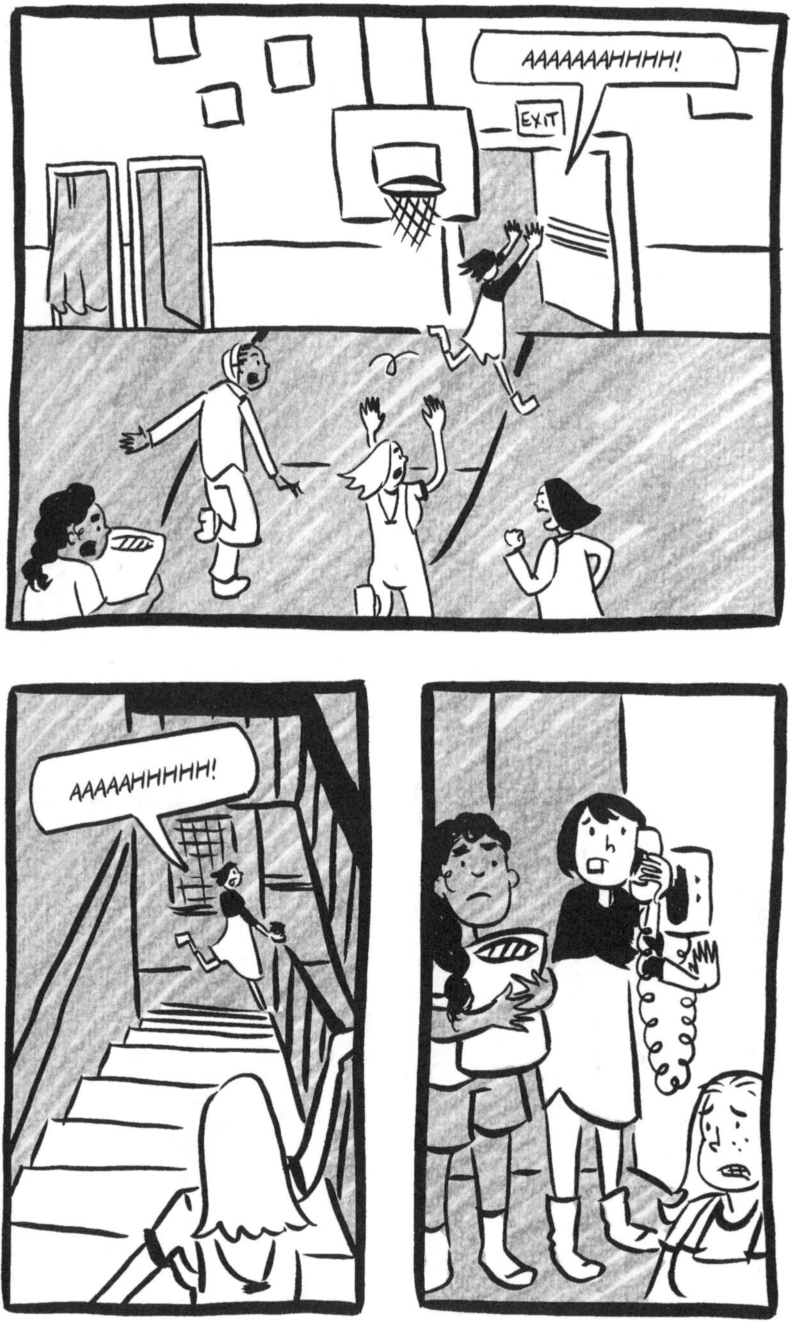
AAAAAAAHHHH!
EXIT
AAAAAHHHHH!

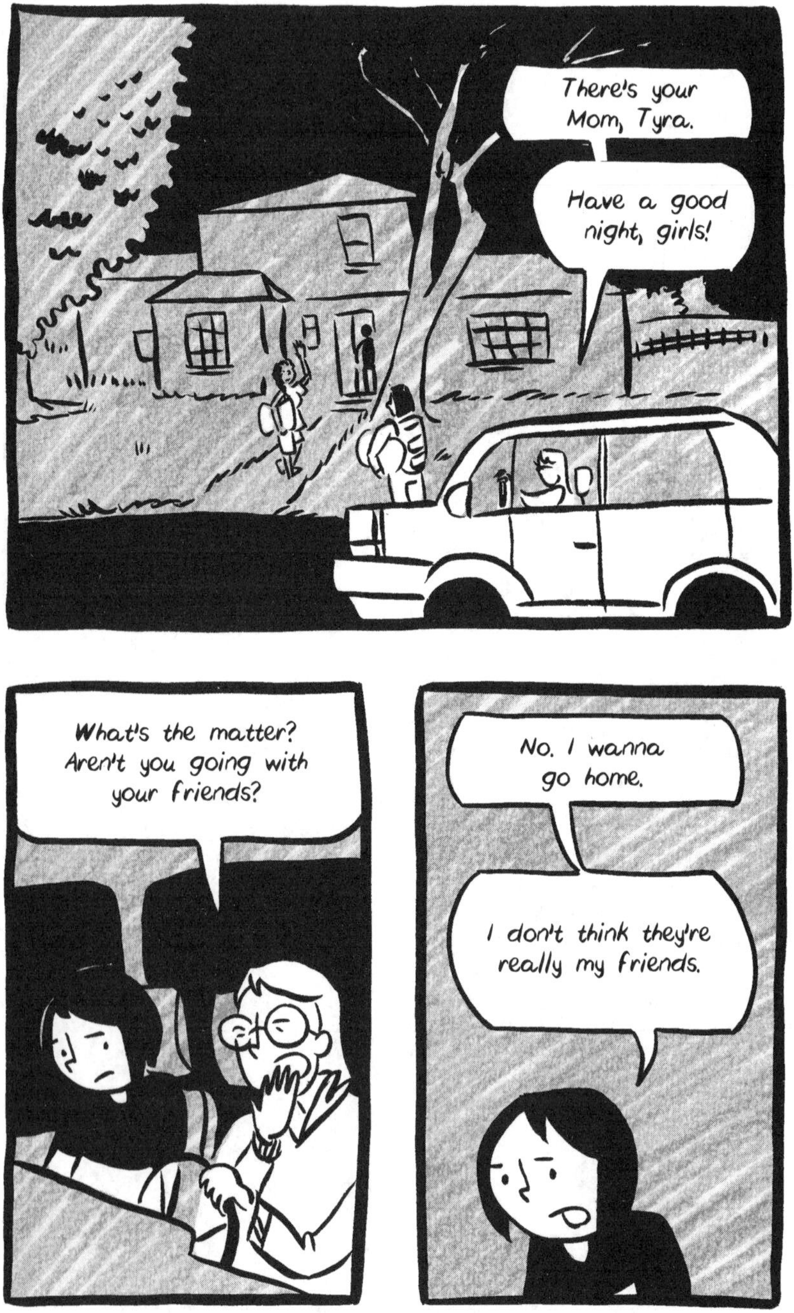
There's your Mom, Tyra.
Have a good night, girls!
What's the matter? Aren't you going with your friends?
No. I wanna go home.
I don't think they're really my friends.

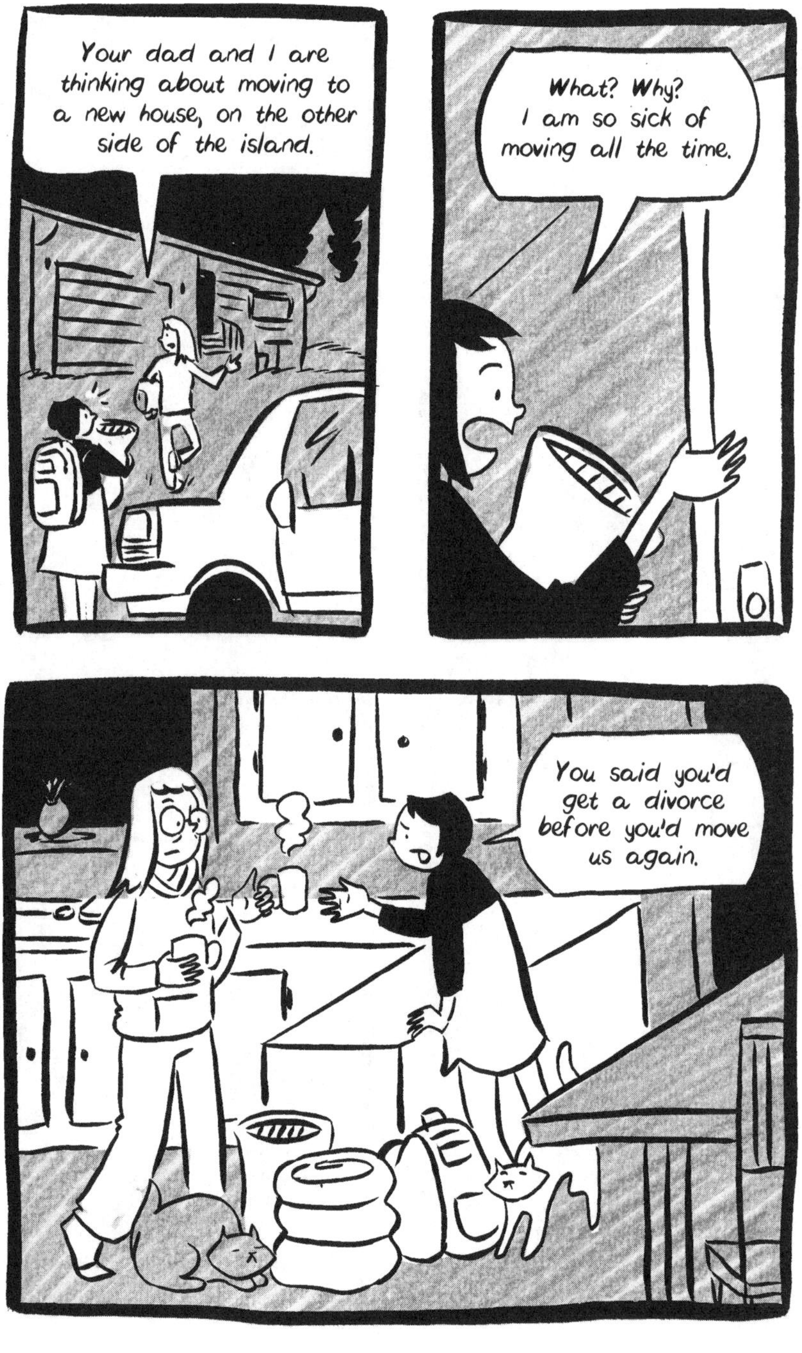
Your dad and I are thinking about moving to a new house, on the other side of the island.
What? Why? I am so sick of moving all the time.
You said you'd get a divorce before you'd move us again.

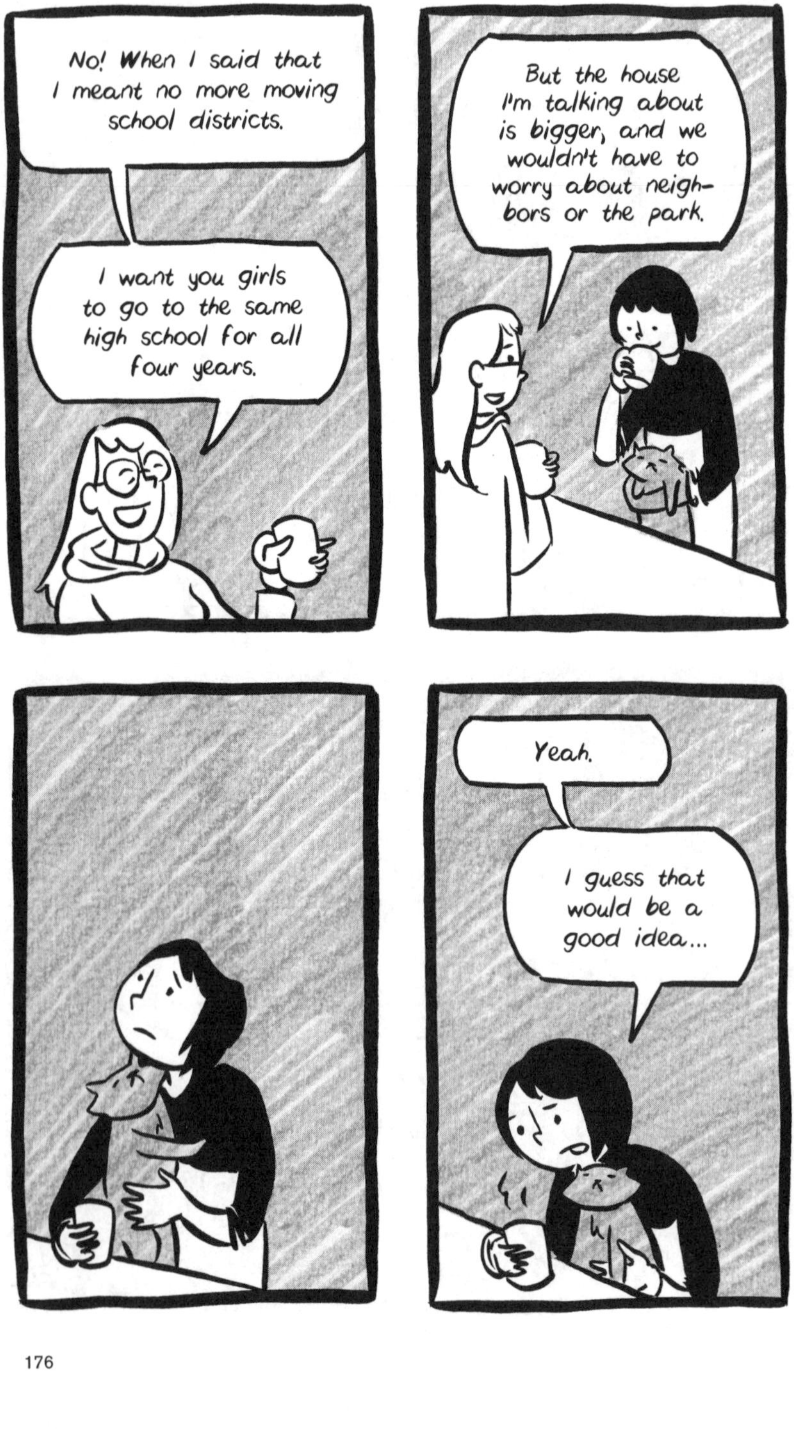
No! When I said that I meant no more moving school districts.
I want you girls to go to the same high school for all four years.
But the house I'm talking about is bigger, and we wouldn't have to worry about neighbors or the park.
Yeah.
I guess that would be a good idea...

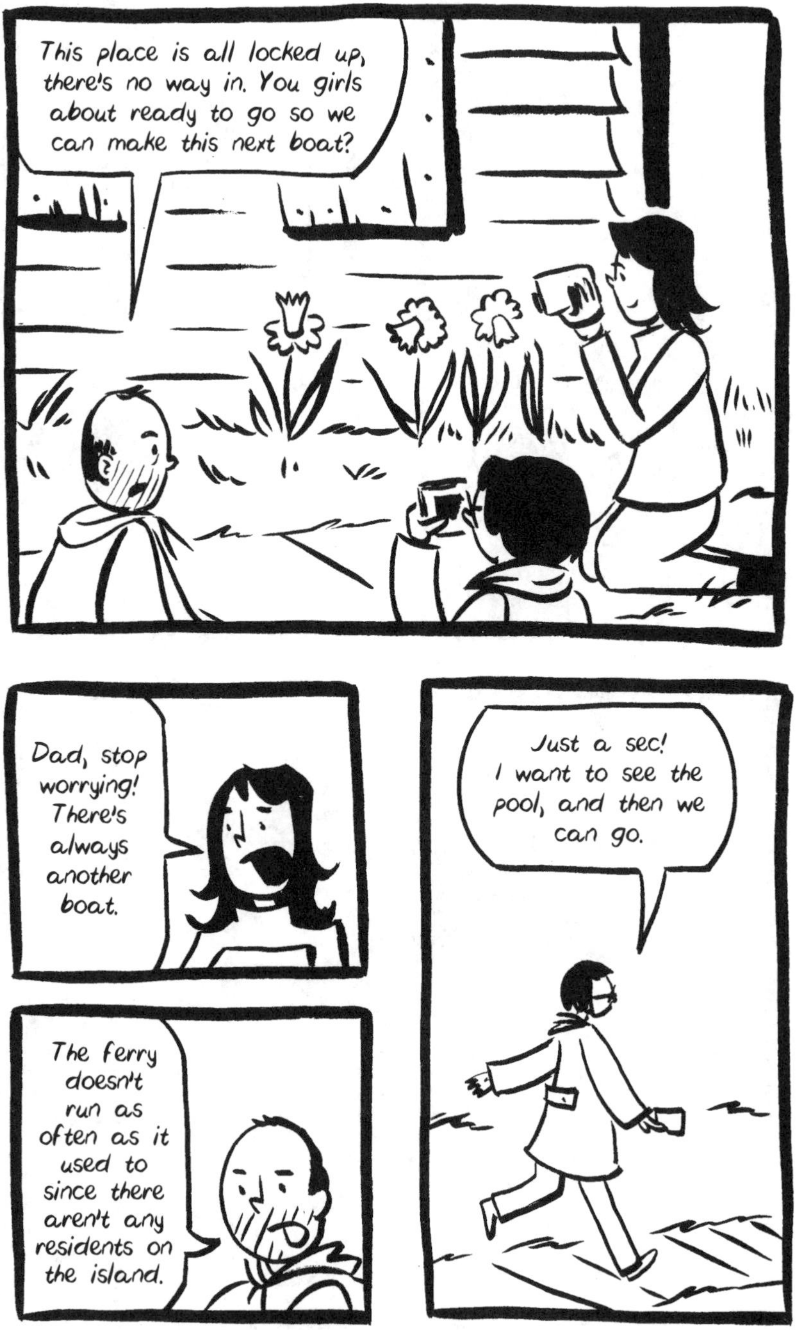
This place is all locked up, there's no way in. You girls about ready to go so we can make this next boat?
Dad, stop worrying! There's always another boat.
The ferry doesn't run as often as it used to since there aren't any residents on the island.
Just a sec! I want to see the pool, and then we can go.

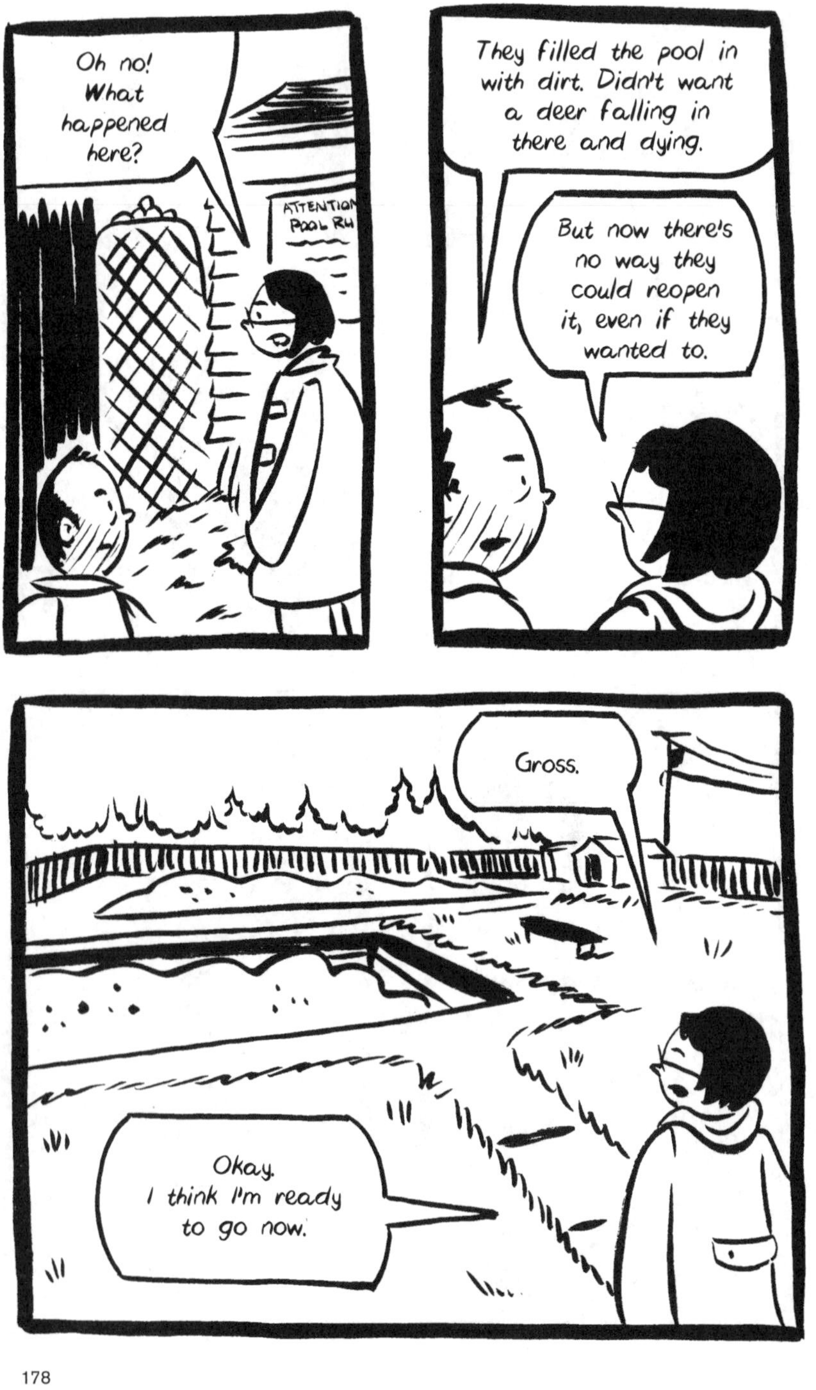
Oh no! What happened here?
They filled the pool in with dirt. Didn't want a deer falling in there and dying.
But now there's no way they could reopen it, even if they wanted to.
Gross.
Okay. I think I'm ready to go now.

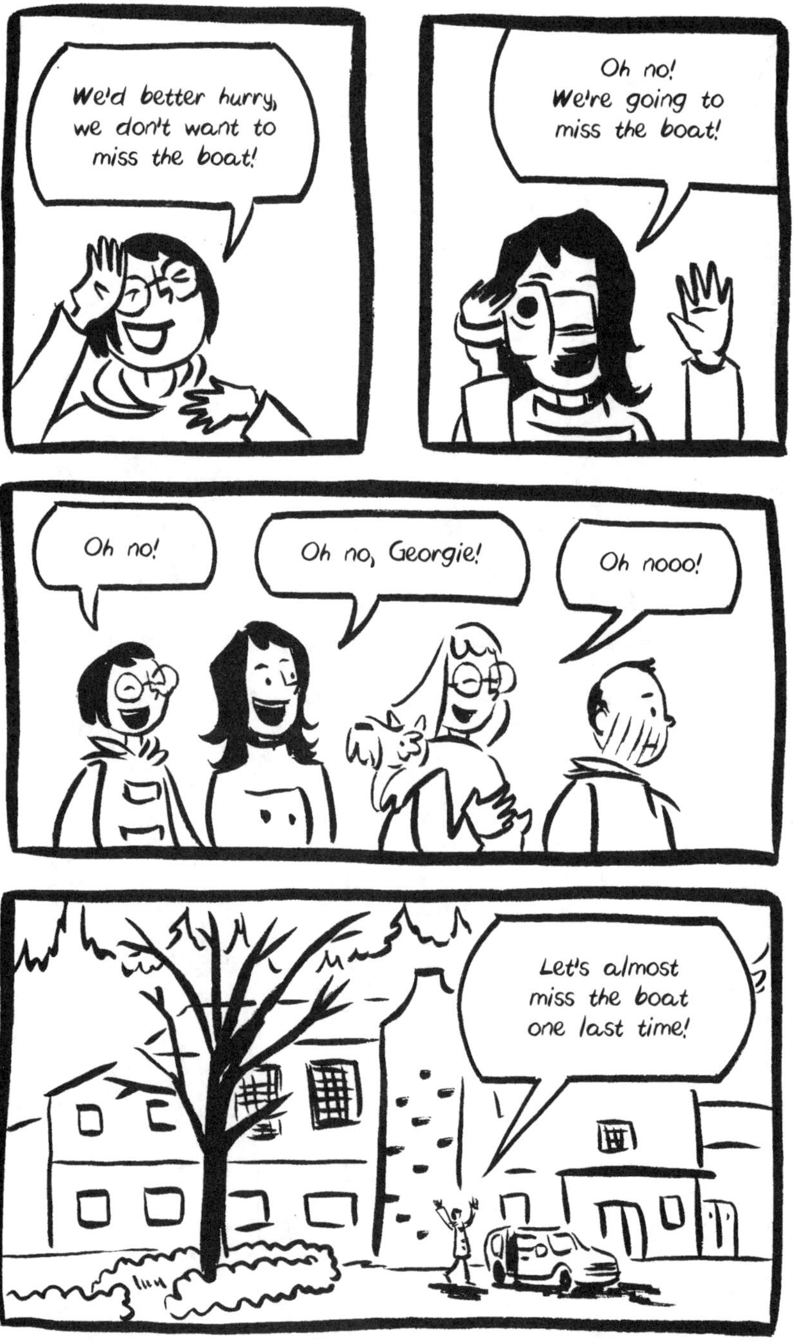
We'd better hurry, we don't want to miss the boat!
Oh no! We're going to miss the boat!
Oh no!
Oh no, Georgie!
Oh nooo!
Let's almost miss the boat one last time!

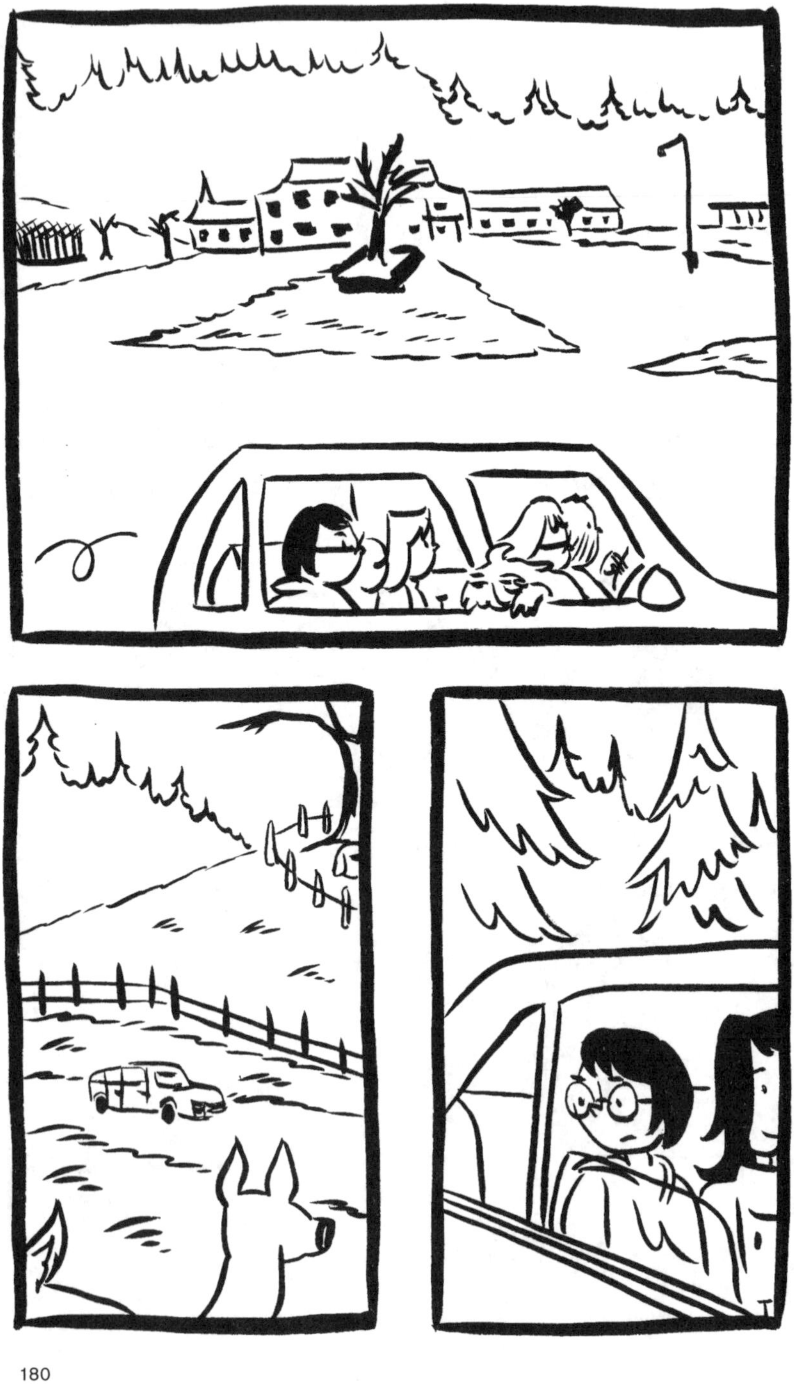

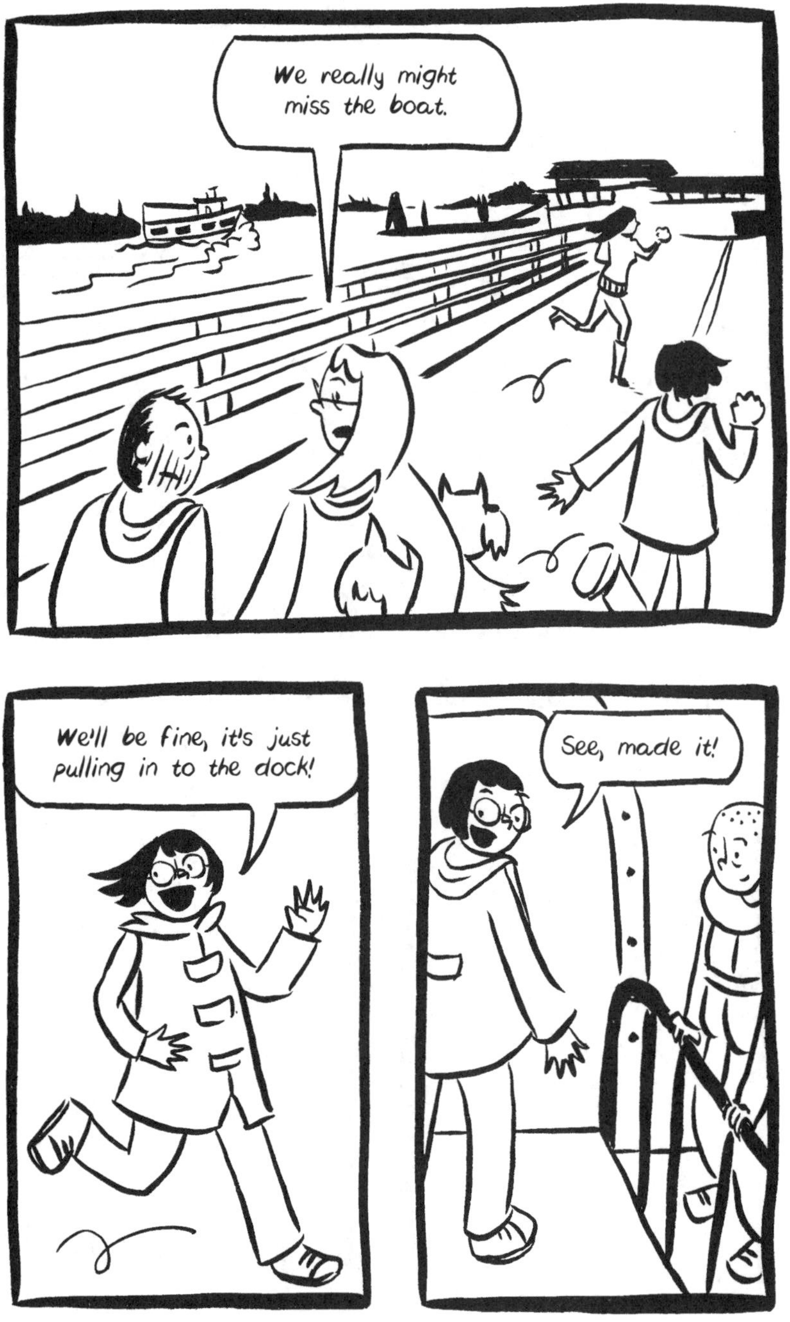
We really might miss the boat.
We'll be fine, it's just pulling in to the dock!
See, made it!

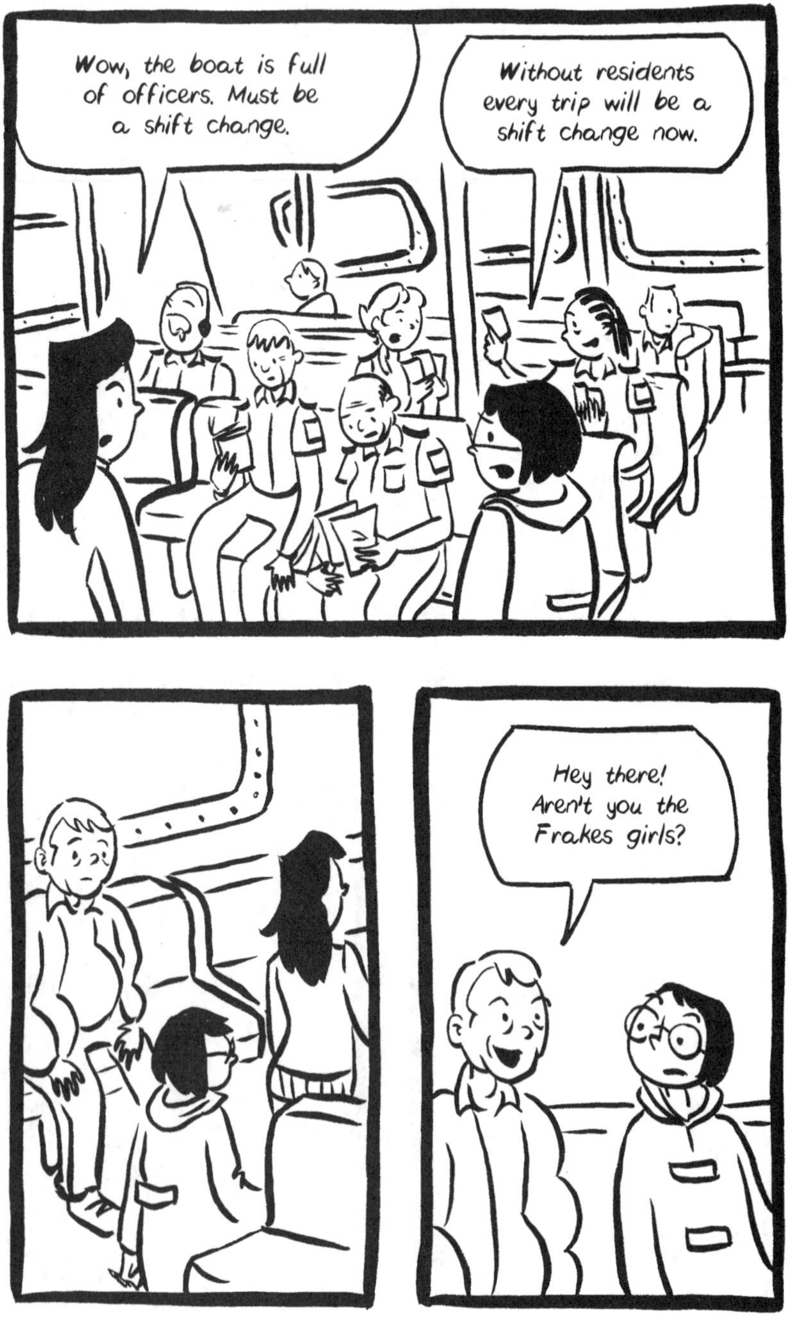
Wow, the boat is full of officers. Must be a shift change.
Without residents every trip will be a shift change now.
Hey there! Aren't you the Frakes girls?

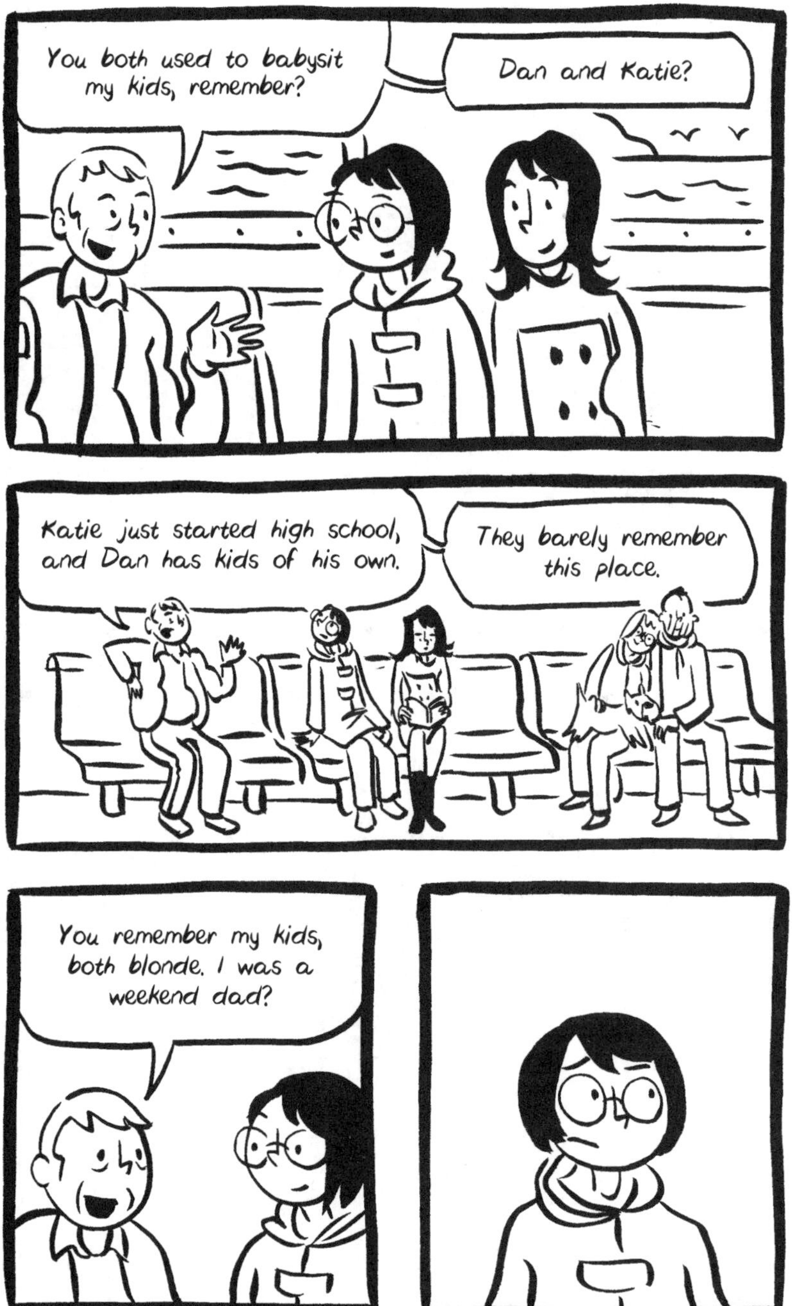
You both used to babysit my kids, remember?
Dan and Katie?
Katie just started high school, and Dan has kids of his own.
They barely remember this place.
You remember my kids, both blonde. I was a weekend dad?

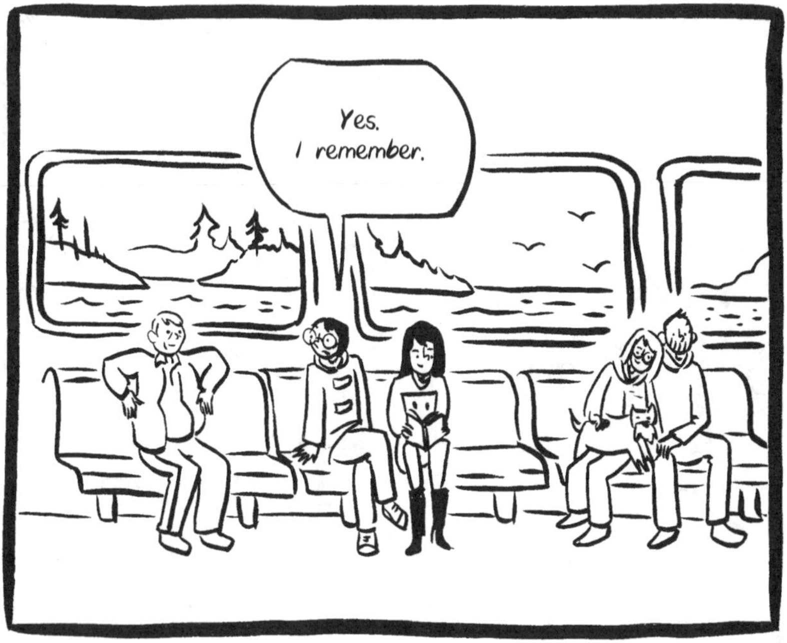
Yes.
I remember.

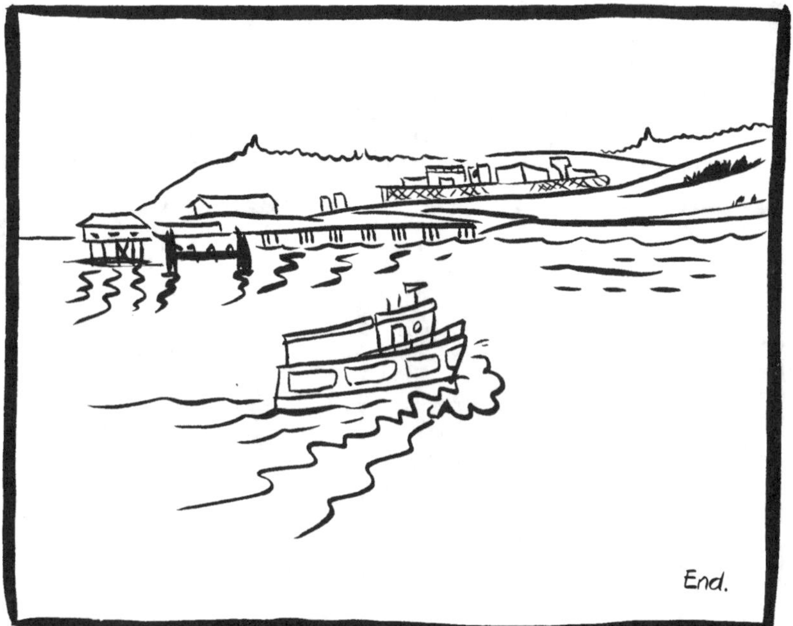
End.

EPILOGUE

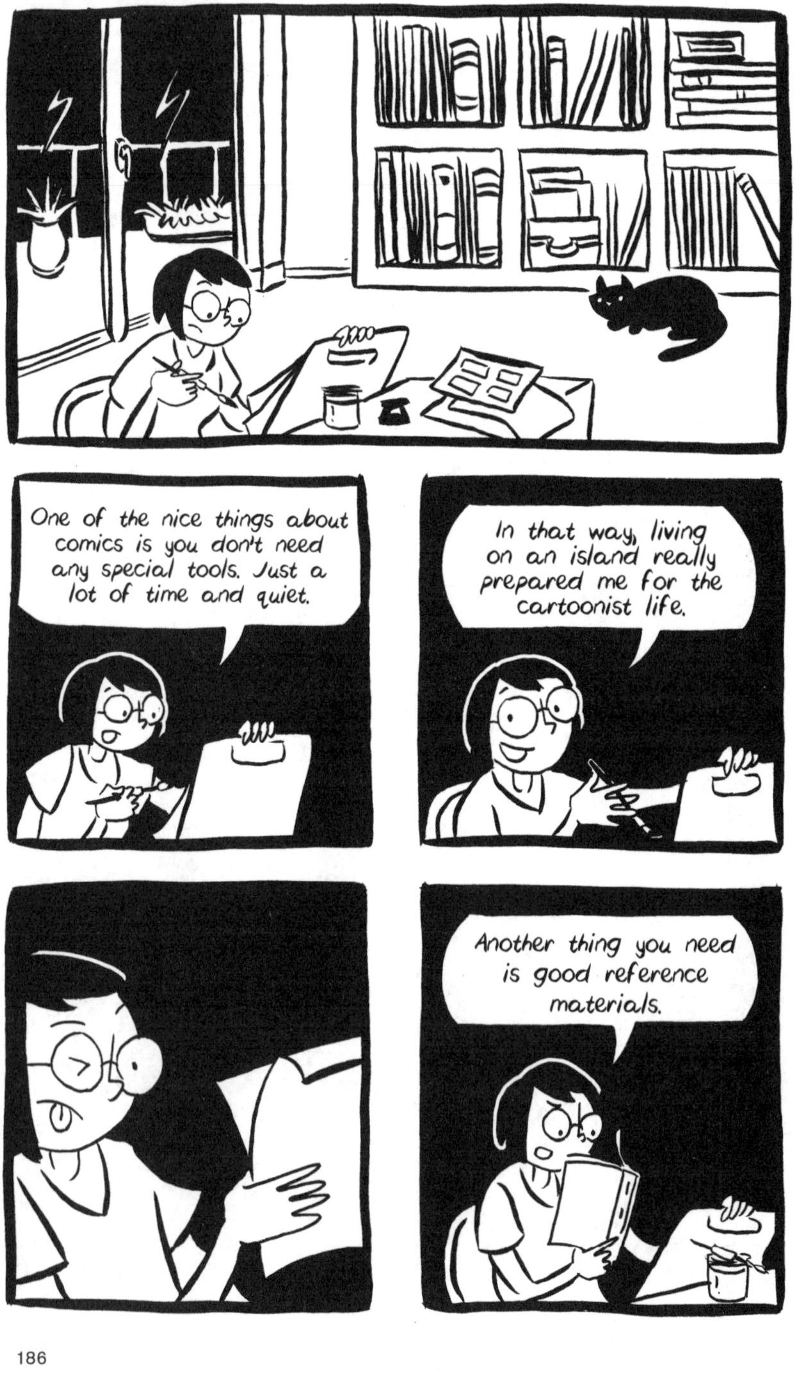

One of the nice things about comics is you don't need any special tools. Just a lot of time and quiet.
In that way, living on an island really prepared me for the cartoonist life.
Another thing you need is good reference materials.

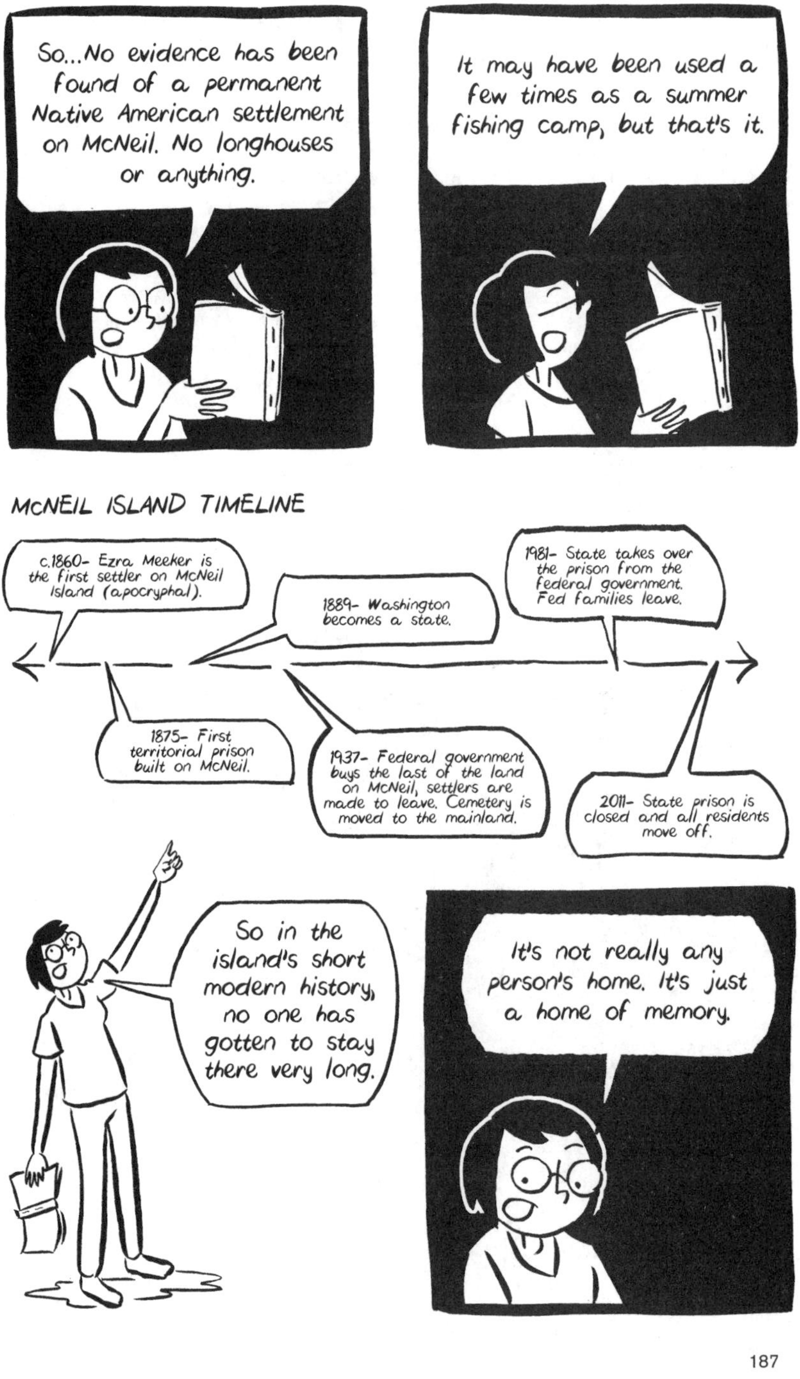
So...No evidence has been found of a permanent Native American settlement on McNeil. No longhouses or anything.
It may have been used a few times as a summer fishing camp, but that's it.
McNEIL ISLAND TIMELINE
c.1860- Ezra Meeker is the first settler on McNeil Island (apocryphal).
1875- First territorial prison built on McNeil.
1889- Washington becomes a state.
1937- Federal government buys the last of the land on McNeil, settlers are made to leave. Cemetery is moved to the mainland.
1981- State takes over the prison from the federal government. Fed families leave.
2011- State prison is closed and all residents move off.
So in the island's short modern history, no one has gotten to stay there very long.
It's not really any person's home. It's just a home of memory.

BIBLIOGRAPHY

Kennedy, Halk., Joan Robinson, Gordon Varey and Lawrence Schwinn. "A Cultural History Resources Survey Reconnaissance and Assessment of McNeil Island," Pierce Co., WA. Seattle: Office of Public Archaeology, Institute for Environmental Studies, University of Washington, 1981.

Kruse, Brandi. "Inmates picking Washington apples on 200-acre orchard." MyNorthwest.com. < http://mynorthwest.com/11/571142/Inmates-picking-Washington-apples-on-200acre-orchard>. Nov. 1, 2011.

Keve, Paul W. "The McNeil Century: The Life and Times of an Island Prison." Chicago: Nelson-Hall, 1984.

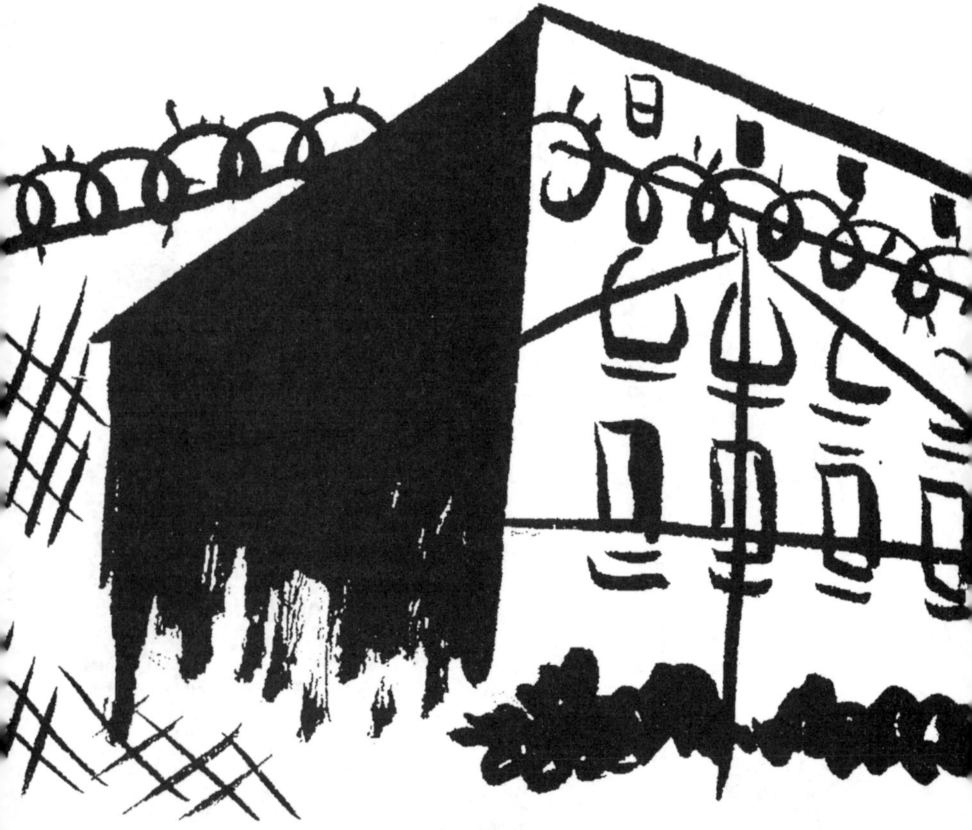

Heckman, Hazel. "Island in the Sound." Seattle, University of Washington Press, 1976.

McNeil Island Historical Society. "Island Houses." Facebook. January 7, 2011. <https://facebook.com/mcneilisland.historicalsociety?v=photos>. Oct. 2014.

Washington State Archives. "Department of Corrections, McNeil Island Photograph Collection, 1855-2010." Digital Archives. Web. <http://www.digitalarchives.wa.gov/>. Oct. 2014.

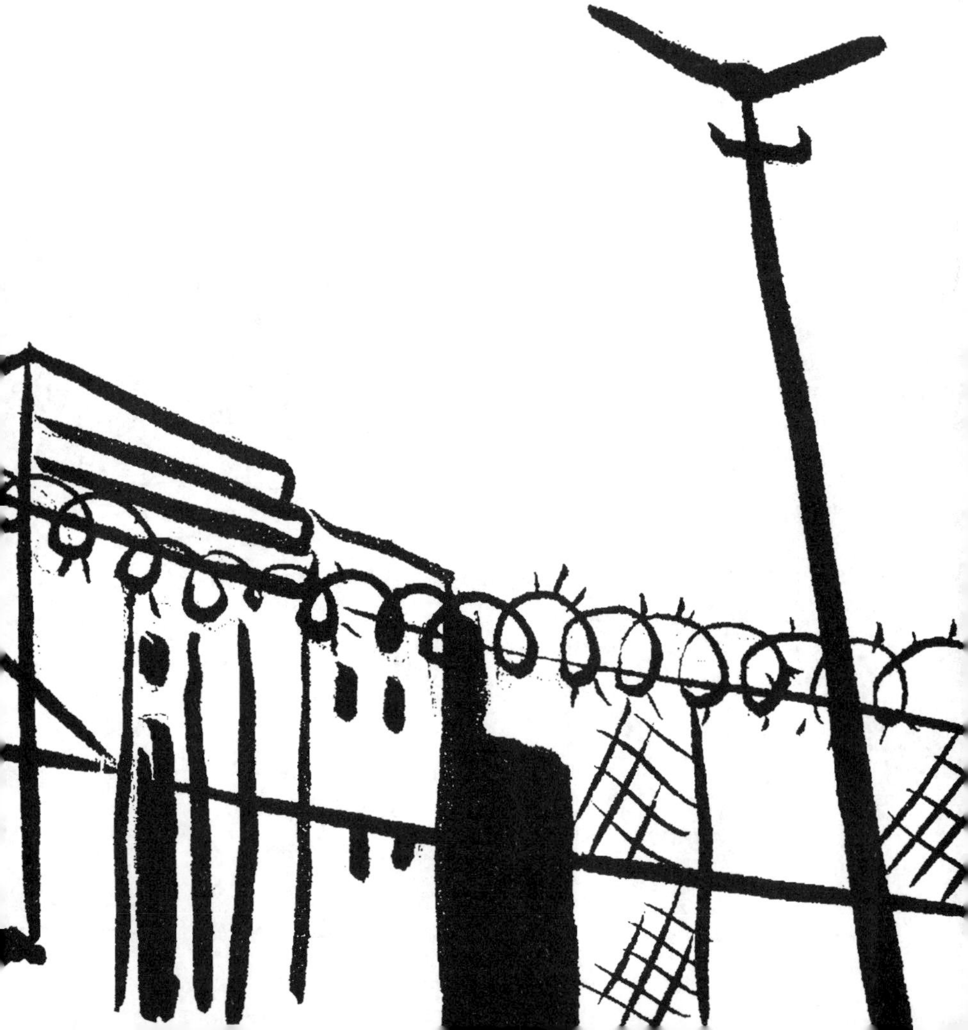

RESOURCES

- McNeil Island Historical Society

  http://www.mcneilisland.net/
  3707 S Asotin St.
  Tacoma, WA 98418

- Post-Prison Education Program

  http://postprisonedu.org/
  810 Third Avenue, Suite 180
  Seattle, WA 98104-1606

- ACLU National Prison Project

  https://www.aclu.org/aclu-national-prison-project

- Vera Institute of Justice

  http://www.vera.org
  233 Broadway, 12th Floor
  New York, NY 1027

- Council for State Government Justice Reinvestment

  http://csgjusticecenter.org

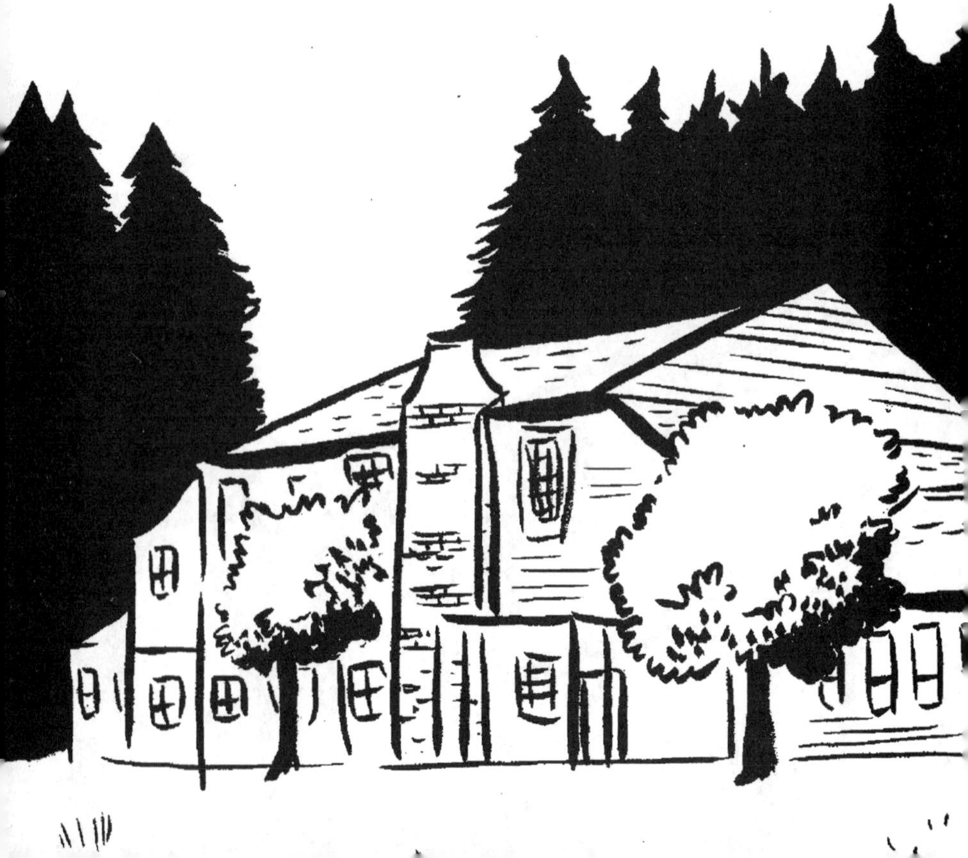

ACKNOWLEDGEMENTS

This project would not have been possible without research assistance from Scott, Kelly and Liz Frakes, Paula Byrne, Judy Hubert, the Loresch family, Eric Heinitz, Ann Burkly, The Seattle Public Library, The Washington State Archives, and the McNeil Island Historical Society.

Thanks to Dan, Adam, and everyone at Zest Books.

Comics typeset in "ColleenHandwriting," designed by Lee Scheinbeim.

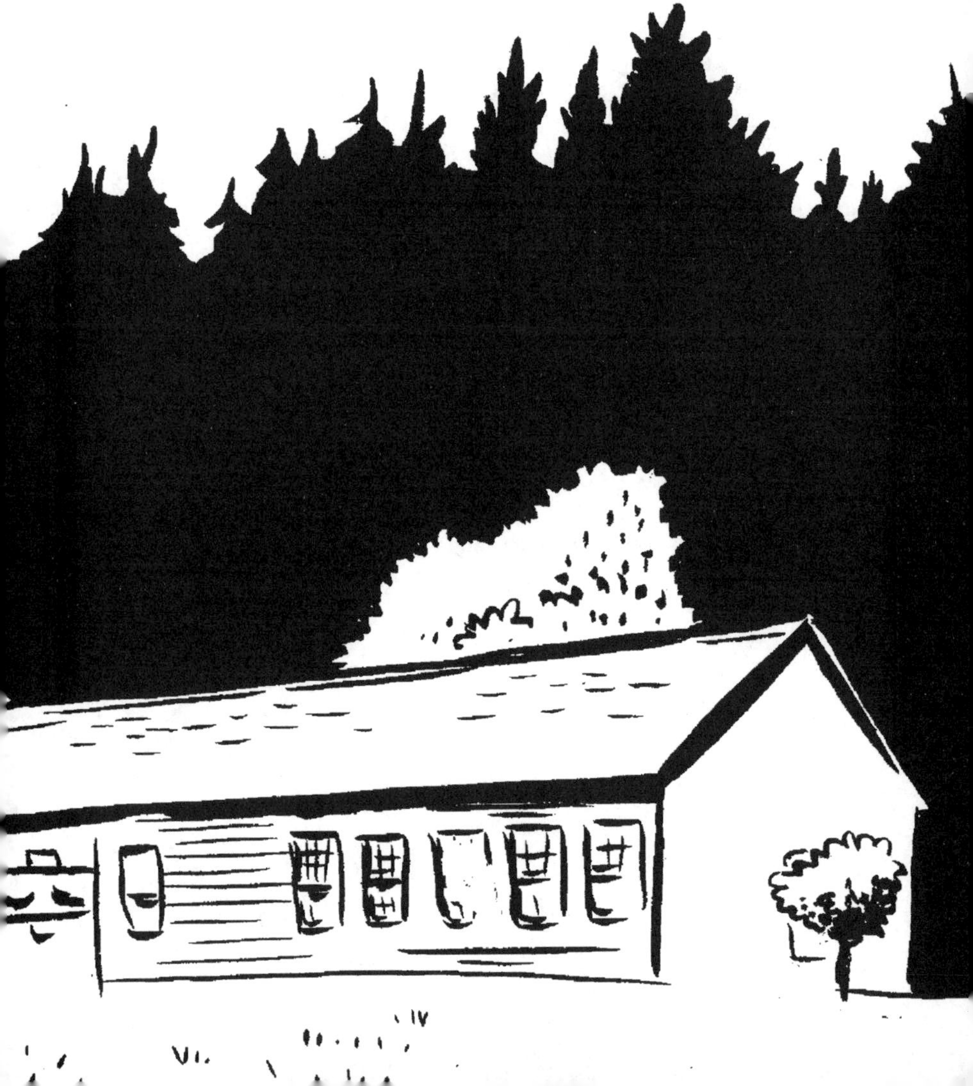

ABOUT THE AUTHOR

COLLEEN FRAKES is a graduate of The Evergreen State College and the Center for Cartoon Studies. In 2007 she received a Xeric Grant for her book *Tragic Relief*. In 2009 she was awarded the Ignatz for "Promising New Talent" for her book *Woman King*. She has since contributed to numerous comic anthologies and drawn dozens of mini comics. She currently lives in Seattle and works in a library.